FINANCIAL INSTITUTIONS AND SERVICES SERIES

REFORMING RISK IN FINANCIAL MARKETS

FINANCIAL INSTITUTIONS AND SERVICES SERIES

Stock Exchanges, IPO's and Mutual funds
E. Klein (Editor)
2004 ISBN: 1-59454-173-6

Global Banking Issues
E. Klein (Editor)
2005 ISBN: 1-59454-172-8

Financial Institutions and Development
E. Klein (Editor)
2005 ISBN: 1-59454-177-9

Capital Formation, Governance and Banking
E. Klein (Editor)
2005 ISBN: 1-59454-191-4

U. S. Coins: The Price of a Penny
Walter M. Carvalho (Editor)
2009 ISBN: 978-1-60692-939-1

Hedge Funds: Regulation and Nonregulation
Yeram E. Torrey (Editor)
2009. ISBN: 978-1-60692-041-1

Reforming Risk in Financial Markets
Melvin R. Turley (Editor)
2009 ISBN: 978-1-60692-445-7

FINANCIAL INSTITUTIONS AND SERVICES SERIES

REFORMING RISK IN FINANCIAL MARKETS

MELVIN R. TURLEY
EDITOR

Nova Science Publishers, Inc.
New York

LIBRARY OF CONGRESS CATALOGING-IN-PUBLICATION DATA
Available upon request

ISBN 978-1-60692-445-7

Published by Nova Science Publishers, Inc. ✢ New York

CONTENTS

PREFACE

This new book deals with the issue of reforming risk in financial markets. This issue has become red hot with the global economic meltdone caused largely by the financial institutions and the practices being followed at the time which rewarded the creation and trading of false financial instruments.

In: Reforming Risk in Financial Markets
Editor: Melvin R. Turley, pp. 1-115
ISBN 978-1-60692-445-7

Chapter 1

CONTAINING SYSTEMIC RISK: THE ROAD TO REFORM. THE REPORT OF THE CRMPG III*

CRM Policy Group

TRANSMITTAL LETTER

The Honorable Henry M. Paulson, Jr.
Secretary of the Treasury, and
Chairman, President's Working Group on Financial Markets
1500 Pennsylvania Ave., NW
Washington, DC 20220

The Honorable Mario Draghi
Governor, Bank of Italy, and
Chairman, Financial Stability Forum
Via Nazionale 91
00184 Rome
Italy

Dear Secretary Paulson and Governor Draghi:

On behalf of CRMPG III we are pleased to convey to you our Report entitled "Containing Systemic Risk: The Road to Reform." As the title of the Report suggests, the Policy Group considers the financial crisis of 2007 and 2008 to be the most severe we have experienced in the postwar period. While this turn of events had multiple causes and contributing factors, the root cause of financial market excesses on both the upside and the downside of the cycle is collective human behavior – unbridled optimism on the upside and fear – bordering on panic – on the downside. As history tells us in unmistakable terms, it is

* This is an edited, excerpted and augmented edition dated August 6, 2008 extracted from www.crmpolicygroup.org

virtually impossible to anticipate when optimism gives rise to fear or fear gives rise to optimism. The last twelve months have been no exception to this sobering reality.

It is this sobering reality that, for centuries, has given rise to the universal recognition that finance and financial institutions must be subject to a higher degree of official oversight than is necessary for virtually all other forms of commercial enterprise. However, official supervision is not a substitute for effective management of financial institutions which is –and should remain – a private function. Yet, here too, there is a dilemma; namely, in a highly competitive marketplace it is very difficult for one or a few institutions to hold the line on best practices or to stand on the sidelines in the face of booming markets. What is needed, therefore, is a form of private initiative that will complement official oversight by insisting on industry practices that will help mitigate systemic risk. The "core precepts" and recommendations in this Report have been framed with that objective in mind.

The Policy Group places particular importance on the five core precepts for containing systemic risk that are discussed in *Section I.* The subsequent four sections of the Report include the following: *Section II* which covers a reconsideration of the standards for consolidation under US GAAP that contemplates a significant shift of currently off-balance sheet status entities to on-balance sheet status; *Section III* which is directed at measures to better understand and manage high-risk complex financial instruments with particular emphasis on (1) the establishment of standards of sophistication that would apply to all participants in the market for high-risk complex financial instruments; (2) enhanced disclosures; (3) improved sales and marketing practices; and (4) strengthened issuer and loan diligence; *Section IV* which focuses on substantial enhancements to risk monitoring and management with particular emphasis on sound corporate governance, risk monitoring, and fostering a single integrated discipline for managing capital adequacy and liquidity and funding; and *Section V* which outlines a series of truly sweeping measures to enhance the resiliency of financial markets generally and the credit markets in particular with special emphasis on the OTC derivatives market and the credit default swap market. The recommendations in *Section* V – including the call for the prompt creation of a clearing corporation that would begin clearing credit default swaps in the fourth quarter of 2008 – are extremely ambitious.

The final section of the Report discusses a number of important "emerging issues". While this section, by its design, does not have recommendations, it does point, in very concrete terms, to subject matter that will require close attention during the period ahead on the part of policy members and practitioners alike.

Achieving the sweeping enhancement and reform set forth in the Report will require collective and concerted industry-wide initiatives, supported by progressive and enlightened prudential supervision conducted in the spirit of the March 6, 2008 Report of the Senior Supervisors Group. In the private sector, greater financial discipline at individual institutions must be reinforced by a renewed commitment to collective discipline in the spirit of elevated "financial statesmanship" that recognizes that there are circumstances in which individual institutions must be prepared to put aside specific interests in the name of the common interest.

Such a commitment may require market participants to (1) make costly investments in infrastructure (human capital and technology) and (2) change business processes, and accept changes to market practices, that in the past have generated sizeable revenues but at the cost of weakening the underlying foundation of the markets. Costly as these reforms will be, those costs will be minuscule compared to the hundreds of billions of dollars of write downs experienced by financial institutions in recent months to say nothing of the economic dislocations and distortions triggered by the crisis.

In an effort to ensure implementation of these enhancements, the Policy Group strongly urges that all major financial institutions should analyze their internal policies, procedures and practices against the recommendations and reforms outlined in this Report. Senior management at these institutions should ensure ongoing monitoring of progress in relation to these reforms.

In closing, we wish to express our gratitude to the Policy Group members and their respective Working Groups for their extraordinary contributions to this Report. We also want to acknowledge that in our work, we have benefited enormously from the earlier efforts of the President's Working Group on Financial Markets and the Financial Stability Forum.

Sincerely,

E. Gerald Comgan
Douglas J. Flint

EXHIBIT I

CRMPG III

Co-chairmen

E. Gerald Corrigan
Managing Director
Office of the Chairman
Goldman, Sachs & Co.

Douglas J. Flint
Group Finance Director
Deputy Head of Global Markets
HSBC Holdings plc

Policy Group Members

Madelyn Antoncic
Managing Director
Global Head of Financial Market Policy Relations
Lehman Brothers

Craig W. Broderick
Managing Director
Chief Risk Officer
Goldman, Sachs & Co.

Ken deRegt
Managing Director
Chief Risk Officer
Morgan Stanley

Andrew Feldstein
Chief Executive Officer
Chief Investment Officer
Blue Mountain Capital Management

Peter Fisher
Managing Director
Co-head of Fixed Income BlackRock, Inc.

Adam Gilbert
Managing Director
JPMorgan Chase & Co.

Christian Lajoie
Head of Group Supervision Issues BNP Paribas

Gary G. Lynch
Executive Vice President Chief Legal Officer
Morgan Stanley

J. Chandler Martin
Executive Vice President Bank of America

Edmond Moriarty Senior Vice President
Co-Chief Risk Officer
Merrill Lynch & Co.

Gavin G. O'Connor
Managing Director
Goldman, Sachs & Co.

Edward J. Rosen, Esq.
Partner
Cleary Gottlieb Steen & Hamilton LLP

Zion Shohet
Treasurer
Head of Corporate Finance
Citigroup

Barry L. Zubrow

Chief Risk Officer
JPMorgan Chase & Co.

Project Secretariat

Darren Littlejohn
Goldman, Sachs & Co.

Manar Zaher
Goldman, Sachs & Co.

Ranbir Hira
Cleary Gottlieb Steen & Hamilton LLP

Jennifer Philbrick
Cleary Gottlieb Steen & Hamilton LLP

EXHIBIT II

Working Groups

I. Standards for Accounting Consolidation

Co-Chairmen

Gary G. Lynch
Executive Vice President
Chief Legal Officer
Morgan Stanley

Gavin G. O'Connor
Managing Director
Goldman, Sachs & Co.

Members

John M. James
Senior Vice President and Corporate Controller
Bank of America

Russell C. Picot
Group Chief Accounting Officer HSBC Holdings plc

Matthew L. Schroeder
Managing Director and Global Head of Accounting
Policy

Goldman, Sachs & Co.

II. High-Risk Complex Financial Instruments

Co-Chairmen

Ken deRegt
Managing Director
Chief Risk Officer
Morgan Stanley

Edmond Moriarty
Senior Vice President
Co-Chief Risk Officer
Merrill Lynch & Co.

Members

Neil Cotty
Chief Accounting Officer
Bank of America

Christian Lajoie
Head of Group Supervision Issues
BNP Paribas

Stephen O'Connor
Managing Director
Head of Counterparty Portfolio
Morgan Stanley

Bruce Petersen
Managing Director
Goldman, Sachs & Co.

Frank Roncey
Head of Risk
Management – Americas
BNP Paribas – NY

Marc Saidenberg
Managing Director
Merrill Lynch & Co.

III. Risk Monitoring and Risk Management

Co-Chairmen

Craig W. Broderick
Managing Director
Chief Risk Officer
Goldman, Sachs & Co.

J. Chandler Martin
Executive Vice President
Bank of America

Zion Shohet
Treasurer
Head of Corporate Finance Citigroup

Members

Michael Alix
Former Member of CRMPG I and II

Madelyn Antoncic
Managing Director
Global Head of Financial Market Policy Relations Lehman Brothers

Liz Beshel
Managing Director
Treasurer
Goldman, Sachs & Co.

Douglas J. Flint
Group Finance Director
Deputy Head of Global Markets HSBC Holdings plc

Christian Lajoie
Head of Group Supervision Issues BNP Paribas

Michael Liberman
Blue Mountain Capital Management

Arrington Mixon
Enterprise Credit Risk Executive Bank of America

Ken Winston

Managing Director Morgan Stanley

IV. Enhanced Credit Market Resiliency

Co-Chairmen

Andrew Feldstein
Chief Executive Officer
Chief Investment Officer
Blue Mountain Capital Management

Peter Fisher
Managing Director
Co-head of Fixed Income BlackRock, Inc.

Barry L. Zubrow
Chief Risk Officer
JPMorgan Chase & Co.

Members

Peter Axilrod
Managing Director
DTCC

Thomas J. Benison
Managing Director
JPMorgan Chase & Co.

Samuel Cole
Chief Operating Officer
Blue Mountain Capital Management

Athanassios Diplas
Managing Director
Deutsche Bank

Adam Gilbert
Managing Director
JPMorgan Chase & Co.

David Inggs
Managing Director
Goldman, Sachs & Co.

Stephen O'Connor
Managing Director
Morgan Stanley

Robert Pickel
Chief Executive Officer
ISDA

Robin Perlen
Managing Director
Bank of America

Don Thompson
Managing Director
JPMorgan Chase & Co.

Doug Warren
Head of US Credit Trading
Managing Director
Barclays Capital

David Weisbrod
Managing Director
JPMorgan Chase & Co.

SECTION I

Introduction

On April 8, 2008 E. Gerald Corrigan, Managing Director, Goldman Sachs, and Douglas Flint, Group Finance Director, HSBC Holdings Plc, announced the formation of the Counterparty Risk Management Policy Group III *(CRMPG III* or the *Policy Group).* This initiative, triggered in part by the guidance of the President's Working Group on Financial Markets, was undertaken in order to provide a private sector response to the credit market crisis of 2007 and 2008 in a manner that complements the published work of a number of official bodies, including the President's Working Group on Financial Markets, the Senior Supervisors Group and the Financial Stability Forum, as well as the efforts of the private-sector based Institute for International Finance.

The scope of the CRMPG III initiative was designed to focus its primary attention on the steps that must be taken by the private sector to reduce the frequency and/or severity of future financial shocks while recognizing that such future shocks are inevitable, in part because it is literally impossible to anticipate the specific timing and triggers of such events.

The CRMPG III effort has focused its attention on four closely related and forward-looking aspects of financial reform and rehabilitation, including: (1) a reconsideration of the standards for consolidation under US GAAP that contemplates a significant shift of currently off-balance sheet entities to on-balance sheet status; (2) measures to better understand and manage complex financial instruments with particular emphasis on their distribution and how their risk sensitivities are disclosed; (3) risk monitoring and risk management with particular emphasis on the role of sound corporate governance and the relationship between liquidity, leverage and capital adequacy; and (4) a series of sweeping measures to enhance the resiliency of credit markets in particular and financial markets more generally with particular attention to strengthening the safeguards associated with the OTC derivatives markets with emphasis on credit default swaps (CDS). Among other things, this section of the Report urges swift industry action to create a clearinghouse for OTC derivatives, starting with CDS.

The Policy Group chose to focus on these four areas in the belief that these are the ones in which it could add the greatest value. In making that judgment, the Policy Group was

mindful that there are other vital areas of inquiry that will not be covered in this Report. Examples of such areas include the need to improve the loan origination and oversight process and the equally obvious need to improve the working of the credit ratings process. In these and other areas, the Policy Group concluded that ample attention is being devoted to these issues by others who are well positioned to identify and implement needed reforms.

The background to this effort is, of course, the chain of events that is now properly labeled the credit market crisis of 2007 and 2008. In retrospect, these events clearly stand out as the most severe financial shock we have witnessed in decades with visible damage not only to the financial sector but extending to the real economy as well. Indeed, the cost of the credit market crisis in economic, financial and human terms has already reached staggering proportions and, even after 12 months, substantial vulnerabilities remain.

The write-downs experienced by large integrated financial intermediaries – especially in the United States and Europe – are also of staggering proportions. It is probably fair to say that, as late as the summer of 2007, virtually none of us would have imagined that, as of July of 2008, financial sector write-offs and loss provisions would approach $500 billion, even as the write-off meter is still running. Fortunately, the starting capital positions of the affected institutions were relatively strong and, even more fortunately, most of these institutions have been able to raise very large amounts of additional capital in recent months.

Even with the benefit of hindsight, there exists a large and troubling question as to the manner in which events unfolded beginning in the July to August interval of 2007. Namely, why were so many, in both the official and private sectors, so slow in recognizing that we were on the cusp of a financial crisis of the magnitude we have experienced? The list of possible explanations is long. For example, it could be that the underlying complexity and risk characteristics of certain financial instruments were so opaque that even some of the most sophisticated financial institutions in the world and their supervisors were simply caught off guard. A much more plausible explanation lies in the fact that the preceding eight to ten years had witnessed multiple financial disturbances with multiple causes – all of which resolved themselves with limited damage and negligible contagion. These experiences undoubtedly gave rise to a false sense of security that the emerging problems of the summer of 2007 would also resolve themselves with little or no systemic damage.

Much has been written and said about the underlying causes of this systematic failure in financial discipline. For that reason, the Policy Group does not wish to repeat that litany in any detail, but it does see some value in briefly highlighting what it considers the most critical of these underlying causes of the credit market crisis:

First: for several years running, global financial markets had been awash with liquidity. This condition reflected in part the recycling of (1) excess savings from Asia in general and China in particular and (2) excess cash from energy producing countries. It may also have reflected the phenomenon of an extended earlier period of very low interest rates, especially in the United States. These factors are also related to global economic and financial macroeconomic imbalances that have long been recognized as potential sources of instability.

There can be no doubt that ample financial market liquidity and relatively low interest rates were an important driving force behind the pervasive "reach for yield" phenomenon of recent years and that the "reach for yield" phenomenon was, in turn, an important factor in driving the surge in demand for and supply of highly complex structured credit products.

Second: reflecting in part the forces discussed above and the intensity of competitive factors in the financial marketplace, it is clear that credit risk had been mispriced for some time. The evidence of this is clear in the terms and conditions of credit extensions in the subprime mortgage market, in the leveraged finance sector, and in the willingness of market participants to acquire highly leveraged structured credit products whose attractiveness relied on a continuation of benign credit conditions for an extended period of time. More generally, the extraordinary tightness of credit spreads across virtually all classes of credit products was widely seen as unsustainable. In these circumstances, it was recognized that, sooner or later, credit spreads and credit terms would inevitably adjust. However, it was all too easy for many, if not most, market participants to conclude that when the correction took place it would be gradual and orderly. Obviously, that conclusion was wrong.

Third: for a variety of reasons – some structural, some technological and some behavioral – contemporary finance has become incredibly complex. We see this in the speed and complexity of capital flows, we see it in the complexity of many classes of financial instruments (some of which contain significant embedded leverage), and we see it in the extraordinary complexity faced by individual financial institutions in their day-to-day risk management activities and in their policies and practices related to valuation and price verification for some classes of financial instruments. Needless to say, the complexity factor is an issue as it pertains to the capacity of the international community of supervisors and regulators to discharge their responsibilities.

The key issue here is not complexity *per se* but rather the extent to which complexity feeds on itself thereby helping to create or magnify contagion risk "hot spots" that may have systematic implications. Thus, we are faced with the pressing need to find better ways to manage and mitigate the risk associated with complexity, a subject that will continue to challenge the best and the brightest among us.

Fourth: reflecting in part the forces described above, the current crisis has witnessed patterns of contagion the speed and reach of which are different in degree, if not kind, from that which we have witnessed in earlier periods of financial instability. The list is long: asset-backed commercial paper, conduits, structured investment vehicles (S IVs), collateralized debt obligations *(CDOs),* quantitative funds, auction rate securities, monolines, and hedge funds. To a considerable extent, the "hot spots" where contagion forces have emerged share at least three common denominators: (1) the contraction in market liquidity, which has been largely driven by a huge shift from risk taking to risk aversion, was itself driven by the fear of the unknown and a limited ability to anticipate with confidence the sensitivity to loss in many financial instruments; (2) greater leverage in balance sheet terms and in the use of off-balance sheet vehicles and the presence of embedded leverage in certain classes of financial instruments; and (3) risk mitigation cushions which were either too thin or were at least partially neutralized by basis risk developments.

Fifth: it is likely that flaws in the design and workings of the systems of incentives within the financial sector have inadvertently produced patterns of behavior and allocations of resources that are not always consistent with the basic goal of financial stability. Often, when the issue of incentives is discussed, the focus is on compensation and, especially, executive compensation. Consistent with the priorities of this Report noted earlier, the Policy Group has chosen not go into the subject of executive compensation in any detail. Having said that, the Policy Group recognizes that more can be done to ensure that incentives associated with compensation are better aligned with risk taking and risk tolerance across broad classes of senior and executive management. Accordingly, and respecting the role and responsibilities of the board of directors in matters relating to executive compensation, the Policy Group believes that compensation practices as they apply to senior and executive management should be (1) based heavily on the performance of the firm as a whole and (2) heavily stock-based with such stock- based compensation vesting over an extended period of time. The long vesting period is particularly important for high risk, high volatility lines of business where short run surges in revenues and profits can be offset if not reversed in the longer term. In broad terms, the Policy Group recognizes that this philosophy of compensation is hardly new, but its importance looms especially large given the events of the past twelve months.

While the linkage between incentives and compensation is obvious for large integrated financial intermediaries, the incentive question has much broader – and no less important – implications. For example, the framework of incentives at the level of individual firms should help to balance business imperatives by ensuring that the resource base and the recognition/reward system for the support and control functions are such that critical tasks, such as risk monitoring and price verification, are performed in a manner that protects the financial integrity and professional reputation of the institution.

While the Policy Group believes that the five factors citied above were the primary underlying forces driving the credit market crisis, there were, of course, many contributing factors. Some observers cite that what they see as the unintended consequences of applying fair value accounting as a contributing factor, particularly as it applies to complex financial instruments that, in periods of stress, tend to be relatively illiquid and difficult to value reliably. Others see fair value accounting as a powerful source of discipline on the risk-taking process. As discussed later, in the "Emerging Issues" section of this Report, there are many facets of the fair value question, not the least of which is framing an alternative to fair value which does not further undermine the already damaged credibility of the financial sector.

Alongside the fair value question, there is an even larger question that the events of the past twelve months have raised. Namely, have changes in the workings of the financial system, such as the ability to "short credit" or the greater importance of the "originate to distribute" model of financial intermediation, made the financial system more accident prone or unstable? This is not an academic question particularly since the period from 1980 has witnessed four or five serious financial shocks that resulted in some form of extraordinary official intervention.

In looking at the post-1980 period (and in looking at the broad sweep of financial history), it is difficult to conclude that the cause of systemic financial shocks can be attributed to particular financial instruments (*e.g.*, the credit default swap) or particular classes of activity (*e.g.*, securitization), even if it can be argued that such factors may have amplified the credit market crisis. Indeed, one of the most striking observations about financial shocks is the fact that each episode tends to have its own unique triggers and dynamics. While the triggers and dynamics are unique, there is evidence of certain common denominators across all the post-1980 financial crises. There are at least four common denominators, with one possible “wild card” looming in the background: (1) credit concentrations, (2) broad-based maturity mismatches, (3) excessive leverage, and (4) the illusion of market liquidity – or the belief that such liquidity will always be present so that the individual instruments or classes of instruments can be bought or sold in an environment of narrow bid-ask spreads. The wild card is periodic macroeconomic imbalances, including such forces as inflation, recession, budget deficits, and large external imbalances. Directly or indirectly, such macroeconomic forces have played a role in contributing to the ebbs and flows of opinion and expectations regarding the outlook for financial market behavior, thus contributing to the tendency for financial markets to overshoot in both directions.

At the end of the day, however, the root cause of financial market excesses on both the upside and the downside of the cycle is collective human behavior: unbridled optimism on the upside and fear on the downside, all in a setting in which it is literally impossible to anticipate when optimism gives rise to fear or fear gives rise to optimism.

The fact that financial excesses fundamentally grow out of human behavior is a sobering reality, especially in an environment of intense competition between large integrated financial intermediaries which, on the upside of the cycle, fosters risk taking and on the downside, fosters risk aversion. It is this sobering reality that has, for centuries, given rise to universal recognition that finance and financial institutions must be subject to a higher degree of official oversight and regulation than is deemed necessary for virtually all other forms of commercial enterprise. However, official oversight is not a substitute for the effective management of financial institutions, which is, and should remain, a private- sector function. Yet here too there is a dilemma; namely, in a competitive marketplace it is very difficult for one or a few institutions to hold the line on best practices, much less for one or a few institutions to stand on the sidelines in the face of booming markets.

What is needed, therefore, is a form of private initiative that will complement official oversight in encouraging industry-wide practices that will help mitigate systemic risk. The recommendations in this Report have been framed with that objective in mind. However, the Policy Group believes there is considerable merit to overlaying these detailed recommendations with five “core precepts” of behavior that all large integrated financial intermediaries should follow in the interest of helping to contain systemic risk factors and promote greater stability.

Mitigating Systemic Risk: Core Precepts for Large Integrated Financial Intermediaries

The complexities of the control and risk management tasks facing large integrated financial intermediaries are extremely difficult to appreciate and understand even for highly sophisticated observers. Indeed, recent experience suggests that senior management of such institutions may not always fully grasp the scale and complexity of these control and risk management challenges. In these circumstances, it is not at all surprising that recent weeks and months have witnessed the publication of thousands of pages of text flowing from dozens of individuals and organizations all devoted to the credit market crisis in general and more specifically to explaining what happened, why it happened and what steps can be taken in the future to reduce the incidence of systemic financial shocks or at least limit or contain the damage associated with such events when they occur.

While there are many good ideas about the future that are now on the table for discussion, the Policy Group is strongly of the view that the focus on the complexity of the subject matter tends to blur the fact that in this world of financial complexity there are certain relatively simple, readily understandable, and forward-looking core precepts upon which the management and supervision of large integrated financial intermediaries must rest. These precepts are relatively easy to communicate to employees, to boards of directors, to investors and to supervisors. Moreover, they lend themselves to relatively straightforward evaluation exercises on the part of boards of directors and supervisory bodies. These precepts are in no way a substitute for the front-line "blocking and tackling" imperatives that are at the center of all control and risk management systems. If anything, they provide the intellectual and policy framework which helps to ensure that the working level, control-related policies and procedures are both robust and flexible over business and credit cycles.

While the Policy Group has developed these core precepts with an eye to their application to large integrated financial intermediaries, systemic risk concerns may arise from institutions that may not seem to fit this description. Thus, while the Policy Group's emphasis is on large integrated financial intermediaries, these core precepts have broader applications.

At the risk of considerable oversimplification and with the recommendations contained in the balance of this Report in mind, the Policy Group believes that these core precepts can be reduced to five categories as discussed below.

Precept I: The Basics of Corporate Governance

Corporate governance is a subject that is often taken largely for granted. However, as described in the March 6, 2008 Report of the Senior Supervisors Group, the culture of corporate governance at individual financial institutions can have a very large bearing on how well or how poorly individual institutions respond to periods of large-scale instability if not outright crisis. For example, risk monitoring and risk management cannot be left to quantitative risk metrics, which by their nature are backward looking. Rather, and particularly in times of stress, risk management must rely heavily on judgment, communication and coordination, spanning the organization and reaching to the highest levels of management. Among other things, this culture of governance will help to break down the silo mentality that can all too easily be associated with individual business units. More broadly, this culture of governance can go a long way to help ensure that critical information on risk profiles, institution-wide exposure and potential channels of contagion are matters of rigorous and continuous attention, not only at the level of risk managers, but also at the highest levels of management.

Of equal importance, the culture of corporate governance must ensure that critical control personnel in such areas as risk monitoring, credit, operations, internal audit, compliance and controllers (with special emphasis on the professionals responsible for position valuations and price verification) are truly independent from front-line business unit personnel, not only in a reporting context but also in a decision-making context. Similarly, corporate governance must ensure that support and control functions have the status and the resources to appropriately sustain the control environment across all risk- taking business units. As an extension of this principle, large integrated financial intermediaries should aggressively seek out opportunities to rotate high-potential individuals between income-producing functions and support/control functions. Finally, the culture of corporate governance must also ensure that incentives – including, but by no means limited to, compensation – are properly aligned so as to foster commercial success over time and discourage short-run excesses in risk taking.

There is no single blueprint for achieving a sound framework of corporate governance, much less a common organizational framework to ensure that result. Many variables – ranging from the business model to the leadership style of top management – enter into the equation for success. However, at the end of the day, corporate governance reduces to behavior and incentives, not the vagaries of organizational charts. Accordingly, the Policy Group recommends that, *from time to time, all large integrated financial intermediaries must examine their framework of corporate governance in order to ensure that it is fostering the incentives that will properly balance commercial success and disciplined behavior over the cycle while ensuring the true decision-making independence of key control personnel from business unit personnel.*

Precept II: The Basics of Risk Monitoring

The most sophisticated risk management models and metrics are only as good as the ability of individual institutions to monitor all positions and risk exposures on a timely basis. For example, large integrated financial intermediaries should have in place the systems to compile, within a matter of hours, estimates of comprehensive counterparty exposure information on a given day based on the prior day's close of business. Timely access to such information helps to ensure that risk metrics are providing the proper signals, but of greater importance, such timely information facilitates meaningful insights into concentrated positions and crowded trades. Such insights help to make better and more informed judgments about contagion and systemic threats and how to better manage counterparty risk in times of stress when models and metrics are most prone to providing false signals. Accordingly, the Policy Group recommends that *all large integrated financial intermediaries must have, or be developing, the capacity (1) to monitor risk concentrations to asset classes as well as estimated exposures, both gross and net, to all institutional counterparties in a matter of hours and (2) to provide effective and coherent reports to senior management regarding such exposures to high-risk counterparties.*

Precept III: The Basics of Estimating Risk Appetite

Estimating risk appetite and finding an adequate risk-reward balance must be a dynamic process that is built on a blend of *qualitative and quantitative factors.* Because judgments about risk appetite and risk-reward must take account of both quantitative and qualitative factors, the determination of risk appetite and risk- reward at a given point in time cannot be estimated by reliance on even a family of highly sophisticated stress tests.

Stress tests and other quantitative tools are necessary, but by no means sufficient, tools for making judgments about risk appetite. In point of fact, stress tests, when combined with carefully constructed scenario analyses, can be helpful, but even under the best of circumstances, stress tests can never anticipate how future events will unfold unless such tests are so extreme as to postulate outcomes that no level of capital or liquidity will provide protections against potential failure. Finally, because risk appetite must also take account of inherently judgmental factors such as compensation systems and the quality of the control environment, excessive reliance on quantitative tools may produce results that lack credibility with top management and boards of directors and are insufficient, if not misleading, as a basis for prudential supervision.

In other words, estimating acceptable thresholds of risk appetite is more an art than a science. Of necessity, the process must rely on multiple classes of quantitative inputs, including a family of scenario analyses and stress tests. At best, however, the quantitative inputs can provide insights into a range of potential loss estimates that help to guide judgments about risk appetite. The more difficult task for senior management, boards of directors and prudential supervisors is how to build into the risk appetite exercise the necessary judgments as to factors such as incentives, the quality of the control environment, the point in the business cycle and other qualitative inputs that should temper the quantitative factors either to a higher or lower appetite for risk. Accordingly, the Policy Group recommends that *all large integrated financial intermediaries must periodically conduct comprehensive exercises aimed at estimating risk appetite. The results of such exercises should be shared with the highest level of management, the board of directors and the institution's primary supervisor.*

Precept IV: Focusing on Contagion

Contagion or the channels and linkages through which local financial disturbances can take on systemic characteristics are by their nature largely unpredictable. However, the basic forces that give rise to contagion are reasonably well known and recognized. That is, in looking at the long history of financial crises, several common denominators are evident, even if the precise triggers that unleash these contagion forces tend to be unique to each individual financial shock. As noted earlier, those common denominators almost always involve most, if not all, of the following: (1) credit concentrations; (2) broad-based maturity mismatches; (3) excessive leverage either in balance sheet terms or in the form of leverage that is embedded in individual classes of financial instruments; and (4) the illusion of market liquidity or the belief that such liquidity will always be present such that individual instruments or classes of instruments can readily be bought or sold in an environment of narrow bid-ask spreads.

While we are unable to anticipate the precise triggers that will unleash contagion forces in future crises, we should be able to do a much better job of building into risk management frameworks ongoing analysis and brainstorming about contagion risks, especially on the upside of the cycle when slippages in financial discipline typically take hold. Clearly, the last twelve months or so have put the spotlight on certain practices that, with the benefit of hindsight, bring into sharp focus the role that the common denominators of contagion played in the credit market crisis.

Looking to the future, the Policy Group recommends that *all large integrated financial intermediaries must engage in a periodic process of systemic "brainstorming" aimed at identifying potential contagion "hot spots" and analyzing how such "hot spots" might play out in the future.* The point of the exercise, of course, is that even if the "hot spots" do not materialize or even if unanticipated "hot spots" do materialize, the insights gained in the brainstorming exercise will be of considerable value in managing future sources of contagion risk.

Precept V: Enhanced Oversight

Large integrated financial intermediaries are subject to oversight by their boards of directors and by official supervisory bodies. While the nature of the oversight functions of boards and supervisors are quite different, the discharge of their respective responsibilities are complementary since both groups share the common goal of seeking to ensure the commercial viability and stability of large integrated financial intermediaries.

The primary responsibility of boards of directors of any public company is to act on behalf of the shareholders. A board must provide an appropriate degree of oversight of the company consistent with the goal of maximizing shareholder value over time. The exercise of these oversight responsibilities in today's business environment is a demanding and time-consuming process, especially for boards of large integrated financial intermediaries. Aside from their oversight duties, boards have certain explicit responsibilities including the authority to hire or to fire the CEO and other executive officers and to approve compensation arrangements for such executive officers. As a part of their responsibility for determining compensation arrangements, boards also need to ensure that compensation- related incentives are properly aligned with the best long-term interests of the company and its shareholders.

The challenges facing directors of large integrated financial intermediaries are formidable since there are limits as to the extent to which outside independent directors can be expected to fully grasp all of the risks associated with the day-to- day activities of such institutions. What they can do, and what management can help them do, is to ask the right questions and insist that they have the information – properly presented – that allows them to exercise their oversight responsibilities.

Prudential supervisors also have oversight responsibilities for financial institutions. However, the authority vested in most supervisory authorities is very broad in that they may prescribe very specific standards of behavior. In addition, in extreme conditions, supervisory authorities typically have the power to, in effect, replace

management, require institutions to raise capital, sell assets or take virtually any necessary steps to preserve the viability of such individual institutions.

As noted above, the oversight roles of boards of directors and supervisors are, in many respects, complementary. That being said, the Policy Group believes that there is a relatively simple way to reinforce the effectiveness of these oversight responsibilities. *Specifically, the Policy Group recommends arrangements whereby the highest-level officials from primary supervisory bodies should meet at least annually with the boards of directors of large integrated financial intermediaries. The purpose of the meeting would be for the supervisory authorities to share with the board of directors and the highest levels of management their views of the condition of the institution with emphasis on high- level commentary bearing on the underlying stability of the institution and its capacity to absorb periods of adversity.* The details of examination and inspection reports should not be discussed except to the extent that such reports relate in a material way to underlying stability issues. Obviously, this format would help to stimulate an exchange of views between the supervisors and the boards, which in turn should help each to better discharge their respective oversight duties. If these arrangements – which already exist in some jurisdictions – are to achieve their objective, it is essential that the spokesperson from the supervisory body be a true policy level executive or, preferably, a principal of the supervisory body. Finally, these high level exchanges of views should minimize the use of quantitative metrics and maximize the use of discussion and informed judgment.

These general recommendations may have to be adapted to the legal and cultural context of the nations and jurisdictions where they apply. Notably, the precise role of the board of directors, on the one hand, and supervisory bodies, on the other, differs somewhat according to country laws and by jurisdiction. The main variation relates to the management responsibility that is borne exclusively by the executive management in countries where the board of directors is a pure oversight body. In such jurisdictions, it may be more appropriate for the supervisory authorities to communicate their conclusions to the full supervisory board through a written assessment and to meet, along with executive management, with the committee of the board best equipped to participate knowledgeably in a discussion of the underlying stability of the institution.

Summary

The core precepts and the recommendations contained in the following sections of this Report are a "package deal". That is, success in achieving any one of the core precepts and recommendations is dependent on achieving success in the others. Moreover, partly because of competitive realities and partly because of practical realities, no one institution can, by itself, accomplish all that needs to be done in restoring the credibility of the industry, much less provide some reasonable assurance that we can better limit or contain the damage associated with future financial shocks.

What is needed to achieve that result, therefore, are collective and concerted industrywide initiatives supported by progressive and enlightened prudential supervision conducted in the spirit of the March 6, 2008 Report of the Senior Supervisors Group. In the private sector, greater financial discipline at individual institutions must be reinforced by a renewed commitment to collective discipline in the spirit of "financial statesmanship" that recognizes that there are circumstances in which individual institutions must be prepared to put aside specific institutional interests in the name of the common good.

The reforms contemplated by this Report (and other similar reports) will not be easy, and they surely will not be inexpensive to implement, especially in the current environment with its extraordinary pressures on the bottom line. However, costly as these reforms will be, those costs will be minuscule compared to the hundreds of billions of dollars in writedowns experienced by financial institutions in recent months, to say nothing of the economic dislocations and distortions triggered by the credit market crisis.

All of this requires leadership which starts with the highest levels of management. There will be occasions when such leaders must be prepared to instruct their subordinates to find "ways to get things done" rather than finding ways to stifle needed change and reform. Nowhere, perhaps, is this imperative more essential than it is regarding the material covered in Section V of this Report regarding financial infrastructure and the need to enhance market resilience.

Finally, financial institutions and their supervisors must avoid the mistakes that were made following the publication of CRMPG II almost three years ago to the day. In some areas, the follow-up and implementation of recommendations in CRMPG II were good. In other areas, the follow-up by individual firms and their supervisors was poor and certainly was not sustained. In some of the areas covered by this Report (notably the material in Section V on Enhanced Credit Market Resiliency), there is a built-in framework for follow-up in the form of ongoing coordination and cooperation between the dealer community, on the one hand, and the Federal Reserve Bank of New York and other official groups, on the other hand.

In an effort to ensure implementation of these enhancements, the Policy Group strongly urges that all major financial institutions should analyze their internal policies, procedures and practices against the recommendations and reforms outlined in this Report. Senior management at these institutions should ensure ongoing monitoring of progress in relation to these reforms.

Executive Summary

This Executive Summary contains a series of excerpts from different parts of this Report, including (1) the five core precepts for mitigating systemic risk discussed in Section I, (2) the specific recommendations of the Policy Group contained in Sections II through V and (3) some highlights of the emerging issues discussion in Section VI of this Report.

With regard to implementation of the core precepts and recommendations, the Policy Group expects that substantial progress will be made over the balance of 2008. However, in some instances, especially the recommendations in Section V relating to Enhanced Credit Market Resiliency, the implementation timetable will stretch out through 2009.

Part I: Mitigating Systemic Risk: Core Precepts for Large Integrated Financial Intermediaries

Precept I: The Basics of Corporate Governance

The Policy Group recommends that, from time-to-time, all large integrated financial intermediaries must examine their framework of corporate governance in order to ensure that it is fostering the incentives that will properly balance commercial success and disciplined behavior over the cycle while ensuring the true decision making independence of key control personnel from business unit personnel.

Precept II: The Basics of Risk Monitoring

The Policy Group recommends that all large integrated financial intermediaries must have, or be developing, the capacity (1) to monitor risk concentrations to asset classes as well as estimated exposures, both gross and net, to all counterparties in a matter of hours and (2) to provide effective and coherent reports to institutional senior management regarding such exposures to high-risk counterparties.

Precept III: The Basics of Estimating Risk Appetite

The Policy Group recommends that all large integrated financial intermediaries must periodically conduct comprehensive exercises aimed at estimating risk appetite. The results of such exercises should be shared with the highest level of management, the board of directors and the institution's primary supervisor.

Precept IV: Focusing on Contagion

Looking to the future, the Policy Group recommends that all large integrated financial intermediaries must engage in a periodic process of systemic "brainstorming" aimed at identifying potential contagion "hot spots" and analyzing how such "hot spots" might play out in the future. The point of the exercise, of course, is that even if the "hot spots" do not materialize or even if unanticipated "hot spots" do materialize, the insights gained in the brainstorming exercise will be of considerable value in managing future sources of contagion risk.

Precept V: Enhanced Oversight

The Policy Group recommends arrangements whereby the highest level officials from primary supervisory bodies should meet at least annually with the boards of directors of large integrated financial intermediaries. The purpose of the meeting would be for the supervisory authorities to share with the board of directors and the highest levels of management their views of the condition of the institution with emphasis on high-level commentary bearing on the underlying stability of the institution and its capacity to absorb periods of adversity. This recommendation may have to be adapted to accommodate local legal and cultural considerations.

Part II: Recommendations

Section II: Standards for Accounting Consolidation

II-1. The Policy Group *endorses,* in principle, the direction of the changes to the US GAAP consolidation rules provided that the changes are (1) principles-based, (2) convergent with International Financial Reporting Standards, and (3) accompanied by suitable disclosure and transition rules regarding regulatory capital which will provide flexibility in the implementation of these rules over a reasonable period of time.

II-2. The Policy Group *recommends* adoption of a single, principles-based global consolidation framework that is based on control and the ability to benefit from that control. The analysis of whether an entity (the investor) has a controlling interest in another entity (the investee) should be based on:

- the investor's power over the investee, including the ability to make decisions that determine the success of the investee;
- the degree of investor exposure to the risks and rewards of the investee, including through guarantees, commitments and all other explicit and implicit arrangements between the two entities; and
- the design and sponsorship of the investee, including the degree to which the activities of the investee expose the investor to commercial, legal, regulatory and reputational risks.

II-3. The Policy Group further *recommends* that the new consolidation framework require a reassessment of the consolidation analysis each reporting period based on changes in the control indicators specified in the preceding recommendation.

II-4. The Policy Group *encourages* standard setters and industry participants to work together toward achieving the goals discussed in this section on a global basis as soon as possible.

II-5. The Policy Group *recommends* that standard setters and industry participants consider a holistic and principles-based approach to disclosure of off-balance sheet activities similar to that found in international standards. The disclosure framework should be fully integrated with enterprise-wide disclosures across the full spectrum of risks: market, credit, liquidity, capital, operational, and reputational.

Enterprise-wide disclosure should be supplemented with detailed information that links to enterprise-wide disclosures and that changes in response to changing risks and uncertainties; for example, in the current environment, disclosures about residential and commercial real estate and leveraged loan exposures.

II-6. The Policy Group *recommends* that firms provide tabular disclosures about the effects of restrictions on the use of consolidated assets, non-recourse liabilities, and minority interests.

Section III: High-Risk Complex Instruments

The Policy Group *strongly recommends* that high-risk complex financial instruments should be sold only to sophisticated investors.

III-1. The Policy Group *recommends* establishing standards of sophistication for all market participants in high-risk complex financial instruments. In recommending specific characteristics and practices for participants, it is guided by the overriding principle that all participants should be capable of assessing and managing the risk of their positions in a manner consistent with their needs and objectives. All participants in the market for high-risk complex financial instruments should ensure that they possess the following characteristics and make reasonable efforts to determine that their counterparties possess them as well:

- the capability to understand the risk and return characteristics of the specific type of financial instrument under consideration;
- the capability, or access to the capability, to price and run stress tests on the instrument;
- the governance procedures, technology, and internal controls necessary for trading and managing the risk of the instrument;
- the financial resources sufficient to withstand potential losses associated with the instrument; and authorization to invest in high-risk complex financial instruments from the highest level of management or, where relevant, from authorizing bodies for the particular counterparty.

Large integrated financial intermediaries should adopt policies and procedures to identify when it would be appropriate to seek written confirmation that the cou nterparty possesses the aforementioned characteristics.

The Policy Group believes that there are opportunities to enhance and strengthen the documentation and disclosures provided to prospective investors in high-risk complex financial instruments, while being mindful that documentation and disclosure practices will (and should) vary somewhat from instrument to instrument and will also vary over time. With that qualification in mind, the Policy Group *recommends* the following as a matter of industry best practice.

III-2a. The documentation of all high-risk complex financial instruments in cash or derivative form should include a term sheet: a concise summary highlighting deal terms and, where appropriate, collateral manager capabilities, and portfolio and deal payment structure. The term sheets for all high-risk complex financial instruments, the full scope of which is outlined in Appendix A, must, among other factors, include the following:

- a clear explanation of the economics of the instrument including a discussion of the key assumptions that give rise to the expected returns; and
- rigorous scenario analyses and stress tests that prominently illustrate how the instrument will perform in extreme scenarios, in addition to more probable scenarios.

III-2b. The documentation associated with *asset-backed high-risk complex financial instruments* should include:

- *A Preliminary and Final Offering Memorandum:* The offering memorandum should include prominently within its first several pages the nature of the economic interest of the underwriter or placement agent (and its affiliates) in the transaction, including a clear statement of the roles to be undertaken and services to be provided by the underwriter or placement agent (or its affiliates) to the transaction, as well as any interests in the transaction (if any) that the underwriter or placement agent (or its affiliates) are required or expected to retain.
- *A Marketing Book:* The marketing book should include an in-depth description of the materials contained in the term sheet. It should especially focus on the collateral manager (in the case of a managed portfolio) and deal structure.
- *Portfolio Stratifications:* This documentation should be in the form of spreadsheets containing bond level information (sector, rating, par balance, etc.), where known, and weighted average loan level information (FICO, service, LTV, % fixed, occupancy, geographic distribution, 2nd liens, *etc.*).
- *Cash Flow/Stress Scenarios:* This documentation should be in the form of spreadsheets and cash flow model outputs. Standard runs should be provided for each tranche offered. The output will typically be in the form of tranche cash flows and default/loss percentages for the tranches and collateral.

III-2c. In addition to the documentation standards covered above, the Policy Group further *recommends* that term sheets and offering memoranda for all financial instruments having one or more of the key characteristics associated with high-risk complex financial instruments as discussed on pages 54, 56 *must have* a "financial health" warning prominently displayed in bold print indicating that the presence of these characteristics gives rise to the *potential* for significant loss over the life of the instrument. The "health warning" should also refer to all risk factors in the offering documents.

The Policy Group further *recommends* that complex bilateral transactions that are privately negotiated between sophisticated market participants are not subject to Recommendations IV-2b and 2c but are subject to Recommendation IV-2a regarding terms sheets. In certain circumstances, however, and by mutual written consent, the term sheet requirement may be waived for bilateral transactions between highly sophisticated market participants or in the context of a repeated pattern of transactions of a particular type.

The Policy Group *recommends* strengthening the relationship between intermediaries and counterparties in sales, marketing, and ongoing communications associated with high-risk complex financial instruments. While its first recommendation calls for establishment of a common standard of sophistication for all market participants in high-risk complex financial instruments, the Policy Group believes there is a responsibility on the part of large integrated financial intermediaries to provide clients with timely and relevant information about a transaction beyond the disclosures discussed in its Recommendation III-2 above.

III-3a. The intermediary and counterparty should review with each other the material terms of a complex transaction prior to execution.

III-3b. Both the intermediary and counterparty must make reasonable efforts to confirm the execution of a complex transaction in a timely manner.

- The counterparty should be promptly notified of any expected delay in the creation of a confirmation.
- The intermediary should disclose whether evidence of agreement, such as a signed term sheet, is binding as to transaction terms. Each party should review the terms and promptly notify the other of any error.

III-3c. When a counterparty requests a valuation of a high-risk complex financial instrument, the intermediary should respond in a manner appropriate to the purpose of the valuation. The intermediary's sales and trading personnel may provide a counterparty with actionable quotes or indicative unwind levels. Only groups independent of sales and trading should provide indicative valuations and only in writing. Where relevant, such indicative valuations should include information describing the basis upon which the valuation is being provided.

III-3d. As a part of the relationship between intermediaries and their counterparties following trade execution, the intermediary should make reasonable efforts on a case-by-case basis to keep the counterparty informed of material developments regarding the performance of key positions.

With respect to high-risk complex asset-backed securitizations, underwriters and placement agents should have in place an ongoing framework for evaluating the performance and reputation of issuers as well as effective and clearly articulated procedures for evaluating the quality of assets. The Policy Group *strongly urges* that underwriters and placement agents redouble efforts to adhere fully to the letter and spirit of existing diligence standards, and seek opportunities to standardize and enhance such standards. These enhancements include the following recommendations:

III-4a. Requiring all firms to follow statistically valid sampling techniques in assessing the quality of assets in a securitization; and

III-4b. Encouraging disclosure to investors of due diligence results, including making the AUP letter publicly available.

Section IV: Risk Monitoring and Risk Management

IV-1a. The Policy Group *recommends* that risk management and other critical control functions be positioned within all large integrated financial intermediaries in a way that ensures that their actions and decisions are appropriately independent of the income producing business units and includes joint approval of key products and transactions. This would generally mean having a Chief Risk Officer (CRO) with a direct line of responsibility to the Chief Executive Officer (CEO) and having the CEO and the board take a highly active role in ensuring that the culture of the organization as a whole recognizes and embraces the independence of its critical control functions. Even without the direct reporting, the CRO should have a clear line of communication to the board.

IV-1b. The Policy Group further *recommends* that institutions ensure that their risk management functions are staffed appropriately for both the upside and the downside and are able to understand and properly size risks in tranquil markets as well as during periods of market stress. The risk management functions must also have the capacity to function effectively in periods of spikes in processing volumes and under various disaster recovery scenarios.

IV-2a. The Policy Group *recommends* that all large integrated financial intermediaries evaluate the manner in which information relating to risk taking, risk monitoring, and risk management is shared with senior management and the board of directors and make necessary improvements to ensure that such information flows are timely, understandable, and properly presented. As a part of this effort, senior management should actively encourage ongoing discussion with board members in order to improve the quality, coverage and utility of information made available to the board. Each institution should evaluate how effective its information flows are as they relate to the intersection of credit, market, operational and liquidity risk.

IV-2b. The Policy Group *recommends* that each institution *ensure that the risk tolerance of the firm is established or approved by the highest levels of management and shared with the board.* The Policy Group further recommends that each institution ensure that periodic exercises aimed at estimation of risk tolerance should be shared with the highest levels of management, the board of directors and the institution's primary supervisor in line with Core Precept III, as discussed on pages 11, 12.

IV- 2c. The Policy Group further *recommends* that large integrated financial intermediaries ensure that their treasury and risk management functions work with each other and with business units to manage balance sheet size and composition in a manner that ensures that the established risk tolerance is consistent with funding capabilities and ongoing efforts to manage liquidity risk.

IV-2d. The Policy Group further *recommends* that each institution review its internal systems of both formal and informal communication across business units and control functions to ensure that such communication systems encourage the *prompt* and *coherent* flow of risk-related information within and across business units and, as needed, the prompt escalation of quality information to top management.

IV-3a. The Policy Group *recommends* that, when schedules permit, the CEO and the second ranking officers of all large integrated financial intermediaries should frequently attend and participate in meetings of risk management-related committees.

IV-3b. The Policy Group further *recommends* that the highest levels of management periodically review the functioning of the committee structure to ensure, among other things, that such committees are appropriately chaired and staffed and there is an appropriate overlap of key business leaders, support leaders, and enterprise executives across committees to help foster firm-wide cooperation and communication.

IV-3c. The Policy Group further *recommends* that for certain classes of firm-wide committees, such as those responsible for the approval of new products – especially new products having high financial, operational or reputational risks – the committee oversight process should include a systematic post-approval review process. This post-approval review process would assess the extent to which new products have, in commercial terms, performed as expected. Equally important, the process would assess whether the risk characteristics of the new product have been consistent with expectations, including the burden of the new products on technology and operating systems. Further, it is particularly appropriate to review at the earliest opportunity outsized profitability and market share gains to ensure that this does not reflect a problem with the original pricing or risk assessment of the product.

IV- 4a. The Policy Group *recommends* that sustained investment in risk management systems and processes, and the careful calibration of such investment to business opportunities being pursued, be a key area of focus for a firm's senior management team.

IV-4b. The Policy Group further *recommends* that each firm's CRO commission a periodic review and assessment of the firm's investments in risk management for presentation to its senior management and the audit committee of its board.

IV-5a. The Policy Group *recommends* that all market participants implement a paradigm shift in credit terms, establishing arrangements that create more stable trading relationships, are less pro-cyclical, and thus reduce systemic risk.

IV-5b. The Policy Group further *recommends* that each firm's senior management commission a periodic review of credit terms extended over a cycle, together with an assessment of the stability of such terms, for discussion with the firm's senior management.

IV-6a. The Policy Group *recommends* that large integrated financial intermediaries ensure that their credit systems are adequate to compile detailed exposures to each of their institutional counterparties on an end-of-day basis by the opening of business the subsequent morning. In addition, the Policy Group recommends that large integrated financial intermediaries ensure their credit systems are capable of compiling, on an *ad hoc* basis and within a matter of hours, detailed and accurate estimates of market and credit risk exposure data across all counterparties and the risk parameters set out below. Within a slightly longer timeframe this information should be expandable to include: (1) the directionality of the portfolio and of individual trades; (2) the incorporation of additional risk types, including contingent exposures and second and third order exposures (for example, Structured Investment Vehicles (SIVs), Asset- Backed Securities (ABS), *etc.*); and (3) such other information as would be required to optimally manage risk exposures to a troubled counterparty. Large integrated financial intermediaries should be able to use exposure aggregation data both prospectively to avoid undue concentrations and, if necessary, in real time to react to unanticipated counterparty credit events.

IV-6b. To demonstrate their compliance with the aforementioned standards, the Policy Group *recommends* that firms conduct periodic exercises for both individual and multiple institutional counterparties, and, to the extent that deficiencies are observed, develop remediation plans as a matter of urgency.

IV-7a. The Policy Group *recommends* that large integrated financial intermediaries' risk analytics incorporate sufficient granularity to reveal less obvious risks that can occur infrequently but that may potentially have a significant impact (for example, basis risks between single name underliers and index hedges). However, risk management professionals and senior management must recognize the limitations of mathematical models, and that the tendency to overly formalize arcane aspects of an analysis can often detract from an understanding of the bigger picture implications of the total risk position. Incremental analytical detail must not be allowed to overwhelm users of the data. The salient risk points must be drawn out and made apparent, especially to senior management. Adequate time and attention by senior management must also be allotted to socializing the implications of the risk data.

IV-7b. The Policy Group *recommends* that large integrated financial intermediaries ensure that assumptions underlying portfolio analyses are clearly articulated and are subject to frequent, comprehensive review. Alternative measures should be presented to demonstrate the sensitivity of the calculated metrics to changes in underlying assumptions.

IV-7c. The Policy Group *recommends* that credit risks be viewed in aggregate across exposures, giving full consideration to the effects of correlations between exposures. Further, counterparty credit risks, including correlations and directionality, should be evaluated based not only on positions within a large integrated financial intermediary, but also considering available data regarding the size and direction of positions the counterparty has at other firms.

IV-7d. The Policy Group further *recommends* that large integrated financial intermediaries work to supplement VaR as the dominant risk measure of market risk and current exposure as the dominant risk measure for credit risk, both for public reporting and for risk discussion purposes. Supplemental measures should include statistical information intended to display the most likely ways a large integrated financial intermediary or a managed portfolio could sustain significant losses, as well as an indication of the potential size of those losses.

IV-8a. The Policy Group *recommends* that firms think creatively about how stress tests can be conducted to maximize their value to the firm including the idea of a *reverse stress test* where the emphasis is on the contagion that could cause a significant stress event to the firm.

IV-8b. The Policy Group further *recommends* that firms incorporate the expanded suite of stress tests into a formalized production schedule, against which trends and developments in key risk factors and exposure amounts can be tracked.

IV-9a. The Policy Group *recommends* that large integrated financial intermediaries adjust quantitative measures of potential credit risk with margined counterparties to take into account exceptionally large positions, as well as position concentrations in less liquid instruments. The adjustment should anticipate potentially protracted unwind periods and the risk of price gapping during unwinds.

IV-9b. The Policy Group further *recommends* that consideration be given to collecting higher initial margin and higher haircuts from counterparties with outsized positions relative to market liquidity. Large integrated financial intermediaries should also evaluate the need to adjust internal pricing for large positions.

IV-10a. The Policy Group *recommends* that large integrated financial intermediaries ensure that they employ robust, consistent pricing policies and procedures, incorporating disciplined price verification for both proprietary and counterparty risk trades. Special attention should be given to bespoke trades, structured products, illiquid products, and other difficult to price assets. A robust monitoring process should be employed to track stale prices and elevate unresolved issues.

IV-10b. The Policy Group further *recommends* that firms and industry groups promote standardized and strengthened dispute resolution mechanisms and encourage the application of higher levels of resources to position pricing. Firms should also promote enhanced understanding of the need for cooperative behavior among firms (for example, when requested to provide indicative bids).

IV-10c. The Policy Group further *recommends* that increased emphasis be given to using, wherever possible, transparent and liquid instruments rather than bespoke products. To incentivize this conduct, large integrated financial intermediaries should consider imposing internal charges against the P & L of hard to value and illiquid transactions, or other methods, such as higher capital charges, higher haircuts to collateralized borrowers, and the imposition of limits on allowed trade volumes. The recommendations incorporated in the section on High-Risk Complex Financial Instruments regarding documents and disclosure are of particular relevance to bespoke products.

IV-11a. The Policy Group *recommends* that large integrated financial intermediaries ensure, in the absence of exceptional circumstances, that when the same instrument is held by different business units, such instrument is marked at the same price in each unit. Large integrated financial intermediaries should restrict those personnel and groups that are authorized to provide marks to internal and external audiences. Any differentials in pricing across applications or units should be carefully considered and the rationale for such differences should be fully documented. Notwithstanding the above, it is recognized that for large integrated financial intermediaries, there are communication walls that are designed to fulfill regulatory requirements for the restriction of information flows. In these instances, it is understood that legitimate differences in pricing may occur.

IV-12a. The Policy Group *recommends* that large integrated financial intermediaries ensure that a review of the systemic risk implications of incentives and consequent remedial actions is an integral component of each firm's risk management practices. Regulators should encourage this proactive review and assessment on a regular periodic basis. Regulators should identify practices that have the potential to destabilize markets during periods of stress and communicate their concerns aggressively.

IV-12b. The Policy Group further *recommends* that, when considering new trade structures, strategies, or other opportunities, systemic risk implications be evaluated by the senior management of large integrated financial intermediaries. Trades or structures which materially add to systemic risk should be subject to particular scrutiny.

IV-13a. The Policy Group *recommends* that all large integrated financial intermediaries should, on a regular basis, conduct liquidity stress tests to measure their Maximum Liquidity Outflow (MLO). Stress tests should be based on scenarios that consider how normal sources of liquidity, both secured and unsecured, could be disrupted for the firm, the markets, or both. The stress test scenarios should focus on potential liquidity outflows, taking into account a firm's particular vulnerabilities.

IV-13b. The Policy Group further *recommends* that, in addition, at a minimum, firms monitor their MLO within the first 30 days and for additional intervals within this timeframe (for example, overnight, one week, two weeks). The MLO is defined as the net loss of liquidity under the firm's most severe scenario from the time of the calculation for the tenors prescribed.

IV-13c. The Policy Group *recommends* that stress scenarios, both for purposes of stress testing and calculation of MLO, should:

- Include both firm-specific and systemic events and their overlapping nature.
- Consider extreme shocks as well as progressive events.
- Take into account implicit as well as explicit risks and potential damage of a firm's actions to its franchise.
- Review the potential for loss of key sources of secured and unsecured funding, including deposits, commercial paper, and other short- and long-term debt. Firms should also consider the impact of funding illiquidity on asset-backed commercial paper conduits and on the ability to securitize pools of assets.
- Analyze the potential outflows related to customer activity, including prime brokerage.

- Examine the impact of on- and off-balance sheet exposures, including the potential outflows related to derivative transactions, liquidity commitments and special purpose vehicles.
- Consider the impact of intra-day liquidity exposures, including the heightened interest of counterparties to accelerate trades and settlements in times of stress and other time-related mismatches in the flow of funds.
- Consider other large cash payments including salaries, taxes and lease payments.
- As with all liquidity practices, evaluate the impact on both individual legal entities, as well as the consolidated firm.
- Consider the availability of central bank facilities. Generally speaking, extraordinary central bank facilities, such as the Federal Reserve System's Primary Dealer Credit Facility, *should not be considered an element of an effective liquidity plan.*

These stress tests, and their results, would be internally classified, confidential documents that would be shared with senior management, boards of directors and primary supervisors on a periodic basis. The information provided by the stress tests should be used to identify funding gaps and assess where gaps are incompatible with the firm's risk appetite. Since the stress test information provided to supervisors would be confidential supervisory information, it would and should be protected from public disclosure.

IV-14. The Policy Group *recommends* that all large integrated financial intermediaries maintain, on an ongoing basis, an unencumbered liquidity reserve of cash and the highest grade and most liquid securities. The liquidity reserve should be sized in relation to the firm's stress tests and MLO and should explicitly reflect the firm's liquidity risk tolerance and desired survival periods.

IV-15. The Policy Group *recommends* that all large integrated financial intermediaries maintain long-term structural liquidity in excess of their illiquid assets. In making this assessment, large integrated financial intermediaries should analyze the term structure of their long-term liabilities, the long-term stable portion of their deposits (where applicable), as well as equity capital. Illiquid assets should include those assets that cannot be converted to cash within a specified horizon and potential growth of those assets, as well as the haircuts necessary to convert generally liquid assets to cash through sale, securitization, or secured financing.

IV-16. The baseline assessment of whether a large integrated financial intermediary has long-term structural liquidity in excess of its illiquid assets should reflect current business conditions. However, the amount of this excess ("the cushion") should reflect an evaluation of the assets and liabilities under stressed conditions. This cushion should be replenished with structured longterm liabilities, with tenors appropriate to market conditions, business strategy, and existing debt maturities.

IV-17. The Policy Group *recommends* that a firm's liquidity plan and any stress tests mentioned above include, in all instances, the full set of on- and off-balance sheet obligations. In addition, they must reflect a clear view of how the firm will address non-contractual obligations that have significant franchise implications. While some non-contractual obligations may not lend themselves to incorporation into the core stress scenarios, an evaluation of how such exposures will play out in different market environments should be an overlay to the core stress scenarios. In addition, a clear assessment of how practices in relevant markets (for example, SIVs and auction rate securities) will affect an individual firm's conduct should be directly factored into liquidity planning. The above liquidity exposures should be fully priced under the firm's transfer pricing policies (see Recommendation V-17).

IV-18. The Policy Group *recommends* that all large integrated financial intermediaries incorporate appropriate pricing-based incentives for the full spectrum of their funding activities. This includes a funds transfer pricing policy that assigns the cost of funding to businesses that use funding and credits the benefits of funding to businesses that provide it. This must encompass both on- and off- balance sheet activities (for example, contingent funding), as well as potential funding needs related to actions that might be taken to preserve the institution's reputation. The funds transfer pricing process should be informed by stress testing efforts that identify potential vulnerabilities and assign the related costs to the businesses that create them. The methodology should provide direct economic incentives factoring in the related liquidity value of assets and behavioral patterns of liabilities. The costs and benefits identified should be assigned to specific businesses and, under all circumstances, used in evaluating the businesses' performance.

IV-19. The Policy Group *recommends* that to manage, monitor, and control funding liquidity risk, treasury officials in particular need to be included in an enterprise-wide risk management process with appropriate channels of communication. The evaluation of the interconnected elements of these risks requires seamless communication across all risk disciplines, as well as between risk management functions, treasury and the underlying businesses. All integrated financial services firms should hold regularly scheduled meetings of an oversight committee represented by the above disciplines to monitor the firm's liquidity positions.

IV-20a. The Policy Group *recommends* that firms explicitly coordinate across their liquidity and capital planning processes and, at a minimum, ensure that critical information flows between the two processes. Executive management must have the capacity to evaluate and incorporate the highly integrated nature of the two disciplines into its planning activities.

IV-20b. The Policy Group re-affirms its *recommendation* that for large integrated banks and investment banks, Basel II should remain the primary capital standard that such institutions, their primary supervisors, and the marketplace generally look to in making judgments about capital adequacy.

IV-20b. The Policy Group *recommends,* at least for the present, that the existing Basel II standards for minimum capital and well-capitalized institutions be maintained. In taking that position, the Policy Group recognizes that the experience of the credit market crisis provides a sobering reminder to individual institutions, their senior management and their supervisors that future judgments about capital adequacy should be more sensitive to downside risks than perhaps has been the case in the past.

IV-20c. The Policy Group further *recommends* that supervisory judgments about capital adequacy for all large integrated banks and investment banks give primary weight to case-by-case evaluations based on the range of criteria contained in Basel II, Pillar II, and, when necessary, such judgments should be promptly shared with individual institutions.

V-20d. The Policy Group *strongly recommends* that every reasonable effort be made by the international community of supervisory authorities to (1) seek to stabilize, at least for a reasonable period of time, the methodology associated with Basel II, (2) move toward a common implementation date across major jurisdictions, and (3) insure a competitive and supervisory level playing field in the application of Basel II across classes of institutions and across national boundaries.

IV-21a. The Policy Group *recommends* that where the use of leverage ratios is compulsory, supervisors monitor such leverage ratios using the Basel II, Pillar II techniques and intervene regarding the adequacy of such leverage ratios only on a case-by-case basis.

IV-21b. The Policy Group *recommends* that efforts be directed at either (1) framing more meaningful leverage ratios where they exist or (2) phasing out their use and implementing alternative risk measures that more effectively fulfill their intended objectives.

Section V: Enhanced Credit Market Resiliency

V-1. The Policy Group *recommends* trade date (T+0) matching for electronically eligible transactions.
Goal: End 2009.

V-2. The Policy Group *recommends* the linkage of confirmation and settlements.
Goal: Dealers early 2009.

V-3. The Policy Group *recommends* a tiered approach to market participation and incentive structure.
Goal: Ongoing.

V-4. The Policy Group *recommends* incentives to buy-side participants.
Goal: Ongoing.

It is important to recognize that buy-side market participants will operate at different volumes. Moderate to large volume participants (more than four trades per month) will be expected to adhere to the same standards as dealer- side firms with respect to transmission standards, trade date confirmation, settlement, and mark-to-market comparisons. As with adoption of the Novation Protocol, dealers should consider limiting trading activity with firms that do not adhere to industry standards. Adherence to industry standards should be part of a routine dealer operational due diligence (side-by-side with the normal credit due diligence).

V-5. The Policy Group *recommends* that market participants should seek to streamline their methods for trade execution and confirmation/affirmation, which should facilitate an end-to-end process flow consistent with same-day matching and legal confirmation.

V-6. The Policy Group *recommends* that senior leaders of trading support functions should clearly articulate to senior management the resource requirements necessary to achieve the same-day standards. Recognizing the expense

management imperatives driven by recent market conditions, senior management should make every effort to help support functions achieve these standards for the overarching benefit of enhancing market resilience.
Goal: Ongoing.

V-7. The Policy Group *strongly urges* that major market participants should deploy a combination of utility and vendor-supplied solutions and should, at a minimum, ensure interoperability of those solutions.
Goal: End of 2009.

V-8. The Policy Group *recommends* that major market participants on both the sell- and buy-sides should make every reasonable effort to speed up the adoption of electronic platform usage. This should entail revisiting the priorities in development and testing schedules.
Goal: End of 2009.

V-9. Consistent with Recommendation V-7 above, the Policy Group further *recommends* that major market participants on both the sell- and buy-sides should hasten their adoption of tools that facilitate standardization in the marketplace. This will in turn facilitate the achievement of the next generation goals for the timeliness and integrity of transaction details.
Goal: End of 2009.

V-10. The Policy Group further *recommends* frequent portfolio reconciliations and mark-to-market comparisons, including on collateralized instruments.
Goal: Weekly end 2008, moving to daily for electronically eligible trades mid 2009.

V-11. ISDA Credit Support Annex documents spell out the bilateral terms of the margin process. While the process is generally standardized, the Policy Group *recommends* that the industry needs to find an effective means to resolve valuations disputes, particularly for illiquid products. Doing so is likely to be a difficult and demanding matter and therefore an industry-wide approach may have to be considered.
Goal: End of 2009.

V-12. The Policy Group *recommends* that, as mark-to-market disputes inevitably surface through the collateral portfolio reconciliation process, the information should be passed to the executing trading desks on a real-time basis to allow for research and resolution. This should, of course, be done with appropriate anonymity of the counterparty's identity, positions, and broader portfolio. A close alignment of the collateral team with trading desks – without violating the fire walls and controls that are critically important to the integrity of the financial system – would facilitate such information sharing. As necessary, significant and large value collateral disputes should promptly be escalated to the appropriate senior officers.
Goal: Immediate.

V-13. The Policy Group *recommends* that dealers, investors and the clearing banks agree on "Best Practices" to govern the tri-party repo market. Components of such Best Practices should include the following:

- tri-party repo program size;
- margin;

- collateral eligibility; and
- collateral valuation.

V-14. The Policy Group *recommends* that market participants actively engage in single name and index CDS trade compression. ISDA has agreed on a mechanism to facilitate single name trade compression with Creditex and Mark-it Partners. Established vendor platforms exist for termination of offsetting index trades, and we urge major market participants to aggressively pursue their use.

V-15. Based on the considerations above, the Policy Group *recommends* that the industry, under the auspices of the current ISDA Portfolio Compression Working Group, commit immediately and with all due speed to achieve consistency of the current product, including potentially:

- utilizing industry preferred Reference Obligations or elimination of Reference Obligations;
- eliminating Restructuring Basis distinctions, recognizing that this needs to be considered in a broader global perspective taking into account regional and national differences; and
- standardizing fee calculations based on a single, common model analytic.

V-16. The Policy Group *recommends* that ISDA should update its Credit Derivative Definitions to incorporate the auction mechanism so that counterparties to new credit default swap trades commit to utilize the auction mechanism in connection with future credit events.

V-17. The Policy Group *recommends* that ISDA should run a protocol (a so-called "big bang" protocol) to provide market participants with an operationally efficient means to amend their existing credit default swap trades to utilize the auction mechanism in connection with future credit events. This protocol should not effect any other changes to the bilateral agreements in effect between adopting counterparties.

V-18. The Policy Group *recommends* that all large integrated financial intermediaries (*e.g.*, the major dealers) should promptly adopt the Close-out Amount approach for early termination upon default in their counterparty relationships with each other. We note that this can be agreed and suitably documented without making any other changes to the ISDA Master. The Policy Group expects that these arrangements will be in place in the very near term.

V-19. The Policy Group *recommends* that a working group should be formed under the auspices of ISDA, with representatives of both dealer and buy-side firms, to review the methodology for counterparty terminations in order to (1) produce a set of best practices and suggested bilateral templates for the transparency of valuation methodologies and parameters, as noted above, for use by all market participants, (2) consider how contractual provisions could reflect prior reconciliation of valuation parameters and (3) seek to reconcile the differing views on what is necessary to evidence agreement that market inputs will be used unless commercially unreasonable. The Policy Group hopes that the working group will be able to report a recommended approach by December 31, 2008.

V-20. The Policy Group *recommends* that all major market participants should periodically conduct hypothetical simulations of close-out situations, including a comprehensive review of key documentation, identification of legal risks and issues, establishing the speed and accuracy with which comprehensive counterparty exposure data and net cash outflows can be compiled, and ascertaining the sequencing of critical tasks and decision-making responsibilities associated with events leading up to and including the execution of a close-out event.

V-21. The Policy Group *recommends* that all market participants should both promptly and periodically review their existing documentation covering counterparty terminations and ensure that they have in place appropriate and current agreements including the definition of events of default and the termination methodology that will be used. Where such documents are not current, market participants should take immediate steps to update them. Moreover, each market participant should make explicit judgments about the risks of trading with counterparties who are unwilling or unable to maintain appropriate and current documentation and procedures.

V-22. The Policy Group *recommends* that the industry should consider the formation of a "default management group", composed of senior business representatives of major market participants (from the buy-side as well as the sell-side) to work with the regulatory authorities on an ongoing basis to consider and anticipate issues likely to arise in the event of a default of a major market counterparty.

V-23. Recognizing the benefits of a counterparty clearing arrangement (CCP) as discussed above, the Policy Group strongly *recommends* that the industry develop a CCP for the credit derivatives market to become operational as soon as possible and that its operations adhere to the BIS Recommendations.

Part III: Emerging Issues Highlights

A. Valuation and Price Verification

"The Policy Group is strongly of the view that under any and all standards of accounting and under any and all market conditions, individual financial institutions must ensure that wholly adequate resources insulated by failsafe independent decision-making authority are at the center of the valuation and price verification process. While the details of approaches and the family of techniques used for these purposes may – and will – differ from time to time and from institution to institution, these efforts should always pass the *two common sense* tests of (1) reasonableness and (2) consistency, both of which apply equally to positions or instruments that have gains and positions or instruments that have losses."

B. Asset Price Bubbles

"This subject matter is highly complex and is one where miscalculation or misjudgment can have serious adverse consequences. Finally, and most importantly, there is no substitute for sustained discipline in both public policy and private action, which remains the best recipe to limit the severity of asset price bubbles and contain their damage when inevitably they occur."

C. Near Banks

"In the current circumstances, some attention has been given to a modified form of direct, but standby supervision. Under this approach, the authorities (*i.e.*, the Federal Reserve in the United States) would step in when problems at one or more hedge funds raise systemic concerns. While such an approach will no doubt be debated in public and official circles, CRMPG III believes that this approach too raises moral hazard questions. Moreover, as a practical matter it would be very difficult to administer such an approach, in part because of the danger that the standby authority might be triggered when it is already too late, or because the triggering of such authority might aggravate the very problem it is seeking to mitigate."

D. Regulatory Structure

"CRMPG III believes that the issue of the role of the central bank in the arena of prudential supervision and financial market oversight requires expedited consideration and resolution."

"In weighing and balancing these factors, the Policy Group would note the following: (1) if the supervisory reach of the Federal Reserve, for example, is to be extended, it must have the direct and ongoing authority to discharge those responsibilities and (2) legitimate moral hazard concerns notwithstanding, there will always be extreme circumstances in which extraordinary interventions by central banks or governments are necessary. However, as witnessed in recent months, extraordinary intervention by the authorities clearly does not mean that financial institutions and their shareholders will be protected from substantial losses."

E. Supervisory Policy and Practice

"The Policy Group believes that the case for devoting greater resources to the supervisory effort is clear and compelling."

"In the arena of supervisory policy one particular subject that is in need of further progress is implementing Basel II capital adequacy standards."

"The Policy Group is under no illusion that there is a quick and easy solution to any of these issues regarding Basel II. Having said that, the Policy Group wishes to urge all deliberate speed on the part of the international community of supervisory authorities in (1) seeking to stabilize, at least for a reasonable period of time, the methodology associated with Basel II, (2) moving toward a common implementation date across major jurisdictions and (3) insuring a competitive and supervisory level playing field in the application of the Basel II across classes of institutions and across national boundaries."

SECTION II: STANDARDS FOR ACCOUNTING CONSOLIDATION

A. Introduction

It is widely recognized that a major contributing factor to the credit market crisis was the manner and extent to which risks associated with certain classes of off-balance sheet activities at many financial institutions may not have been adequately encompassed within firms' risk monitoring and risk mitigation frameworks. Thus, when contingent risks arising from such off-balance sheet activities were triggered, this gave rise to elevated contagion risk and large write-downs at many financial institutions.

To a very considerable extent, both the demand for and the supply of the structured credit products that were often housed in off-balance sheet special purpose vehicles were driven by the "reach for yield" investment phenomenon, which characterized the three to four year period leading up to the credit market crisis. In some cases (for example, securitizations), regulatory arbitrage was a factor since Basel I (the prevailing capital standard when the build-up of these activities occurred) called for little or no explicit capital charges for certain arrangements with off-balance sheet vehicles.

A similar phenomenon existed for loan commitments. In the cases of conduits and SIVs, substantial maturity mismatches were common as long-term assets were being financed by short-term asset-backed commercial paper, encouraged by the implicit belief that ready access to such financing would always be there. And, in the case of many bank- sponsored conduits there were explicit arrangements whereby the sponsoring bank was committed to provide back-up financing in the event that commercial paper financing was not available. In other cases, these arrangements were regarded by market participants as implicit and based on the belief that reputational risks were such that sponsors would provide back-up financing even in the absence of an explicit arrangement.

Clearly, an important contributing factor was the idiosyncratic consolidation rules under U.S. Generally Accepted Accounting Principles *(US GAAP)*. There are various relevant accounting standards under US GAAP which determine whether an entity is on or off the balance sheet. These rules are extraordinarily complex and their interpretation can only be mastered by highly skilled and experienced professionals. The discussions on pages 41, 47 of this Report provide several examples of the workings of US GAAP consolidation rules. These examples are designed to provide insight into the application of these rules for readers who are not experts in this field.

For the purpose of this introduction, it is sufficient to note that securitization vehicles considered to be "Qualifying Special Purpose Entities" *(QSPEs)* receive off-balance sheet treatment even if the sponsoring entity provides credit enhancements by retaining a significant residual interest in the securitization trust (*i.e.*, the sponsor is expected to absorb the majority of the risks and rewards). The rationale for off-balance sheet treatment is that the vehicle is passive and therefore the sponsor does not control it.

Currently, the Financial Accounting Standards Board *(FASB)* is in the very advanced stages of preparing to issue for public comment further revisions to the current consolidation rules. It is widely expected that the proposed revisions will substantially modify the existing rules in ways that will require many vehicles that currently qualify for off-balance sheet treatment under current US GAAP to come onto the balance sheet of sponsoring institutions.

As an extension of this discussion, it should be noted that for banks and other financial institutions that operate under International Financial Reporting Standards (IFRS), the International Accounting Standards Board (IASB) is also re-examining its consolidation standards. The Policy Group encourages the FASB and the IASB to work together on cross-border convergence of accounting standards with a more principles-based orientation in this area.

Obviously, the new US GAAP consolidation rules – assuming they take the general form that is expected – will have profoundly important implications for many institutions in terms of balance sheet size and may have a material impact on regulatory capital requirements for certain institutions. However, the consolidation of off-balance sheet vehicles will not, in most circumstances, have a major impact on regulatory capital requirements for institutions using risk-based capital standards such as Basel II. This is because the risk absorbed by the sponsors, for example via their retention of the residual interests in a securitization trust, is already appropriately captured in explicit capital charges under Basel II.

For affected institutions, the accounting changes will have an impact on reported leverage ratios which will, in many cases, rise appreciably. This will be consequential to institutions that are subject to regulatory leverage constraints, notwithstanding the fact that risks carried by these institutions may already be subject to capital charges. This result is peculiar since, by definition, changes in accounting conventions are not economic and therefore should not generally have economic consequences. This is still another example of the fact that leverage ratios tell us a lot about arithmetic but little about financial and economic reality.

The Policy Group is mindful of the profoundly important and demanding implications of the likely revisions to the US GAAP consolidation rules. Nevertheless, the Policy Group endorses, in principle, the direction of these changes provided they are (1) principles- based, (2) convergent with IFRS, and (3) accompanied by suitable disclosure and transition rules regarding regulatory capital which will provide flexibility in the implementation of these rules over a reasonable period of time.

The following is a technical discussion on accounting consolidation, its effects on financial reporting, and the Policy Group's recommendations for improvements to consolidation accounting and disclosure. In formulating its recommendations on accounting consolidation, and as discussed in other parts of this Report, the Policy Group elected not to address the issue of fair value accounting.

B. Basics of Consolidation

Consolidation is the process by which the financial statements of a parent are combined with those of its subsidiaries, as if they were a single economic entity. Consolidated results are considered more useful in the decision-making process of users of financial statements, such as investors and creditors. For example, consolidation of a traditional operating subsidiary provides more accurate information on the revenues and expenses

of the parent so that users have a better understanding of how net earnings were achieved. Consolidation of a securitization vehicle provides information on the use of leverage in financing a securitization. Because consolidation policies determine when an enterprise's involvement with another entity gives rise to a parent-subsidiary relationship, consolidation principles become vitally important to financial statement reporting.

Consolidation can, however, obscure those assets and liabilities that are truly impacting the economic performance and financial position of the consolidated enterprise. For example, the assets and liabilities, revenues and expenses, and cash flows of a subsidiary are typically reported in the financial statements of the parent, as if the parent is at risk for the entire change in value of those assets and liabilities, even though this may not be true as an economic matter. Additionally, assets financed via non-recourse debt are often aggregated with assets for which the enterprise is fully exposed to risk. Moreover, as consolidation increases the size of the balance sheet, the aggregation of similar items can obscure individual amounts. Consequently, transparent display, reporting, and footnote disclosures in the financial statements are crucial to providing a clear picture of the consolidated enterprise.

C. US GAAP Consolidation Rules

Under US GAAP, there currently are three consolidation models for determining when a parent-subsidiary relationship is present, each based on the type of entity an enterprise is involved with. The three types of entities are: (1) voting entities, (2) variable interest entities (such as special purpose entities (SPEs)), and (3) QSPEs.

1. Voting Entities

Consolidation policy under US GAAP for voting entities was codified in 1959 with the issuance of a standard that requires an enterprise to consolidate an entity it unilaterally controls through majority voting interests. If no investor has the ability to control a voting entity, no one consolidates.

To illustrate the consolidation analysis under US GAAP for a voting entity, consider the following example:

Example 1 – Traditional Business

Facts:

An entity is a business with employees, assets and activities that produce revenues and expenses.

The entity is sufficiently capitalized with equity and its owners have the ability to make decisions in proportion to their ownership interests.

The owners are exposed to first loss and have the rights to receive any residual returns

Analysis:

Under US GAAP, this entity is analyzed for consolidation under a control model as described above. An owner having majority control (typically, through ownership of voting common stock) would consolidate in this example.

The standard for voting entities was written for traditional businesses, long before the advent of structured finance and special-purpose entities. Therefore, no guidance existed for consolidation of structured finance or special purpose entities for which voting power was not meaningful in determining control. Over time, practice developed and certain bright-line rules were enacted that related to specific fact patterns involving SPEs.[1] In practice, these brightlines were analogized to many different situations, and sometimes inappropriately used by enterprises to structure entities to avoid consolidation. This created the need for specific rules governing SPEs or, as they later became known, "variable interest entities".

2. Variable Interest Entities

The concept of a variable interest entity was introduced in 2003, in the wake of Enron. At the time, regulators were pressing for updated accounting guidance that would address the abuses observed in the accounting for SPEs. In response, the FASB issued an interpretation of the 1959 standard, which effectively created a new model for consolidation. The model identified the characteristics of what the FASB termed a "variable interest entity" (VIE), an entity consolidated based on risks and rewards, to differentiate it from a "voting entity" – an entity that would continue to be evaluated for consolidation based on "voting control".

A VIE is a separate legal entity that has any of the following characteristics: (1) insufficient US GAAP equity to absorb "expected" losses, that is, not "actual" losses, (2) owners are shielded from losses or returns are capped, or (3) an inability by owners to make substantive decisions that drive the success of the entity.

A variable interest holder has an interest in a VIE that absorbs some or all of the expected losses or gains of the entity. Examples of variable interests include common and preferred shares, partnership interests, subordinated debt, guarantees, and certain derivative instruments. A variable interest holder absorbing the majority of expected losses or gains of a VIE consolidates the entity. The determination of expected losses or gains is based on a formula[2] and requires scenario analysis of projected cash flows or changes in fair value. The analysis can be performed on a qualitative basis when the facts are clear and conclusive. However, in other cases (for example, multi-seller Asset- Backed Commercial Paper conduits *(ABCP Conduits))* the analysis can require calculations involving complex models that generate thousands of scenarios.

The VIE analysis is performed at the date of initial involvement with an entity and reconsidered only upon certain events. Actual losses in excess of expected losses are not a "reconsideration event," even if losses significantly reduce the value of equity. Examples of reconsideration events include additional investments into the entity, refinancing of existing debt, and significant changes to governing documents or business activities. CDOs, SIVs, and ABCP Conduits are examples of entities that are typically structured as VIEs.

---

[1] A common example of a bright-line rule created during this period relates to off-balance sheet leasing transactions where a minimum of 3% of third party equity was determined to be substantive for purposes of analyzing whether an SPE should be consolidated. Enterprises would transfer real property to an SPE, obtain third party financing, and obtain 3% equity from a third-party investor. The resulting accounting analysis would enable the enterprise to report the real property and financing as an operating lease, that is, off-balance sheet rather than an on-balance sheet financing.

[2] To illustrate the formula for calculating expected losses with a simple example, consider an investment of $100 with only two expected outcomes: the investment can return $200 or zero. Each outcome has a 50% probability. The expected (probability-weighted) cash flows from the investment are therefore $100 [($200 x 50%) + ($0 x 50%)]. The expected loss and gain from the investment (probability-weighted variance around the mean) is negative $50 [($0 - $100) x 50%] and positive $50 [($200 - $100) x 50%], respectively. If the fair value of US GAAP equity is less than $50, then the equity of the entity would be "insufficient" and the entity would be deemed a VIE. A variable interest holder absorbing the majority of the $50 of expected losses would consolidate the VIE. If no variable interest holder absorbs the majority of the $50 of expected losses or gains, no one consolidates the VIE.

To illustrate the consolidation analysis under US GAAP for a VIE, consider the following example:

Example 2 – Asset-Backed Commercial Paper Conduit ("ABCP Conduit")

Facts:

A company sells receivables to an ABCP Conduit managed by a sponsoring bank.

The ABCP Conduit issues commercial paper (CP) to investors to finance the acquisition of the receivables. Repayment of the CP is dependent on receivable collections and the issuance of new CP upon maturity.

The sponsoring bank's responsibilities can include serving as the ABCP Conduit's administrative agent, CP placement agent, program-wide credit support provider (for example, a guarantee or letter of credit) and, importantly, as the CP backstop liquidity provider.

The sponsoring bank arranges the sale of "first loss notes" to third party investors. These notes are insignificant in size (generally 10 basis points) and are structured to absorb a majority of the ABCP Conduit's expected losses. These notes would not be recognized as US GAAP equity.

Analysis:

Under US GAAP, the ABCP Conduit would be considered a VIE because it lacks sufficient US GAAP equity. Initially, the sponsoring bank would not consolidate the ABCP Conduit because it does not have a majority of the expected losses and gains as a result of the sale of the first loss notes to third parties. The sponsoring bank's power to control the ABCP Conduit would not be considered in the analysis because the VIE model is based solely on an analysis of risk and rewards. Because of the revolving nature of the CP issuance, the sponsoring bank may be required to reconsider, on at least a quarterly basis, whether it holds a majority of the expected losses and gains through its program- wide credit support and backstop liquidity facilities.

The VIE model contains several scope exceptions, none more significant than the exception for QSPEs.

3. *Qualifying Special Purpose Entities*

SPEs are generally used in securitizations to achieve legal isolation in the event of bankruptcy. These entities are generally created with a single purpose and have very limited operational duties and discretionary powers, that is, they generally are passive in nature. The operations of SPEs are generally limited to collections of principal and interest on passive assets and distributions of the cash flows to the beneficial interest holders in the entity based on a predefined formula.

In connection with an accounting standard issued in 1996, the FASB decided that transfers of financial assets to SPEs that meet the above description and certain other "qualifying" criteria, would receive off-balance sheet or "sale accounting" treatment. Although QSPEs generally have several characteristics of VIEs, QSPEs were specifically excluded from the VIE consolidation model, given their passive nature. As a result, no party consolidates a QSPE. In practice, securitization vehicles that hold credit card receivables, automobile loans, residential mortgages and commercial mortgages are generally structured as QSPEs so as to benefit from the off-balance sheet treatment.

To illustrate the consolidation analysis under US GAAP for a QSPE, consider the following example:

Example 3 – Residential Mortgage Securitization

Facts:

A sponsoring bank sells a pool of residential mortgage loans to a bankruptcy remote securitization trust (Trust).

The sponsoring bank provides credit enhancement through the retention of a residual interest in the Trust.

The residual interest is expected to absorb the majority of the risks and rewards of the mortgage loans. The sponsoring bank also retains the right to service the mortgage loans, but the entity is otherwise passive.

The Trust issues tranched debt securities to finance the purchase of the mortgage loans. There is no substantive equity issuance.

Principal and interest collections on the mortgage loans are distributed to holders based on a predetermined formula designed to achieve specified credit risk profiles for each tranche.

Analysis:

US GAAP currently states that no party consolidates a QSPE. If the Trust is a QSPE (as is typically the case for residential mortgage securitizations), the sponsoring bank would receive off-balance sheet treatment, irrespective of its ability to service the assets and its holding of the residual interest. If the Trust is not deemed a QSPE, the Trust would be deemed a VIE, and the sponsoring bank generally would consolidate the Trust because, as the holder of the residual interest, the sponsoring bank has a majority of the risks and rewards of the Trust.

A significant issue raised in the development of the QSPE model was the level of discretion required to service the assets held by a QSPE. The issue of servicer discretion was highlighted during the current subprime residential mortgage crisis as assets defaulted at higher than expected rates and greater discretion was required to service what were previously deemed "passive" assets. The possibility of heightened servicer discretion has called into question the QSPE model.

D. US GAAP Disclosure Rules

There currently is no single framework for disclosure of off-balance sheet activities in US GAAP. Rather, disclosure rules are promulgated on a standard by standard basis, usually in response to a perceived weakness highlighted by an event in the marketplace. Current disclosure requirements, although numerous and complex, are heavily prescriptive and generally rules-based. Therefore, disclosures are generally not applied by analogy to situations that do not have a specific "rule" for disclosure. Disclosure requirements also tend to overlap in certain areas (generally, where more accounting guidance was provided by standard setters), and gap in other areas. This creates unnecessary complexity and is not conducive to providing clear and transparent disclosures.

Consider the following example of the limitations associated with current disclosure rules under US GAAP:

Example 4 – Disclosure of Retained Interests in Securitizations

Disclosure Requirement:

The disclosure requirements for retained interests from securitization activities include disclosure of the fair value of such retained interests at the reporting date, the weighted average maturities and sensitivities to changes in key valuation assumptions, disaggregated by type of instrument (for example, mortgages vs. corporate debt).

Disclosure Limitations:

This disclosure does not provide a comprehensive view of enterprise-wide risk. Particularly, the scope focuses only on retained interests and does not consider an enterprise's purchased interests. Retained interests are generally a small subset of total assets for a financial institution. Further, the scope specifically excludes related hedges, and fair value sensitivities do not account for simultaneous changes in inputs.

Similar limitations exist in various other standards that require specific disclosures about financial instruments and related risks, such as, but not limited to, disclosure regarding VIEs and derivative guarantees.

E. Current Developments in US GAAP Consolidation and Disclosure Rules

The FASB is in the process of amending its consolidation standard for VIEs and QSPEs, with a goal of issuing final standards with an effective date in 2010. Additionally, disclosure requirements will be enhanced with an effective date as soon as possible.

The FASB is proposing to eliminate the concept of QSPEs. Moreover, the consolidation model for VIEs is expected to become more qualitative in nature, specifically related to the assessment of whether a variable interest holder has control over a VIE, either through substantive decision-making power or exposure to a majority of the risk and rewards. This assessment will no longer be limited to inception and specific reconsideration events but will be analyzed each reporting period. The amended US GAAP consolidation model is expected to generally align with the current IFRS model,[3] that is, an assessment of control and risk and rewards.

---

[3] IFRS has a single model for consolidation: the control model. The IFRS control model has two parts, both of which must be met in order to conclude that one entity controls another. A controlling entity must have the power to govern the financial and operating policies of an entity, so as to obtain benefits from its activities. IFRS provides additional control indicators to consider when determining whether control over an SPE exists. These indicators include the concept of control described above as well as a consideration of which party

The result of these changes is expected to significantly increase the recognized balance sheets of financial institutions that sponsor and underwrite securitizations. This will be primarily due to the elimination of the QSPE model. The increase in balance sheet size will highlight the need for adequate financial statement presentation and disclosures to disaggregate and explain the consolidated balance sheet, for example, linking consolidated assets with related consolidated liabilities.

There also will be income statement effects, as consolidation will increase reported revenues and expenses. Consolidation could also impact reported earnings if it results in the elimination of previously recognizable profits or losses, which would now be viewed as intercompany in nature and therefore not recognizable under US GAAP. Additionally, these changes are expected to have broad implications for many other areas outside of financial reporting such as regulatory capital ratios, debt covenants, and other contractual obligations.

F. Recommendations for Consolidation and Related Disclosure Principles

The current consolidation rules under US GAAP have not been wholly effective at providing decision-useful information to the capital markets. Moreover, the current financial statement disclosure rules have been inadequate in bridging the gap between the consolidated financial statement and an enterprise's economic exposure to risks.

The current US GAAP consolidation rules lack a single principles-based model for consolidation. Rather, an enterprise is required to first assess which consolidation model is applicable to its interest in an entity and then determine whether an entity should be consolidated based on the rules within the applicable model. The rules for consolidation across those models are not symmetrical: one model is based solely on control, one model is based solely on risk and rewards, and the third is a scope exception for passive SPEs. It is understandable, therefore, that users of US GAAP consolidated financial statements are confused about the meaning of reported amounts in consolidated financial statements.

Additionally, the framework for each of the models is rules-based and at times focuses less on the substance of an enterprise's involvement with an entity and more on its form. A clear example of this would be the rule for calculating expected losses under the VIE model, where a quantitative outcome determines control without any further qualitative analysis of other known control factors. Moreover, the VIE model does not require reconsideration of the consolidation analysis at each reporting period. Therefore, a VIE remains off-balance sheet under an initial consolidation conclusion, even if the assumptions initially applied were not predictive of actual results.

US GAAP has prescriptive disclosure requirements on exposure to VIEs, retained interests in QSPEs, and derivative instruments. However, each rule does not build on a principle that requires a holistic look at the reporting enterprise. Therefore, these rules have not been entirely successful in providing users of the consolidated financial statements with a complete picture of a financial institution's exposure to risks. Looking ahead, the developing

absorbs a majority of the risks or rewards. The indicators are considered in the context of all relevant factors. Judgment is used to conclude which party in substance has control over the SPE. Acknowledging current events in the financial markets, the IASB is also in the process of updating its standard on consolidation. The changes are expected to endorse and clarify the current stated principles and focus on application guidance to improve comparability.

changes to the consolidation rules are expected to result in a significant increase to the balance sheets of financial institutions. As a result, robust and holistic disclosures will be required to enable users to dissect the information reported in the consolidated financial statements.

Recognizing the pressing need for changes to the US GAAP consolidation and disclosure rules, the Policy Group *recommends* as follows:

Recognition Framework Recommendations

II-1. The Policy Group *endorses,* in principle, the direction of the changes to the US GAAP consolidation rules provided that the changes are (1) principles-based, (2) convergent with IFRS, and (3) accompanied by suitable disclosure and transition rules regarding regulatory capital which will provide flexibility in the implementation of these rules over a reasonable period of time.

II-2. The Policy Group *recommends* adoption of a single, principles-based global consolidation framework that is based on control and the ability to benefit from that control. The analysis of whether an entity (the investor) has a controlling interest in another entity (the investee) should be based on:

- the investor's power over the investee, including the ability to make decisions that determine the success of the investee;
- the degree of investor exposure to the risks and rewards of the investee, including through guarantees, commitments and all other explicit and implicit arrangements between the two entities; and
- the design and sponsorship of the investee, including the degree to which the activities of the investee expose the investor to commercial, legal, regulatory, and reputational risks.

II-3. The Policy Group further *recommends* that the new consolidation framework require a reassessment of the consolidation analysis each reporting period based on changes in the control indicators specified in the preceding recommendation.

II-4. The Policy Group *encourages* standard setters and industry participants to work together toward achieving the goals discussed in this section on a global basis as soon as possible.

Disclosure Framework Recommendations

II-5. The Policy Group *recommends* that standard setters and industry participants consider a holistic and principles-based approach to disclosure of off-balance sheet activities similar to that found in international standards. The disclosure framework should be fully integrated with enterprise-wide disclosures across the full spectrum of risks: market, credit, liquidity, capital, operational, and reputational.

Enterprise-wide disclosure should be supplemented with detailed information that links to enterprise-wide disclosures and that changes in response to changing risks and uncertainties; for example, in the current environment, disclosures about residential and commercial real estate and leveraged loan exposures.

II-6. The Policy Group *recommends* that firms provide tabular disclosures about the effects of restrictions on the use of consolidated assets, non- recourse liabilities, and minority interests.

The following are some examples of consolidated assets and liabilities for which additional disclosure may be necessary in order to bridge the gap between the amounts reported in the consolidated financial statements and an enterprise's economic exposure to risk:

- risk exposure to consolidated assets absorbed by minority investors;
- linking of consolidated assets to non-recourse financings on a disaggregated basis; and
- hedges and other risk management tools used to limit or participate in exposure to consolidated assets or liabilities.

SECTION III: HIGH-RISK COMPLEX FINANCIAL INSTRUMENTS

A. Introduction

As discussed elsewhere in this Report, throughout the credit market crisis, the behavioral characteristics of several classes of structured credit instruments have accounted for a significant fraction of the write-downs and losses incurred by large integrated financial intermediaries, hedge funds, specialized financial institutions and other market participants. Moreover, there is almost universal agreement that, even with optimal disclosure in the underlying documentation, the characteristics of these instruments and the risk of loss associated with them were not fully understood by many market participants. This lack of comprehension was even more pronounced when applied to CDOs, CDOs squared,[4] and related instruments, reflecting a complex array of factors, including a lack of understanding of the inherent limitations of valuation models and the risks of short-run historical data sets. As a consequence, these instruments displayed price depreciation and volatility far in excess of levels previously associated with comparably rated securities, causing both a collapse of confidence in a very broad range of structured product ratings and a collapse in liquidity for such products.

In light of these circumstances, the Policy Group has devoted considerable emphasis and resources to the subject of complex financial instruments and has developed specific recommendations designed to reform and improve market practices in response to the credit market crisis. The Policy Group has not addressed the activities of rating agencies in the credit market crisis, nor has it made recommendations concerning their role going forward. Instead, the Policy Group believes that it is vital for every market participant to understand risk and make independent credit judgments even when ratings are available. As such, the Policy Group's analysis focuses on the instruments, the participants, the practices, and the flow of information in the markets for high-risk complex financial instruments.

[4] The risk characteristics of CDOs were spelled out in great detail in the CRMPG II Report. That analysis is appended as Appendix B to this Report.

A natural starting point for this analysis centers on the attributes of high-risk complex financial instruments recognizing that *not all complex financial instruments are necessarily high-risk.* The definition of a high-risk complex financial instrument is itself a complex subject. For example, while it is easy enough to say that subprime CDOs are a high-risk complex financial instrument, it is impossible to solve the definitional issue by compiling a list of such high-risk instruments, if for no other reason than any such list would be almost immediately out of date.

Additionally, the Policy Group's focus has not been limited to discussing the characteristics and practices associated with specific instruments in the credit market crisis. Its aim, instead, is to provide recommendations that may be applied in a forward- looking manner to transactions in high-risk complex financial instruments – including both cash and derivatives – in all markets. Thus, the effort to cope with the definitional challenge is better framed by identifying the key characteristics of classes of high-risk complex financial instruments that warrant special treatment in terms of sales and marketing practices, disclosure practices, diligence standards, and, more broadly, the level of sophistication required for all market participants, including issuers and investors.

The first and perhaps the most important characteristic of high-risk complex financial instruments is leverage. However, recognizing the role of leverage is one thing, while understanding that leverage can take several forms is quite another matter. Leverage may refer to borrowing money to finance the purchase of securities or other financial instruments. It may also refer to so-called embedded leverage often associated with derivatives and asset tranching. An example of this is an investment in subordinated tranches of asset-backed or corporate credit derivative contracts. In the case of these instruments, the market exposure is magnified relative to an investment in the underlying instrument and gains and losses are experienced more quickly, sometimes much more quickly, than in an un-leveraged investment. Unlike leverage generally associated with borrowing, losses associated with embedded leverage are generally limited to the size of the initial investment; however, the risk of loss to which investors found themselves exposed far exceeded most, if not virtually all, stress scenario modeling they had performed.

The multiplier effect of embedded leverage may also be compounded. For example, mezzanine tranches of mortgage securitizations (which, themselves, have embedded leverage) were often purchased by CDOs, which, in turn, issued senior and subordinated tranches, creating embedded leverage on leverage in the subordinated pieces. Some of these CDOs in turn found their way into CDOs squared, compounding the leverage even further. Exposures to rising delinquency rates were, as a result, greatly magnified for investors in these instruments. On certain occasions, these highly leveraged CDO-related instruments were acquired by various forms of investment vehicles that were themselves highly leveraged.

The magnitude of this embedded leverage was in itself often model-derived value which depended, for example, on projections of mortgage delinquency and default rates. In other words, investors could not always be certain about the degree to which their exposures to the mortgage market were leveraged at the time of investment. When delinquency assumptions associated with the mortgage securitizations of 2005, 2006 and early 2007 proved to be far too low, the leverage and losses experienced by investors in these secondary and tertiary repackagings were far greater than anticipated.

The second key characteristic of high-risk complex financial instruments is that, by their nature, they are prone to periods of sharply reduced market liquidity. As witnessed during the credit market crisis, market liquidity for many of these instruments was not merely reduced but in some instances virtually evaporated. In this environment, risk reductions – including de-leveraging – were nearly impossible, and hedging was very expensive and often imperfect, introducing basis risk. Needless to say, in these circumstances, valuations and price verification for these instruments had limited evidential support, although this did not obscure the fact that *some positions* and *some trades* had lost much, if not essentially most, of their value, with little prospect for material future recovery.

The third characteristic of high-risk complex financial instruments is that they may be characterized by a lack of price transparency. These instruments are often bespoke, and their valuations depend on proprietary financial models and the inputs that drive those models. Frequently, the inputs for these models are not directly observable in the market. In addition, even a valid model with accurate inputs will not always capture the immediate supply and demand profile of the market, meaning that the model price will not always determine the price at which a transaction will occur. In this circumstance, buyers and sellers of high-risk complex financial instruments may achieve price discovery only through actual transactions, but these may not occur because of the aforementioned illiquidity.

It is possible that an instrument which would otherwise be high-risk and complex is not regarded as such because of its liquidity and price transparency. Large capitalization common stocks are generally considered neither high-risk nor complex, avoiding the label because of their visibility in the market and liquidity. If stocks were priced in a vacuum based only on a model of one's own design, such shares would probably be considered both high-risk and complex. Conversely, price transparency does not always preclude an instrument from being labeled high-risk and complex. There are, for example, futures markets in high-risk complex financial instruments that are so labeled despite the transparency provided by the futures markets.

While issues surrounding leverage, market liquidity, and price transparency are the key characteristics in identifying high-risk complex financial instruments, other factors have contributed to the problems witnessed during the credit market crisis. For example, in some investment vehicles the high-risk factors of leverage and market illiquidity were amplified by substantial maturity mismatches, where illiquid long-term assets were funded with short-term liabilities. Additionally, for many high-risk instruments, disclosure information was limited, or to the extent it was provided, it could have been more "user friendly" in its presentation. Finally, many high-risk complex financial instruments presented significant challenges for risk monitoring and management systems, which struggled to keep up with the complexities of product design and development and, in particular, encompass the risk that hedging strategies were ineffective, so generating additional, and sizeable, exposure in the form of basis risk.

The aforementioned characteristics are neither an exhaustive list nor should they be assumed to provide a strict definition of high-risk complex instruments, which the Policy Group believes should be avoided. Instead, market participants should establish procedures for determining, based on the key characteristics discussed above, whether an instrument is to be considered high-risk and complex and thus require the special treatment outlined in this section.

In the wake of the obvious problems presented by high-risk complex financial instruments, the Policy Group has developed a series of measures and recommendations that it believes address the shortcomings that surfaced during the credit market crisis while not unduly suppressing the beneficial role of innovation in the financial marketplace. The four broad areas of reform recommended by the Policy Group are as follows:

1. refining and elevating standards of sophistication for market participants;
2. enhancing the level and usefulness of disclosure;
3. strengthening intermediary-client relationships in such areas as sales and marketing practices; and
4. ensuring consistent diligence standards for issuers and placement agents of high-risk complex financial instruments.

B. Standards of Sophistication

The Policy Group *strongly recommends* that high-risk complex financial instruments should be sold only to sophisticated investors. Having said that, the practicalities of making this doctrine operational are both subtle and complex. The Policy Group further recommends that a standard of behavior and consistent practice be introduced for all market participants. While there are clearly delineated roles for originators, underwriters, managers, trustees, investors, and others, the Policy Group recommends that involvement in the market for high-risk complex financial instruments in any of these roles requires:

- education and training in the nuances of these instruments;
- systems and models sufficient for tracking performance, managing risk, and running stress scenarios;
- strong governance procedures and internal controls; and
- financial resources sufficient to withstand potential losses associated with high- risk complex financial instruments.

While these standards must apply to participants at every stage in the process, perhaps the most vital point of application is the investor. The starting point is the assurance that the investor has a high level of financial sophistication. It is therefore necessary to develop a workable definition of a "sophisticated investor". One such approach followed in the United States is Securities and Exchange Commission (SEC) Rule 144A, which is itself quite complex to administer. In essence, Rule 144A lists and defines various types of entities which are called "Qualified Institutional Buyers" (QIBs). At the risk of considerable oversimplification, QIBs are entities that own and invest in at least $100 million in securities of issuers that are not affiliated with the QIB. Similar regulatory definitions are employed in other jurisdictions, including under the European Union Markets in Financial Instruments Directive *(MiFID)* in Europe.

Any definition of a sophisticated investor should reflect at a minimum the definition provided by the relevant regulatory jurisdiction. The details of regulatory requirements, however, are such that entities may pass the quantitative (or objective) tests of the relevant regulations but may not be appropriate buyers of high-risk complex financial instruments as discussed above.

Recommendations

III-1. The Policy Group *recommends* establishing standards of sophistication for all market participants in high-risk complex financial instruments. In recommending specific characteristics and practices for participants, it is guided by the overriding principle that all participants should be capable of assessing and managing the risk of their positions in a manner consistent with their needs and objectives. All participants in the market for high-risk complex financial instruments should ensure that they possess the following characteristics and make reasonable efforts to determine that their counterparties possess them as well:

- the capability to understand the risk and return characteristics of the specific type of financial instrument under consideration;
- the capability, or access to the capability, to price and run stress tests on the instrument;
- the governance procedures, technology, and internal controls necessary for trading and managing the risk of the instrument;
- the financial resources sufficient to withstand potential losses associated with the instrument; and
- authorization to invest in high-risk complex financial instruments from the highest level of management or, where relevant, from authorizing bodies for the particular counterparty.

Large integrated financial intermediaries should adopt policies and procedures to identify when it would be appropriate to seek written confirmation that the counterparty possesses the aforementioned characteristics.

C. Disclosure

As discussed in the prior section, it is critical that participants in the markets for high-risk complex instruments must understand the risks that they face. An investor or derivative counterparty should have the information needed to make informed decisions. While the Policy Group has recommended that each participant must develop a degree of independence in decision-making, large integrated financial intermediaries have a responsibility to provide their counterparties with appropriate documentation and disclosures. Disclosures must meet the standards established by the relevant regulatory jurisdiction. The Policy Group believes that appropriate disclosures should often go beyond those minimum standards, both through enhancement for instruments currently requiring disclosure, and by establishing documentation standards for instruments that currently require little or none.

Risk information should be available to participants in a format that makes it easily accessible. The format should clearly identify the factors that influence day-to-day price changes in the instrument, as well as making a clear statement of the factors and influences that might lead to significant or catastrophic losses. While no intermediary or counterparty can literally predict the outcome of an investment or forward looking market conditions, appropriate disclosures should anticipate the factors and market conditions that will cause the instrument to experience losses. Disclosure should also identify, to the extent possible, the sensitivities of the instrument to those factors and conditions, as well as the approximate magnitude of the losses the instrument will likely experience in such an environment.

For instruments requiring disclosure, the depth and breadth of information required may contribute to the difficulty of accessing the most useful information concerning risk. This information is in the disclosure documents, but the Policy Group believes that a document containing a brief discussion of significant risks will contribute to increased transparency. For instruments currently requiring little or no disclosure, this document will serve as a means of communicating relevant risk information to counterparties. For instruments requiring disclosure, this summary should not be viewed as a substitute for the often lengthy disclosures, but rather as a supplement. Ideally, it will highlight significant risks and encourage a more thorough examination of the relevant sections of the full disclosure document.

Recommendations

The Policy Group believes that there are opportunities to enhance and strengthen the documentation and disclosures provided to prospective investors in high-risk complex financial instruments, while being mindful that documentation and disclosure practices will (and should) vary somewhat from instrument to instrument and will also vary over time. With that qualification in mind, the Policy Group *recommends* the following as a matter of industry best practice.

III-2a. The documentation of all high-risk complex financial instruments in cash or derivative form should include a term sheet: a concise summary highlighting deal terms and, where appropriate, collateral manager capabilities, and portfolio and deal payment structure. The term sheets for all high-risk complex financial instruments, the full scope of which is outlined in Appendix A, must, among other factors, include the following:

- a clear explanation of the economics of the instrument including a discussion of the key assumptions that give rise to the expected returns; and
- rigorous scenario analyses and stress tests that prominently illustrate how the instrument will perform in extreme scenarios, in addition to more probable scenarios.

III-2b. The documentation associated with *asset-backed high-risk complex financial instruments* should include:

- *A Preliminary and Final Offering Memorandum:* The offering memorandum should include prominently within its first several pages the nature of the economic interest of the underwriter or placement agent (and its affiliates) in the transaction, including a clear statement of the roles to be undertaken and services to be provided by the underwriter or placement agent (or its affiliates) to the transaction, as well as any interests in the transaction (if any) that the underwriter or placement agent (or its affiliates) are required or expected to retain.

- *A Marketing Book:* The marketing book should include an in- depth description of the materials contained in the term sheet. It should especially focus on the collateral manager (in the case of a managed portfolio) and deal structure.
- *Portfolio Stratifications:* This documentation should be in the form of spreadsheets containing bond level information (sector, rating, par balance, *etc.*), where known, and weighted average loan level information (FICO, service, LTV, % fixed, occupancy, geographic distribution, 2nd liens, *etc.*).
- *Cash Flow/Stress Scenarios:* This documentation should be in the form of spreadsheets and cash flow model outputs. Standard runs should be provided for each tranche offered. The output will typically be in the form of tranche cash flows and default/loss percentages for the tranches and collateral.

III-2c. In addition to the documentation standards covered above, the Policy Group further *recommends* that term sheets and offering memoranda for all financial instruments having one or more of the key characteristics associated with high-risk complex financial instruments as discussed on pages 54, 56 *must have* a "financial health" warning prominently displayed in bold print indicating that the presence of these characteristics gives rise to the *potential* for significant loss over the life of the instrument. The "health warning" should also refer to all risk factors in the offering documents.

The Policy Group *recommends* that complex bilateral transactions that are privately negotiated between sophisticated market participants are not subject to Recommendations IV-2b and 2c but are subject to Recommendation IV-2a regarding term sheets. In certain circumstances, however, and by mutual written consent, the term sheet requirement may be waived for bilateral transactions between highly sophisticated market participants or in the context of a repeated pattern of transactions of a particular type.

D. Intermediary-Client Relationships

Although all market participants must be sophisticated, high-risk complex financial instruments involving a financial intermediary and an end-user or counterparty require special clarity with respect to the nature of the relationship between the parties and the obligations of each in connection with these transactions. These obligations start with the communication prior to and during the execution of a trade and often extend well beyond trade execution. This is particularly, but not exclusively, true for high-risk complex OTC

derivatives. Since these transactions will often remain outstanding for a significant period of time, it is in the interests of both parties to have a firm and clear understanding of the principles that should guide the parties over the course of their relationship. These principles are intended as a complement to the standards of sophistication for market participants and disclosure enhancements outlined earlier. A sophisticated participant in possession of clear and concise risk information and a thorough understanding of its counterparty relationships will be in a better position to evaluate high-risk complex financial instruments and manage the associated risks. These principles are intended to complement, rather than substitute for, compliance by large integrated financial intermediaries with their express contractual undertakings and with applicable legal and regulatory requirements relating to the offer or sale of such products.

Recommendations

The Policy Group *recommends* strengthening the relationship between intermediaries and counterparties in sales, marketing and ongoing communications associated with high-risk complex financial instruments. While its first recommendation calls for establishment of a common standard of sophistication for all market participants in high-risk complex financial instruments, the Policy Group believes that large integrated financial intermediaries should provide clients with timely and relevant information about a transaction beyond the disclosures discussed in its Recommendation III-2 above.

III-3a. The intermediary and counterparty should review with each other the material terms of a complex transaction prior to execution.

III-3b. Both the intermediary and counterparty must make reasonable efforts to confirm the execution of a complex transaction in a timely manner.

- The counterparty should be promptly notified of any expected delay in the creation of a confirmation.
- The intermediary should disclose whether evidence of agreement, such as a signed term sheet, is binding as to transaction terms. Each party should review the terms and promptly notify the other of any error.

III-3c. When a counterparty requests a valuation of a high-risk complex financial instrument, the intermediary should respond in a manner appropriate to the purpose of the valuation. The intermediary's sales and trading personnel may provide a counterparty with actionable quotes or indicative unwind levels. Only groups independent of sales and trading should provide indicative valuations and only in writing. Where relevant, such indicative valuations should include information describing the basis upon which the valuation is being provided.

III-3d. As a part of the relationship between intermediaries and their counterparties following trade execution, the intermediary should make reasonable efforts on a case-by-case basis to keep the counterparty informed of material developments regarding the performance of key positions.

E. Issuer Diligence

One area of focus in the creation and distribution of high-risk complex financial instruments is the responsibility of underwriters for understanding and ensuring proper documentation of the quality of assets in a securitization. Underwriters engage in a process known as "due diligence" when agreeing to bring a transaction to market. Due diligence in both the real estate and non-real estate asset-backed markets takes place on three levels: (1) due diligence of originators, (2) due diligence of the assets being securitized, and (3) due diligence of offering documents. The section that follows describes the current due diligence process in the securitization markets and offers several recommendations for improvements in practices and in communicating results. The description is quite detailed and outlines a very thorough process, but the Policy Group feels that there is room for some improvement. It also believes that the process as described along with the Policy Group's suggested improvements should be the standard by which all underwriters conduct their due diligence activities.

1. Due Diligence of Originators

Due diligence of originators in both the real estate and non-real estate asset-backed markets is driven by the following scenarios: (1) when a new or infrequent issuer comes to market, (2) when a frequent originator forms a new relationship with an underwriter, and (3) each time a frequent issuer plans to securitize a pool of loans. The process of due diligence involves developing an understanding and comfort level with respect to the business practices, background, creditworthiness, and historical performance data of an originator. When a new or infrequent issuer comes to market, the due diligence process involves a detailed examination of their business, involving a number of professionals from the underwriter representing the asset-backed business, credit risk management, and legal/compliance areas. For frequent issuers, due diligence generally occurs multiple times a year, often immediately prior to a transaction or on a fixed quarterly basis.

Once a relationship is established between an originator and an underwriter, the due diligence is largely confirmatory and relies on representations from the originator that nothing material has changed in its business practices as well as an ongoing examination of the originator's performance data in an attempt to determine if in fact there have been material changes. The due diligence conference call is a primary form of diligence of regular issuers and is composed of business and legal questions. Business questions are posed by the underwriter and focus on revealing any material issues related to the portfolio performance and forecast, changes in asset underwriting, the status of the servicer, competition within the relevant industry and any general corporate issues. Legal questions are asked by the underwriters' counsel and are meant to highlight material litigation, potential material legislation, regulatory issues and accounting concerns. Call participants include business and legal representatives from the issuer, all underwriters and their respective legal counsel. This "bring-down" acts as a confirmation of prior due diligence and is often undertaken immediately prior to a transaction, both to ensure that information is current as well as to accommodate a tight securitization schedule.

When a frequent issuer establishes a new relationship with an underwriter (*i.e.*, one with whom it has not previously been involved in a transaction), due diligence may involve the more detailed approach described above, but the underwriter may, depending on the circumstances, rely in part on the due diligence performed by another underwriter familiar with the issuer. Generally, an underwriter in the co-manager role relies on the due diligence performed by the lead managers while the lead manager(s) undertake a more thorough examination. Since there is general agreement among underwriters about the characteristics of an acceptable originator, the reliance has not been considered problematic.

2. Due Diligence of Assets

Due diligence of assets is the process by which an underwriter familiarizes itself with the assets to be securitized and establishes a comfort level as to the quality and disclosure of process and information provided by the originator. Asset due diligence is often conducted on behalf of the underwriter by third-party vendors specializing in this activity.

In the real estate and non-real estate asset-backed markets, due diligence involves the issuer or underwriter hiring an accounting firm to check data integrity. A formal "agreed upon procedures" (AUP) letter from the accountant reports the findings of this confirmatory analysis. In the United States, this letter is mandated by SEC Regulation AB, the SEC's regulatory framework for publicly issued asset-backed securities (ABS), which took effect on January 1, 2006. All publicly registered ABS are subject to Regulation AB, which dictates registration, disclosure and reporting requirements. The AUP letter diligence occurs in two parts: (1) verification of the accuracy of historical data; and (2) comparison of the data tape to the actual loan files through "tape-to-file" procedures. The issuer provides the accountants with sample documents and data related to the transaction pool of receivables. These documents and data may include: (1) a preliminary and final pool of receivables data file; (2) a prospectus supplement; (3) selection criteria; (4) the composition of receivables, distribution of the receivables split by APR, payment frequency, current balance, geography, *etc.*; (5) the managed portfolio losses and delinquencies; (6) copies of the receivables files; (7) the servicer reports; (8) the pool file cash flows; and (9) the methodology used to project various payment speeds. Much of this information is made available to investors.

To verify historical data, the accountants recalculate a selection of key data and performance metrics and compare their findings with those of the issuer to ensure accuracy. In tape-to-file analysis, the accountants will perform statistical sampling of the

pool of assets and compare the information provided on the tape to underwriters with the information contained in the loan files or on the originator's or servicer's systems. If exceptions are found they are investigated by the underwriter with the originator and accounting firm to determine what caused the data discrepancy. Exceptions will generally result in the need for additional (or more targeted) sampling in order to determine whether there are systemic problems within the pool of assets and, a determination made, whether to proceed with a transaction. *The accountants provide the results of their review via letter to the issuer and underwriter, but this is not shared with investors. AUP letters are also customary in nonpublic (e.g., Rule 144A) underwritten transactions.*

In the real estate asset-backed market the due diligence involves random sampling of loans with a detailed examination of the loans in the sample. Here again, if exceptions are found, they are investigated and an additional (and larger) sample is taken. This process may be repeated. If problems persist in the larger samples, the underwriter may determine that the transaction should not proceed.

In both markets there is a tension in the sampling process between the desire for thorough review and the desire to respond quickly to an originating client's desire to come to market quickly. The sample size is sometimes a point of negotiation between the issuer and the underwriter with whom it is considering transacting.

3. Due Diligence on Disclosure

Regulation AB specifies disclosure requirements in four key categories: static pool data, credit enhancement, transaction parties, and pool assets. Static pool performance data on delinquencies, losses, prepayments and residual realization must be provided for the past five years or for such shorter period during which the sponsor has been securitizing, originating or purchasing the same type of assets as those in the subject transaction. Such detailed performance data disclosure is mandated at the time of sale and the initial data are available throughout the life of the transaction on the issuer's static pool performance website, a link to which is typically provided in the prospectus. The prospectus should describe internal credit enhancement, including applicable subordination, overcol lateral ization and reserve accounts. The prospectus must articulate the experience of and material concerns regarding transaction parties, specifically the sponsor, originator(s) and servicer.

Regulation AB also contains extensive disclosure guidelines regarding the securitized asset pool. For example, the "credit underwriting process" description must include: (1) details of any internal credit grading scales such as FICO or an equivalent internal scoring metric; (2) a description of any economic or other factors that may effect the pool assets; and (3) definitions of delinquencies, charge-offs and uncollectible accounts that address the effect of any grace period, re-aging, restructuring, partial payments considered current or other practices on delinquency experience.

Underwriters examine the disclosure documents to ensure that they accurately reflect the characteristics of the pool of assets. This includes a review by accountants and attorneys. The accountants undertake to comfort the portfolio statistics in the disclosure document and include this in their AUP letter referenced above. The attorneys ensure that the disclosure is not only accurate, but that it also does not omit any material facts. This review is generally thought to be quite thorough. While there are differences among disclosure documents there are no questions or recommendations for changing this due diligence procedure.

The Policy Group has some recommendations concerning due diligence, but is left with the question of what went wrong in the process and how diligence practices might have contributed to the unexpected nature of the losses associated with a number of asset- backed securitizations. This problem appears to have arisen more from a general reliance by all market participants – including, perhaps, the rating agencies – on historical information in assessing the potential for losses, rather than systemic shortcomings in due diligence. While the Policy Group has identified some areas for enhancement of diligence and strongly urges all underwriters to adhere to rigorous standards like those described above, it does not believe these changes would have materially changed performance expectations in the market at the time of the bubble. For this reason, the Policy Group recommended elsewhere in this Report more imaginative use of stress tests and so-called "reverse stress tests" to better inform potential investors and counterparties of the risks they face.

Recommendations

With respect to high-risk complex asset-backed securitizations, underwriters and placement agents should have in place an ongoing framework for evaluating the performance and reputation of issuers as well as effective and clearly articulated procedures for evaluating the quality of assets. The Policy Group *strongly urges* that underwriters and placement agents redouble efforts to adhere fully to the letter and spirit of existing diligence standards, and seek opportunities to standardize and enhance such standards. These enhancements include the following recommendations:

- III-4a. Requiring all firms to follow statistically valid sampling techniques in assessing the quality of assets in a securitization; and
- III-4b. Encouraging disclosure to investors of due diligence results, including making the AUP letter publicly available.

SECTION IV: RISK MONITORING AND RISK MANAGEMENT

A. Introduction

As is now widely recognized, the events leading up to the credit market crisis and the crisis itself have demonstrated shortcomings in risk monitoring and risk management across many institutions and classes of institutions. To some extent, these shortcomings reflect the fact that virtually all risk management tools are unable to model/present the most severe forms of financial shocks in a fashion that is credible to senior management. In addition, these shortcomings reflect "technical" limitations associated with risk management tools, including the fact that most quantitative models are, to some extent, backward-looking. That is to say, they are in essence a disciplined framework for the analysis of historic data and, as such, they implicitly assume that the future will look like the past. As another example of technical limitations, many hedges are far less than perfect, giving rise to basis risk; for example, when historic correlations, or default rates, or other parameters move materially away from modeled outcomes, which on occasion has resulted in substantial write downs or losses. Finally, and perhaps most importantly, there have been shortcomings regarding the full appreciation of the tight linkages and interdependencies between capital adequacy and liquidity – both market liquidity and funding liquidity.

While these and other shortcomings in risk monitoring and risk management can, with the benefit of hindsight, be explained, there is a larger and more profound issue at work in this context. That is, despite all of the complexities of risk management, the essence of risk monitoring and risk management is quite straightforward. Specifically, risk monitoring and management reduces to the basics of getting the right information, at the right time, to the right people, such that those people can make the most informed judgments possible.

Looked at in that light, several things stand out. Risk management assumes that risk monitoring is effective and that critical information flowing into and out of risk monitoring processes can be distilled and compiled in a coherent and timely manner and made available, not only to the risk managers, but to key business leaders across the institution and to top management. Only when this logical sequence of conditions is present and is supported by a rigorous but flexible framework of corporate governance will there be reasonable prospects that business judgments can better anticipate and respond to contagion and systemic events. This is the fundamental reason why the Policy Group has placed so much emphasis on the core precepts outlined in Section I.

This same philosophy has also shaped the content of this section with its emphasis on (1) corporate governance, (2) enhanced tools and techniques in risk monitoring and management, (3) the use of the "maximum liquidity outflow" technique to substantially upgrade liquidity management, and (4) the linking together of the conceptual frameworks for analysis of capital adequacy, leverage and liquidity. Indeed, to the extent that capital adequacy and rigorous stress testing of liquidity are viewed *as a single discipline,* concerns about leverage and leverage ratios will be substantially mitigated.

B. Governance Background and Recommendations

The Policy Group has identified corporate governance as a core precept for large integrated financial intermediaries. Because effective risk monitoring and risk management are so tightly linked to sound corporate governance, this part of Section IV includes discusses and makes recommendations regarding corporate governance. These recommendations are designed to reinforce Core Precept I relating to corporate governance in Section I. The recommendations discussed below cover the following aspects of governance:

1. structure;
2. internal communication; and
3. the roles of committees.

1. Structure

Large integrated financial intermediaries by definition take risk. The goal of risk management is not to eliminate that risk, but to manage it effectively to provide the stakeholders of the institution with long-term returns commensurate with the risk. Riskmanagement – in the broadest possible meaning of that term – must be deeply rooted in the culture of individual institutions. However, culture is easy to recognize but hard to define. Thus, to a large extent, the practice of sound corporate governance must rely, in part, on the organizational structure of the firm.

Good governance begins with the Chief Executive Officer (CEO). The message that the CEO conveys to the firm's employees about the importance of corporate governance as it applies to the firm's risk taking and the way in which that risk taking is discussed with the board sets the tone for the overall corporate governance process.

Effective corporate governance is realized when the many facets of an organization work closely together to properly identify, monitor, price and mitigate (or intentionally accept on an unmitigated basis) all of the risks inherent in the business model of the organization, including financial, operational and reputational risk. Success depends importantly on the highest levels of the organization having information that is clear, timely and actionable.

To create the link between corporate governance and risk management, some firms use the concept of "three lines of defense". In this model, the business unit is the first line of defense and is accountable for identifying, assessing, taking and mitigating the risks of its business. The second line of defense includes the business support functions, such as risk management, legal, compliance, human resources, finance, operations, and technology. Each of these groups independently and collectively works closely with the business units to ensure that the business has appropriately identified, measured, priced, and managed the risk in the business. It is expected that the business support functions will work closely in helping to shape strategy, implementing company policies and procedures, and collecting information across the business units to create company-wide views of risk. The third line of defense includes the audit function that independently tests the efficacy of the processes created by senior business leaders and top management and the judgments made by these officials.

There is a widespread consensus about the need for a strong, independent risk management function. This is usually achieved by having a role, such as Chief Risk Officer (CRO), with a strong reporting relationship that reinforces the importance of the function. However, the reporting relationship is not sufficient by itself. The CEO and board of directors need to ensure that the individual performing the CRO role is a clear and visible member of the firm's top management team and is able to independently influence risk taking, risk appetite, and risk mitigation. The members of the risk management organization should have shared responsibility for approving new business, products, and transactions along with the business line. The risk management team must work closely with other independent support and control functions, such as controllers, operations and internal audit, to ensure seamless control of risk taking and mitigation across the family of control functions.

The CRO function must have human and infrastructure resources available to it commensurate with the level of sophistication of the institution. As businesses are started or continue to develop, senior management needs to ensure that the business support functions are staffed with individuals capable of understanding the business's risk as it evolves and relating it to other risks within the institution. Consideration needs to be given to rotating business leaders into business support functions in order to deepen their understanding of risk and to provide additional experience and expertise to the support functions. Information systems and processes must allow for a robust and timely assessment of the risks of the firm.

Recommendations

IV-1a. The Policy Group *recommends* that risk management and other critical control functions be positioned within all large integrated financial intermediaries in a way that ensures that their actions and decisions are appropriately independent of the income producing business units and includes joint approval of key products and transactions. This would generally mean having a CRO with a direct line of responsibility to the CEO and having the CEO and the board take a highly active role in ensuring that the culture of the organization as a whole recognizes and embraces the independence of its critical control functions. Even without the direct reporting, the CRO should have a clear line of communication to the board.

IV-1b. The Policy Group further *recommends* that institutions ensure that their risk management functions are staffed appropriately for both the upside and the downside and are able to understand and properly size risks in tranquil markets as well as during periods of market stress. The risk management functions must also have the capacity to function effectively in periods of spikes in processing volumes and under various disaster recovery scenarios.

2. Communication

While far from being universally true, much of the writings from the events of the last 12 months have focused on the inability of firms to see the totality of the risk they faced. This problem was the result of several causes, including: (1) inadequate risk aggregation systems, (2) systems or processes that did not pull together all exposures because they were viewed as outside the scope of the firm's risk, (3) siloed business or risk management units, and (4) simply a lack of understanding.

As described above, the creation of a specific governance structure will not, by itself, solve these problems. Firms which were able to work across their organizations with common language and measures of risk had a greater chance of success during times of market stress.

All personnel in risk taking and risk mitigation business units must understand all aspects of risk – strategic, credit, market, liquidity and operational risk. During the credit market crisis, credit risks became market risks, which then became liquidity risks in very short order. Officials across the organization need to understand those connections and the potential for contagion, just as they must understand the implications of those connections for risk appetite even though there is no single metric that will measure the risk of contagion or express that appetite.

In the complex world of large integrated financial intermediaries, there are a myriad of risks and measures of those risks. It is the responsibility of risk management to distill that information into a very understandable and concise format. Risk transparency is not measured by the quantity of information considered in committees, but by the ease of understanding of that information by someone who is not experienced in that field. This is true of information presented to all committees within the company, including information submitted to senior management and, when appropriate, to the board of directors.

Recommendations

IV-2a. The Policy Group *recommends* that all large integrated financial intermediaries evaluate the manner in which information relating to risk taking, risk monitoring, and risk management is shared with senior management and the board of directors and make necessary improvements to ensure that such information flows are timely, understandable, and properly presented. As a part of this effort, senior management should actively encourage ongoing discussion with board members in order to improve the quality, coverage and utility of information made available to the board. Each institution should evaluate how effective its information flows are as they relate to the intersection of credit, market, operational and liquidity risk.

IV-2b. The Policy Group *recommends* that each institution *ensure that the risk tolerance of the firm is established or approved by the highest levels of management and shared with the board.* The Policy Group further recommends that each institution ensure that periodic exercises aimed at estimation of risk tolerance should be shared with the highest levels of management, the board of directors and the institution's primary supervisor in line with Core Precept III, as discussed on pages 11, 12.

IV-2c. The Policy Group further *recommends* that large integrated financial intermediaries ensure that their treasury and risk management functions work with each other and with business units to manage balance sheet size and composition in a manner that ensures that the established risk tolerance is consistent with funding capabilities and ongoing efforts to manage liquidity risk.

IV-2d. The Policy Group further *recommends* that each institution review its internal systems of both formal and informal communication across business units and control functions to ensure that such communication systems encourage the *prompt* and *coherent* flow of risk-related information within and across business units and, as needed, the prompt escalation of quality information to top management.

3. The Roles of Committees

All large integrated financial intermediaries must, as a practical matter, rely on a number of senior level institution-wide committees to facilitate communication, coordination, and, in some instances, collective or consensus-based decision-making. While the names and mandates of such institution-wide committees will vary from one institution to another, the subject matter covered by these committees is fairly common and typically includes areas such as (1) financial risk management including funding and liquidity, (2) large commitments of the firm's own capital, (3) operational and reputational risk, (4) business practices, and (5) new product approvals. Recognizing the vital roles of these committees as an integral part of governance arrangements at large integrated financial intermediaries, the Policy Group believes that there are opportunities to strengthen the functioning of the committee structure. Specifically:

IV-3a. The Policy Group *recommends* that, when schedules permit, the CEO and the second ranking officers of all large integrated financial intermediaries should frequently attend and participate in meetings of risk management-related committees.

IV-3b. The Policy Group further *recommends* that the highest levels of management periodically review the functioning of the committee structure to ensure, among other things, that such committees are appropriately chaired and staffed and there is an appropriate overlap of key business leaders, support leaders, and enterprise executives across committees to help foster firm-wide cooperation and communication.

IV-3c. The Policy Group further *recommends* that for certain classes of firm- wide committees, such as those responsible for the approval of new products – especially new products having high financial, operational or reputational risks – the committee oversight process should include a systematic post-approval review process. This post-approval review process would assess the extent to which new products have, in commercial terms, performed as expected. Equally important, the process would assess whether the risk characteristics of the new product have been consistent with expectations, including the burden of the new products on technology and operating systems. Further, it is particularly appropriate to review at the earliest opportunity outsized profitability and market share gains to ensure that this does not reflect a problem with the original pricing or risk assessment of the product.

C. Risk Measurement and Monitoring and Recommendations

CRMPG I and CRMPG II incorporated a number of recommendations that were broadly grouped into "Transparency and Counterparty Risk Assessment" (CRPMG I), "Internal Risk Measurement, Management and Reporting" (CRMPG I) and "Risk Management and Risk-Related Disclosure Practices" (CRMPG II) sections. As a result of significant individual firm and broader industry attention and investment, substantial progress has been made in fulfilling a preponderance of these initial recommendations. However, as a result of a more complex business environment and other factors, including an increasing variety of structures giving rise to basis and liquidity risk, required standards for risk management have increased substantially.

One component of these standards, without which effective risk management is not possible, is the accurate measurement and monitoring of credit and market risks. Building on the recommendations of the CRMPG I and II Reports, the following reflects additional or updated recommendations, which are essential, in the current environment, to the measurement and monitoring of these risks.

1. Investment in the Risk Management Process

Recent events have highlighted limitations and weaknesses in the risk management processes and infrastructures of many large integrated financial intermediaries and their clients. In some cases, reliance on other "smart" players to vet trades has been considered sufficient to allow other firms to do "copy cat" trades. In other cases, excessive reliance on rating agencies without an independent and detailed analysis of the rating agencies' rating criteria has led to complacency in building large positions of highly- rated but complex and illiquid financial instruments. In yet other cases, risk management teams have engaged in sophisticated theoretical modeling with limited connection to practical risk-taking activity. As a result, these teams' relevance and efficacy have been limited.

These and other causes contributed to risk management systems and processes that were inadequate for the task of managing risk in the volatile, stressed environment of the credit market crisis.

Recommendations

Large integrated financial intermediaries need to make serious and sustained investment in their risk management teams and infrastructures. This activity must be at the core of the risk taking process. Large integrated financial intermediaries who choose not to make such investments, or who cannot afford to develop a comprehensive, sophisticated knowledge of the products in which they propose to trade, would be prudent to refrain from significant involvement in these areas.

Building these risk capabilities is not inexpensive. Nor can they be assembled "just in time" for large incremental market positions or new initiatives. Firms must make significant and sustained commitments during both tumultuous and quiet markets. Moreover, risk management infrastructure cannot be quickly discarded if the product or industry sector is no longer an area of opportunity; it must remain in place as long as the risk positions remain in place.

IV-4a. The Policy Group *recommends* that sustained investment in risk management systems and processes, and the careful calibration of such investment to business opportunities being pursued, be a key area of focus for a firm's senior management team.

IV-4b. The Policy Group further *recommends* that each firm's CRO commission a periodic review and assessment of the firm's investments in risk management for presentation to its senior management and the audit committee of its board.

2. Stability of Credit Terms

Credit terms, including initial and variation margin for derivatives, haircuts for margin loans, and similar terms have been a key means by which large integrated financial intermediaries compete for client business. During benign market periods, it is not uncommon for credit terms to be negotiated down to levels that could expose large integrated financial intermediaries to material risk (relative to the credit of the counterparty) in the event of a counterparty default. Conversely, when market conditions deteriorate, large integrated financial intermediaries are often inclined to tighten credit terms to levels providing greater resilience against credit issues.

As the events that create stress in one counterparty may also impact others, the combined impact of multiple counterparties simultaneously coming under stress can undermine the stability of the financial system by setting off rounds of cascading liquidations and accelerating price declines.

While incentives for pro-cyclical credit loosening and credit tightening actions are readily understandable, the effect of these actions is to increase financial stress on a counterparty when that counterparty – and sometimes the entire financial system – is most vulnerable. Consequences include straining systemic liquidity, requiring the sales of positions on an immediate or other accelerated basis, and potential promulgation of adverse rumors.

Large integrated financial intermediaries and other market participants can also adversely affect counterparties through other means, including: (1) requesting (or not accepting when requested) assignments or novations of trades, (2) requesting that a counterparty close out derivatives transactions (especially those that are in-the-money to the counterparty and thus require the return of collateral), and (3) withdrawing funding lines. These decisions can have the same effects as tightening credit terms, not only in terms of draws on liquidity, but also on the ability of the counterparty to maintain its desired portfolio composition.

The effect of these actions can both increase the stress on individual counterparties, as well as increase the risk of systemic disruption.

Recommendations

Large integrated financial intermediaries and their clients must mutually recognize the value of stable credit terms and work together to create sustainable arrangements. Such credit terms should be analyzed to estimate their adequacy during stress periods. Those that are likely to prove inadequate should be identified so the parties can consider strengthening them. The term and haircuts of a financing should be sized to the anticipated time required for an orderly liquidation during periods of market stress, while at the same time incorporating the uncollateralized credit quality of the counterparty. For example, a large integrated financial intermediary would have less onerous terms and haircuts than a small, standalone fund. Large integrated financial intermediaries and their clients should be aware of the consequences of requesting and setting credit terms that are not resilient to changing market conditions, and clients should prepare contingency plans to deal with adverse developments in credit terms.

IV-5a. The Policy Group *recommends* that all market participants implement a paradigm shift in credit terms, establishing arrangements that create more stable trading relationships, are less pro-cyclical, and thus reduce systemic risk.

IV-5b. The Policy Group further *recommends* that each firm's senior management commission a periodic review of credit terms extended over a cycle, together with an assessment of the stability of such terms, for discussion with the firm's senior management.

3. Credit Risk Systems – Exposure Aggregation Capabilities

To *manage* risk effectively, large integrated financial intermediaries must have the capability to *monitor* risk comprehensively. However, the range of large integrated financial intermediaries and client products, markets and businesses, together with the volumes and varieties of trades, and the disparate risk metrics applicable to these products, makes this difficult. Further complicating the compilation of accurate exposure information is the variety of collateral and other limit- and trade-specific terms used, and the multitude of contract forms that are used to document trades and their associated credit terms.

Large integrated financial intermediaries need to maximize their ability to take appropriate actions to deal with counterparties before, during, and after the time the counterparty experiences problems. To do this, it is essential that large integrated financial intermediaries have the ability to rapidly compile aggregated counterparty information. This information should incorporate exposures across all related legal entities, on a global basis, with adjustments to reflect the effect of enforceable netting and collateral arrangements.

Recommendations

IV-6a. The Policy Group *recommends* that large integrated financial intermediaries ensure that their credit systems are adequate to compile detailed exposures to each of their institutional counterparties on an end-of-day basis by the opening of business the subsequent morning. In addition, the Policy Group recommends that large integrated financial intermediaries ensure their credit systems are capable of compiling, on an *ad hoc* basis and within a matter of hours, detailed and accurate estimates of market and credit risk exposure data across all counterparties and the risk parameters set out below. Within a slightly longer time frame this information should be expandable to include: (1) the directionality of the portfolio and of individual trades; (2) the incorporation of additional risk types, including contingent exposures and second and third order exposures (for example, SIVs, ABS, *etc.*); and (3) such other information as would be required to optimally manage risk exposures to a troubled counterparty. Large integrated financial intermediaries should be able to use exposure aggregation data both prospectively to avoid undue concentrations and, if necessary, in real time to react to unanticipated counterparty credit events.

IV-6b. To demonstrate their compliance with the aforementioned standards, the Policy Group *recommends* that firms conduct periodic exercises for both individual and multiple institutional counterparties, and, to the extent that deficiencies are observed, develop remediation plans as a matter of urgency.

4. Portfolio Metrics

Consistent with the recommendations of CRMPG I and II, market participants have expanded the range of risk metrics they use to include a range of stress tests, scenario analyses and other measures that are useful in revealing portfolio risk characteristics.

However, in many cases during the recent market disruption, these risk metrics were not effective in capturing the totality of risks that were actually incurred. Deficiencies included: (1) insufficiently extreme modeling of adverse price moves; (2) unanticipated deterioration in liquidity (which stretched out closeout periods); (3) unfavorable position correlations; and (4) the incomplete capture of contingent risks.

Risk reports may also be materially affected by the incorporation of underlying assumptions that are not fully apparent to users, but which can have a profound effect on calculated exposures. Examples include underlying assumptions about: (1) the effectiveness of market and credit hedges; (2) collateral valuations; (3) collateral enforceability; (4) trade valuations; and (5) prepayment, default, delinquency, and severity.

Despite the range of available metrics, public disclosure has remained focused on VaR and on current exposure as the major measures of market and credit risk, respectively. This has contributed to the market's lack of understanding of the size and nature of risks being taken by large integrated financial intermediaries and other market participants.

Recommendations

IV-7a. The Policy Group *recommends* that large integrated financial intermediaries' risk analytics incorporate sufficient granularity to reveal less obvious risks that can occur infrequently but that may potentially have a significant impact (for example, basis risks between single name underliers and index hedges). However, risk management professionals and senior management must recognize the limitations of mathematical models, and that the tendency to overly formalize arcane aspects of an analysis can often detract from an understanding of the bigger picture implications of the total risk position. Incremental analytical detail must not be allowed to overwhelm users of the data. The salient risk points must be drawn out and made apparent, especially to senior management. Adequate time and attention by senior management must also be allotted to socializing the implications of the risk data.

IV-7b. The Policy Group *recommends* that large integrated financial intermediaries ensure that assumptions underlying portfolio analyses are clearly articulated and are subject to frequent, comprehensive review. Alternative measures should be presented to demonstrate the sensitivity of the calculated metrics to changes in underlying assumptions.

IV-7c. The Policy Group *recommends* that credit risks be viewed in aggregate across exposures, giving full consideration to the effects of correlations between exposures. Further, counterparty credit risks, including correlations and directionality, should be evaluated based not only on positions within a large integrated financial intermediary, but also considering available data regarding the size and direction of positions the counterparty has at other firms.

IV-7d. The Policy Group further *recommends* that large integrated financial intermediaries work to supplement VaR as the dominant risk measure of market risk and current exposure as the dominant risk measure for credit risk, both for public reporting and for risk discussion purposes. Supplemental measures should include statistical information intended to display the most likely ways a large integrated financial intermediary or a managed portfolio could sustain significant losses, as well as an indication of the potential size of those losses.

5. Stress Tests

Considerable emphasis has recently been given by risk practitioners, regulators, internal and external auditors, and other constituents to the practice of using stress tests as an essential metric in measuring risk. As conventionally performed, financial institutions select one or multiple stress scenarios and then evaluate their portfolio against the stresses incorporated in the selected scenario(s). They then draw conclusions based on the resulting loss levels relative to the capital, earnings capacity, or other determinants of the ability of the institution to incur such losses, as well as the returns expected and other such considerations.

One limitation of this approach is that it has, as a starting point, assumptions about the underlying markets and other parameters. To the extent that users of stress tests consider these assumptions to be unrealistic, too onerous, not strenuous enough, incorporating unlikely correlations or having similar issues which detract from their credibility, the stress tests can be dismissed by the target audience and its informational content thereby lost.

Additional ways of running and analyzing the data from stress tests may be useful. One approach which might draw out additional information would include the use of so-called "reverse stress tests". The starting point in the analysis would be an assumption that over a short period of time an institution incurs a very large multi-billion dollar loss. The analysis would then work backward to identify how such a loss could occur given actual positions and exposures prevailing when the stress test is conducted. If the assumed loss were truly large, it is highly likely that the possible sequence of events producing such a loss would have to entail elements of contagion or systemic forces. Thus, the reverse stress test is likely to require institutions to address issues that are not normally captured in stress tests. Done properly, the conduct of such a reverse stress test would be a very challenging exercise, requiring the engagement of senior personnel from both the income- producing and the control functions in a context in which the results of such exercises would be shared with senior management. Finally, the use of reverse stress tests would be very much in keeping with Core Precept III, as discussed in Section I.

Recommendations

IV-8a. The Policy Group *recommends* that firms think creatively about how stress tests can be conducted to maximize their value to the firm including the idea of a *reverse stress test* where the emphasis is on the contagion that could cause a significant stress event to the firm.

IV-8b. The Policy Group further *recommends* that firms incorporate the expanded suite of stress tests into a formalized production schedule, against which trends and developments in key risk factors and exposure amounts can be tracked.

6. Risk Metrics and Liquidity Parameters

Among parameters incorporated into risk metrics in particular and risk management in general, current and prospective position liquidity is arguably the least developed. This is not because the importance of liquidity is not recognized. For example, CRMPG II specifically recommended that greater attention be focused on identifying and mitigating crowded trades.

However, despite best intentions, little progress has been made in systematically or broadly capturing liquidity information. This is due in part to its volatility and lack of transparency.

Recent experience has demonstrated that the range of trades and entire markets that can become illiquid is very broad, and that illiquidity events can occur rapidly and with little warning. For example, recently, markets saw illiquidity in the "usual suspects" of popular but crowded trades and bespoke trades with limited numbers of potential counterparties. But, previously unrecognized product deficiencies were also revealed as there was rapid loss of liquidity in the commercial paper, asset-backed commercial paper, and municipal and student loan auction rate markets.

As a result, risk analytics and metrics that are based on "normal market" price volatility, unwind periods and other parameters can materially understate the risks inherent in trades or portfolios during periods of illiquidity. This is the case regardless of whether such illiquidity occurs as a result of crowded trades, market technical factors or other causes.

The use of "normal market" risk analytics and metrics permits (and perhaps even encourages) the development and use of structures that appear to be low risk but that in fact have unrevealed tail risk during periods of systemic stress (for example, SIVs and quantitative strategies-oriented hedge funds).

In addition to resulting in the potential understatement of the amount of risk being taken by a large integrated financial intermediary to its counterparties, the absence of liquidity information also has the potential to obscure the large integrated financial intermediary's understanding of its counterparties' credit quality. From a risk of loss perspective this is a toxic combination.

Recommendations

IV-9a. The Policy Group *recommends* that large integrated financial intermediaries adjust quantitative measures of potential credit risk with margined counterparties to take into account exceptionally large positions, as well as position concentrations in less liquid instruments. The adjustment should anticipate potentially protracted unwind periods and the risk of price gapping during unwinds.

IV-9b. The Policy Group further *recommends* that consideration be given to collecting higher initial margin and higher haircuts from counterparties with outsized positions relative to market liquidity. Large integrated financial intermediaries should also evaluate the need to adjust internal pricing for large positions.

Additional transparency in fixed income markets and their trade flows should be encouraged to permit market participants to better understand market activity. Initiatives like TRACE reporting of transactions and prices on a timely basis will improve understanding of the markets and permit participants to better manage their risks. In aggregate, this will reduce systemic risk.

Industry groups and regulators need to support and sponsor additional academic and applied research on developing analytics for measuring, and procedures for disseminating, information on illiquid trades of all forms.

7. Pricing of Trades

Over the past year, one of the more public indications of market turmoil was the prevalence of significant valuation disputes. Mortgages, leveraged finance, and structured credit generally were among the markets where pricing disagreements were frequent and often substantial. This led to protracted periods of wide bid-ask spreads, and lack of consistent (or even non-existent) price information. This was true even among products and trade structures that had historically evidenced substantial trading volumes and strong price discovery.

In addition to differences in valuation methodologies, causes of pricing discrepancies included a lack of adequate infrastructure by some industry participants. As a result, some large integrated financial intermediaries were not able to analyze positions on a timely or comprehensive basis.

Among other consequences, there was a rise in levels of collateral disputes to magnitudes that contributed materially to systemic risk and that compromised risk management effectiveness. This increase also imposed additional burdens on stressed counterparties, for whom non-payment of collateral was sometimes construed as an indication of financial distress.

Recommendations

IV-10a. The Policy Group *recommends* that large integrated financial intermediaries ensure that they employ robust, consistent pricing policies and procedures, incorporating disciplined price verification for both proprietary and counterparty risk trades. Special attention should be given to bespoke trades, structured products, illiquid products, and other difficult to price assets. A robust monitoring process should be employed to track stale prices and elevate unresolved issues.

IV-10b. The Policy Group further *recommends* that firms and industry groups promote standardized and strengthened dispute resolution mechanisms and encourage the application of higher levels of resources to position pricing. Firms should also promote enhanced understanding of the need for cooperative behavior among firms (for example, when requested to provide indicative bids).

IV-10c. The Policy Group further *recommends* that increased emphasis be given to using, wherever possible, transparent and liquid instruments rather than bespoke products. To incentivize this conduct, large integrated financial intermediaries should consider imposing internal charges against the P & L of hard to value and illiquid transactions, or other methods, such as higher capital charges, higher haircuts to collateralized borrowers, and the imposition of limits on allowed trade volumes. The recommendations incorporated in the section on High- Risk Complex Financial Instruments regarding documents and disclosure are of particular relevance to bespoke products.

8. Consistency of Position Prices across Applications

The challenges associated with pricing illiquid and highly structured positions are compounded by the multiple outlets through which such prices are used inside and outside of a large integrated financial intermediary. Firm books and records, customer statements, collateral calls, and regulatory filings are but some of the applications for these valuations.

Many large integrated financial intermediaries acknowledge providing, externally, or using internally, different valuations for identical underlying products. This can lead to legal, reputational, regulatory and other potential issues, which can lead to financial and non-pecuniary losses. It can also lead to inaccurate information being used for internal and external decision making. Finally, it contributes to, and may be indicative of, a lack of discipline and financial control within a firm.

Recommendations

IV-11a. The Policy Group *recommends* that large integrated financial intermediaries ensure, in the absence of exceptional circumstances, that when the same instrument is held by different business units, such instrument is marked at the same price in each unit. Large integrated financial intermediaries should restrict those personnel and groups that are authorized to provide marks to internal and external audiences. Any differentials in pricing across applications or units should be carefully considered and the rationale for such differences should be fully documented. Notwithstanding the above, it is recognized that for large integrated financial intermediaries, there are communication walls that are designed to fulfill regulatory requirements for the restriction of information flows. In these instances, it is understood that legitimate differences in pricing may occur.

9. Incentive Structures – Impact on Risk (Including Systemic Risk)

Large integrated financial intermediaries and other market participants manage their businesses within a complex framework of rules, norms, and practices established by regulators, auditors, legal departments, equity and debt investors, and a variety of other constituents.

Large integrated financial intermediaries typically attempt to optimize performance subject to liquidity, rating agency, regulatory capital, accounting, and other parameters. This can encourage behavior which, when taken across an industry as a whole, can prove highly pro-cyclical. This is particularly the case given industry participants' tendency to mirror each other's trading strategies, and their requirement to unwind positions on a simultaneous basis during periods of market stress.

Recommendations

IV-12a. The Policy Group *recommends* that large integrated financial intermediaries ensure that a review of the systemic risk implications of incentives and consequent remedial actions is an integral component of each firm's risk management practices. Regulators should encourage this proactive review and assessment on a regular periodic basis. Regulators should identify practices that have the potential to destabilize markets during periods of stress and communicate their concerns aggressively.

IV-12b. The Policy Group further *recommends* that, when considering new trade structures, strategies, or other opportunities, systemic risk implications be evaluated by the senior management of large integrated financial intermediaries. Trades or structures which materially add to systemic risk should be subject to particular scrutiny.

D. Liquidity Background and Recommendations

The recent market dislocation has demonstrated the critical need for individual firms to adopt liquidity practices that are appropriate for the scope of their businesses, their geographic footprint, and their risk profile. Maintenance of a strong liquidity position, combined with effective risk management and monitoring practices, is essential to the financial condition of individual firms and, more broadly, the health of the financial system.

As demonstrated by the recent events surrounding Bear Stearns, few institutions can withstand extreme funding and liquidity dislocations involving both secured and unsecured financing sources. At a minimum, these events demonstrated several threats to firms that have become more prevalent over the preceding ten years: (1) the unwillingness of counterparties to provide funding, even against certain high quality assets, in a time of severe stress; (2) the rapid loss of funding from prime brokerage clients; and (3) dislocations related to CDS. Although it is not possible to anticipate the precise evolution of financial markets and innovation over the next ten years, our recommendations reflect the belief that new vulnerabilities will undoubtedly appear.

The immediate instinct, after the extreme liquidity dislocation experienced recently, is to mandate a prescriptive, target-based approach to liquidity management. While convenient, that approach will wholly miss the mark of what will be effective. The Policy Group believes that liquidity should be monitored by supervisors in the context of the Basel II, Pillar II process *via* an evaluation of a firm's liquidity risk management processes and models, as well as the assessment of a broad set of liquidity metrics. Firms' liquidity needs, strategies, and processes vary widely for entirely legitimate business reasons. Therefore, to effectively supervise liquidity is to recognize the unique product and geographic nature of different firms and the related set of factors that make for a well- functioning liquidity program.

In that context, the role of an effective liquidity manager is to identify a firm's full set of potential liquidity fault lines, to build a nuanced understanding of the dynamic behavior of different liquidity levers in stress events, and to develop a thoughtful set of expectations around outcomes and survival periods under these stress events. These activities, of course, must incorporate any regulatory or jurisdictional restrictions on the use of liquidity for a firm's different legal entities and reflect the sometimes very complex structure of legal entities comprising large integrated financial intermediaries.

A number of recent efforts, including the draft Basel Committee on Banking Supervision, "Principles for Sound Liquidity Risk Management and Supervision," provide broad-based views on effective liquidity management in the context of the credit market crisis. CRMPG III objectives in this area are not to present a comprehensive policy view of effective liquidity management, but rather to highlight the most critical lessons from the recent dislocation and make related recommendations.

1. Maximum Liquidity Outflow (MLO) Stress Testing

Over the past nine to twelve months, unprecedented market disruptions have combined with a deterioration of the financial condition of firms to place significant pressure on the funding of individual firms, as well as on the system as a whole. These events, and the resulting funding pressures, have exposed weaknesses in firms' approaches to stress testing and the connection between these stress tests and "business as usual" liquidity management. Many firms had sound approaches to idiosyncratic and systemic funding

liquidity disruptions but did not forecast the likely overlap of these events and their related maximum liquidity outflows in any given period of time. In addition, many firms' stress testing and contingency planning were designed with relatively short survival horizons under the assumption that a crisis would be of moderate duration and that within this timeframe confidence in the institution and the system would be restored.

Recommendations

IV-13a. The Policy Group *recommends* that all large integrated financial intermediaries should, on a regular basis, conduct liquidity stress tests to measure their MLO. Stress tests should be based on scenarios that consider how normal sources of liquidity, both secured and unsecured, could be disrupted for the firm, the markets, or both. The stress test scenarios should focus on potential liquidity outflows, taking into account a firm's particular vulnerabilities.

IV-13b. The Policy Group further *recommends* that, in addition, at a minimum, firms monitor their MLO within the first 30 days and for additional intervals within this timeframe (for example, overnight, one week, two weeks). The MLO is defined as the net loss of liquidity under the firm's most severe scenario from the time of the calculation for the tenors prescribed.

IV-13c. The Policy Group *recommends* that stress scenarios, both for purposes of stress testing and calculation of MLO, should:

- Include both firm-specific and systemic events and their overlapping nature.
- Consider extreme shocks as well as progressive events.
- Take into account implicit as well as explicit risks and potential damage of a firm's actions to its franchise.
- Review the potential for loss of key sources of secured and unsecured funding, including deposits, commercial paper, and other short- and long-term debt. Firms should also consider the impact of funding illiquidity on asset-backed commercial paper conduits and on the ability to securitize pools of assets.
- Analyze the potential outflows related to customer activity, including prime brokerage.
- Examine the impact of on- and off-balance sheet exposures including the potential outflows related to derivative transactions, liquidity commitments, and special purpose vehicles.
- Consider the impact of intra-day liquidity exposures, including the heightened interest of counterparties to accelerate trades and settlements in times of stress and other time-related mismatches in the flow of funds.

- Consider other large cash payments including salaries, taxes and lease payments.
- As with all liquidity practices, evaluate the impact on both individual legal entities, as well as the consolidated firm.
- Consider the availability of central bank facilities. Generally speaking, extraordinary central bank facilities, such as the Federal Reserve System's Primary Dealer Credit Facility, *should not be considered an element of an effective liquidity* plan.

These stress tests, and their results, would be internally classified, confidential documents that would be shared with senior management, boards of directors, and primary supervisors on a periodic basis. The information provided by the stress tests should be used to identify funding gaps and assess where gaps are incompatible with the firm's risk appetite. Since the stress test information provided to supervisors would be confidential supervisory information, it would and should be protected from public disclosure.

2. Availability of Unencumbered Highly-Liquid Reserves

Recent events have demonstrated that firms may experience a rapid reduction in the availability of both unsecured and secured funding. This experience requires a reexamination of the types of assets that would be available for incremental funding in a liquidity event. Pools of lower quality unencumbered assets may not provide incremental funding if the firm cannot convert assets into same day liquidity through sale, repo, or pledge to a central bank. Further, recent experience has indicated that firms may lose secured funding from lower quality assets that are currently providing liquidity.

Recommendations

IV-14. The Policy Group *recommends* that all large integrated financial intermediaries maintain, on an ongoing basis, an unencumbered liquidity reserve of cash and the highest grade and most liquid securities. The liquidity reserve should be sized in relation to the firm's stress tests and MLO and should explicitly reflect the firm's liquidity risk tolerance and desired survival periods.

3. Structural, Long-Term Liquidity

Long-term, structural liquidity shortfalls translate, over time, into short-term funding needs or vulnerabilities. This is particularly the case under more prolonged periods of dislocation. A comprehensive view of a firm's liquidity requires utilizing measures to address both the short-term and long-term liquidity position of the firm. To enable an effective liquidity program, there is a need to regularly assess the structural, longer-term liquidity position of the firm.

Recommendations

IV-15. The Policy Group *recommends* that all large integrated financial intermediaries maintain long-term structural liquidity in excess of their illiquid assets. In making this assessment, large integrated financial intermediaries should analyze the term structure of their long-term liabilities and the long-term stable portion of their deposits (where applicable), as well as equity capital. Illiquid assets should include those assets that cannot be converted to cash within a specified horizon and potential growth of those assets, as well as the haircuts necessary to convert generally liquid assets to cash through sale, securitization, or secured financing.

The baseline assessment of whether a large integrated financial intermediary has long-term structural liquidity in excess of its illiquid assets should reflect current business conditions. However, the amount of this excess ("the cushion") should reflect an evaluation of the assets and liabilities under stressed conditions. This cushion should be replenished with structured long-term liabilities, with tenors appropriate to market conditions, business strategy, and existing debt maturities.

4. A More Encompassing Approach to Liquidity Management

Strategic planning and new product development processes have not consistently taken into account their initial and ongoing impact on liquidity. In addition, firms systematically have not fully incorporated into their liquidity planning the full extent of on- and off-balance sheet obligations, including non-contractual, reputational and franchise related exposures. In particular, the growth and nature of off-balance sheet liquidity exposures have not been consistently factored into liquidity plans, subjected to adequate stress tests, priced in a manner commensurate with their expected risks, or consistently factored into risk capital models. The incorporation of these risks into the broader thinking of liquidity managers has often been gradual and in some instances lagged market events.

Recommendations

IV-16. The Policy Group *recommends* that a firm's liquidity plan and any stress tests mentioned above include, in all instances, the full set of on- and off-balance sheet obligations. In addition, they must reflect a clear view of how the firm will address non-contractual obligations that have significant franchise implications. While some non-contractual obligations may not lend themselves to incorporation into the core stress scenarios, an evaluation of how such exposures will play out in different market environments should be an overlay to the core stress scenarios. In addition, a clear assessment of how practices in relevant markets (for example, SIVs and auction rate securities) will affect an individual firm's conduct should be directly factored into liquidity planning. The above liquidity exposures should be fully priced under the firm's transfer pricing policies (see Recommendation V-17).

5. Comprehensive Funds Transfer Pricing

One of the foundations for business performance evaluation and the management of a firm's balance sheet is a comprehensive funds transfer pricing mechanism that assigns the cost of funding to businesses that make use of it and credits the benefits of funding to businesses that generate it. Many of today's issues around liquidity and funding at individual firms can be traced back to a failure to adequately price for both on- and off- balance sheet funding exposures.

Recommendations

IV-17. The Policy Group *recommends* that all large integrated financial intermediaries incorporate appropriate pricing-based incentives for the full spectrum of their funding activities. This includes a funds transfer pricing policy that assigns the cost of funding to businesses that use funding and credits the benefits of funding to businesses that provide it. This must encompass both on- and off-balance sheet activities (for example, contingent funding), as well as potential funding needs related to actions that might be taken to preserve the institution's reputation.

The funds transfer pricing process should be informed by stress testing efforts that identify potential vulnerabilities and assign the related costs to the businesses that create them. The methodology should provide direct economic incentives factoring in the related liquidity value of assets and behavioral patterns of liabilities. The costs and benefits identified should be assigned to specific businesses and, under all circumstances, used in evaluating the businesses' performance.

6. Integration of Liquidity Risk Management into a Firm-Wide Risk Management Approach

Recent market events and the resulting stress on individual financial institutions and on the system, more broadly, exposed shortfalls in the communication processes between risk disciplines within firms and between the risk functions and the respective business managers. Regardless of a firm's formal organizational structure, communication processes often fell short of that necessary to ensure identification and mitigation of the comprehensive set of risks faced by firms. The President's Working Group on Financial Markets' March 6, 2008 "Policy Statement on Financial Market Developments" appropriately notes that firms that suffered extensive losses exhibited "inadequate communications among senior management, business lines and risk management functions". Further, the Financial Stability Forum, in its April 2008 report, "Enhancing Market and Institutional Resilience," observes that firms did not adequately address the links between funding, market, liquidity, and credit risk. Failure to link these disciplines in a seamless way contributed to liquidity blind spots within firms, resulted in inadequate evaluation of liquidity buffers and contributed to dislocations in the money markets.

Recommendations

IV-18. The Policy Group *recommends* that to manage, monitor, and control funding liquidity risk, treasury officials in particular need to be included in an enterprise-wide risk management process with appropriate channels of communication. The evaluation of the interconnected elements of these risks requires seamless communication across all risk disciplines, as well as between risk management functions, treasury and the underlying businesses. All integrated financial services firms should hold regularly scheduled meetings of an oversight committee represented by the above disciplines to monitor the firm's liquidity positions.

7. Capital and Liquidity Planning

As part of the liquidity planning process, firms regularly collect information (for example, levels, rates, maturities) about the entirety of the balance sheet. This information allows them to manage the inherent interest rate risk and to evaluate any maturity mismatches that may exist. At the same time, capital planning information related to asset levels and sensitivities is critical for effective liquidity planning. The events of the past year have made it clear that the liquidity and capital planning processes need to be more coordinated.

Recommendations

IV-19. The Policy Group *recommends* that firms explicitly coordinate across their liquidity and capital planning processes and, at a minimum, ensure that critical information flows between the two processes. Executive management must have the capacity to evaluate and incorporate the highly integrated nature of the two disciplines into its planning activities.

E. Capital Adequacy and Recommendations

Strong levels of capitalization are essential to ensuring confidence in financial institutions. The turmoil in credit and money markets over the last year has reemphasized this. Firms that have experienced substantial losses in connection with subprime, leveraged loan, or other write-downs have found it imperative to replenish their capital bases. Failing to do so risked a further erosion of confidence in these firms as going concerns by investors, counterparties, customers, and supervisors. The capital raising completed over the last year – in the hundreds of billions of dollars – has helped strengthen firms' abilities to absorb future potential losses and repositioned them to invest in more attractive business segments as opportunities present themselves. Reflecting upon the issue of capital adequacy in the context of the recent market stresses, two important considerations emerge:

First, while strong capital levels are critical to future financial performance, they alone do not ensure a financial institution can or will remain a going concern. Both Bear Stearns and Northern Rock appeared to have reasonable levels of capitalization as measured by their respective regulatory regimes. However, neither firm was able to maintain the necessary liquidity to fund their operations on a continuing basis, resulting in their effective insolvency. *Therefore, it is evident that capital management and liquidity management are complementary disciplines that must be addressed together.*

Second, the adequacy of capital is best determined by employing robust measures of the economic risks of the assets the capital is funding. Accounting measures of capital leverage and blunt risk-based measures such as Basel I provide potentially misleading signals about capital adequacy – particularly in periods of market stress – because they do not properly recognize material risk factors applicable to underlying assets (including their liquidity characteristics) or the structural features of business activity, such as dynamic collateral requirements. This consideration underscores the

Policy Group's belief that the risk-sensitive regime in Basel II is preferable to both Basel I and leverage ratio measures.

Recommendations

IV-20a. The Policy Group re-affirms its *recommendation* that for large integrated banks and investment banks, Basel II should remain the primary capital standard that such institutions, their primary supervisors, and the marketplace generally look to in making judgments about capital adequacy.

IV-20b. The Policy Group *recommends,* at least for the present, that the existing Basel II standards for minimum capital and well-capitalized institutions be maintained. In taking that position, the Policy Group recognizes that the experience of the credit market crisis provides a sobering reminder to individual institutions, their senior management and their supervisors that future judgments about capital adequacy should be more sensitive to downside risks than perhaps has been the case in the past.

IV-20c. The Policy Group further *recommends* that supervisory judgments about capital adequacy for all large integrated banks and investment banks give primary weight to case-by-case evaluations based on the range of criteria contained in Basel II, Pillar II, and, when necessary, such judgments should be promptly shared with individual institutions.

IV-20d. The Policy Group *strongly recommends* that every reasonable effort be made by the international community of supervisory authorities to (1) seek to stabilize, at least for a reasonable period of time, the methodology associated with Basel II, (2) move toward a common implementation date across major jurisdictions, and (3) insure a competitive and supervisory level playing field in the application of Basel II across classes of institutions and across national boundaries.

F. Leverage

The Policy Group is strongly of the view that leverage ratios are a seriously flawed measure of capital adequacy, except in highly unusual circumstances. The limitations that are inherent to leverage ratios were spelled out in the CRMPG I Report in 1999 and repeated in the CRMPG II Report in 2005.

As set out in detail in Appendix A of the CRMPG I Report, traditional measures of leverage, such as total on-balance sheet assets to equity, are misleading because they inadequately capture the relationship between the real risk of loss and the capital available to absorb it. A gross on-balance sheet leverage measure (1) does not take into account the potential variability in the value of off-balance sheet assets, (2) does not capture the risk dynamics of assets with embedded leverage, (3) does not give credit for hedging (including when matched book assets are perfectly hedged with offsetting liabilities), and (4) most importantly, *fails to distinguish between assets with the same balance sheet value but widely differing risk.* All balance sheet measures of leverage share a critical flaw in that a firm that appears to have relatively low leverage can nonetheless be taking substantial risks, while a firm that looks relatively highly leveraged may well be taking little risk. Viewed in isolation without greater understanding of the risk characteristics of portfolio assets, balance sheet measures of leverage can send false signals about a firm's financial and risk condition. Appendix A to the CRMPG I Report explored these flaws and offered progressively more sophisticated measures of leverage to address them. In the end, CRMPG I concluded there is no single right measure of leverage. The challenge for financial institutions is to ensure that there is deep understanding and management of how asset liquidity and funding liquidity interact dynamically for a given portfolio of assets and sources of financing, including capital.

Notwithstanding the Policy Group's view as to the shortcomings of leverage ratios, the Policy Group does recognize that (1) in some circumstances they can provide useful information and (2) in the aftermath of the credit market crisis they cannot be dismissed out of hand.

Recommendations

IV-21a. The Policy Group *recommends* that where the use of leverage ratios is compulsory, supervisors monitor such leverage ratios using the Basel II, Pillar II techniques and intervene regarding the adequacy of such leverage ratios only on a case-by-case basis.

IV-21b. The Policy Group *recommends* that efforts be directed at either (1) framing more meaningful leverage ratios where they exist or (2) phasing out their use and implementing alternative risk measures that more effectively fulfill their intended objectives.

SECTION V: ENHANCED CREDIT MARKET RESILIENCY

A. Introduction

A sound foundation and sturdy frame – unseen by the casual observer – underlie the integrity of any structure, making it safe for ordinary use, preventing it from collapsing in on itself, and supporting it against unexpected, external shocks. In short, strong foundations and sturdy frames ensure structural resilience.

The recent, seismic shock to the financial markets has thrown into sharp focus some of the flaws and deficiencies in the foundation and frame that support the credit markets and the credit derivatives market in particular. The goal in this section of the Report is to highlight some of the most important structural flaws and make specific recommendations to remediate those deficiencies. The analysis does not undertake an inquiry into the macro- or microeconomic benefits or costs of particular financial instruments. Rather, it assumes that the credit derivatives market will continue to be a large, growing and important part of the global financial landscape and we therefore seek to expeditiously reinforce the weak structural elements of the market architecture.

While the focus of this section is on the credit markets, we would expect that many of the observations and recommendations are transferable to other markets characterized by rapid growth, innovation and complexity, including (but not limited to) interest rate derivatives, equity derivatives, and commodity derivatives. This section also incorporates several specific recommendations related to the fixed income tri-party repo market given its importance to the financing by dealers of a significant share of their inventories.

A resilient credit derivatives market requires the ongoing commitment of major market participants to support the talent, technology, business process, market practice and legal architecture integral to a strong market foundation. That foundation should be designed and operated to (1) avoid systemic risk that would arise from operational malfunction during ordinary markets, and (2) absorb, rather than amplify, shocks created by extraordinarily stressed markets.

Such a commitment may require market participants to (1) make costly investments in infrastructure (in both human capital and technology), (2) change business processes, and (3) accept changes to market practices that in the past have generated sizable revenues but have done so at the cost of not investing in more scalable infrastructure. This reinforcement of the market structure will fail if not explicitly mandated and monitored by the senior-most executives of major market participants (buy-side as well as sell-side) and actively encouraged and supported by senior officials of central banks and other official institutions.

This section highlights six interrelated areas of weakness in need of immediate improvement and enhancement. They are:

I. *Timeliness and integrity of transaction details,* including the economic terms of the transaction and subsequent transfer, assignment or novation of the transaction.
II. *Daily reconciliation of collateral valuations,* including trade population reconciliation, valuation methodology and market inputs to that methodology.
III. *Operationally manageable number and gross notional of outstanding trades in the market,* including compression of the current market outstandings and the subsequent avoidance of regrowth.
IV. *Credit Event settlement,* including greater efficiency and certainty of the process.
V. *Close-out of defaulting counterparty,* including adoption of a viable method for timely and orderly close-out and general preparedness to execute a close-out of a major counterparty.
VI. *Central Clearing Mechanism.*

The Policy Group makes specific recommendations for strengthening each of these six areas of weakness, including:

- Improvements to the infrastructure that processes trade confirmation and reconciliation of transaction details, and suggested timeline for implementation.
- Enhancements to the daily valuation and collateral management process.
- Endorsement of an industry initiative to compress outstanding trade populations.
- Formal adoption of the auction-based, net physical settlement procedure for Credit Events as a part of standard ISDA documentation.
- Rapid bilateral adoption, which has already begun, amongst major banks/dealers of the Close-out Amount methodology, and the creation of a close-out ISDA supplement that would bridge the gap between the Market Quotation method and the Close-out Amount method and thereby facilitate a more general, wide-scale adoption of a more resilient close-out method without prejudicing the rights of a defaulting party.

- A central counterparty helps address many of the deficiencies of the current market foundation, and the Policy Group recommends that the industry move with deliberate speed toward the creation of one or more such counterparties in a manner that does not compromise the integrity or robustness of the marketplace.

In making the recommendations in the sections below, the Policy Group is cognizant of the fact that some of them are very ambitious in light of existing market practices. Nevertheless, the Policy Group firmly believes that these recommendations are more than just aspirational in nature. Rather, they are concrete goals that, if implemented by major market participants, will substantially enhance the credit market's resilience to stress events and conditions, including the failure of one or more major counterparties. Therefore, the Policy Group strongly urges major market participants to make substantial progress toward implementing the recommendations by the targeted dates, recognizing that progress is likely to vary across firms. The Policy Group also recognizes the need for the support of official institutions, especially the Federal Reserve Bank of New York, in implementing these recommendations in line with the target dates.

The Policy Group is mindful of the enormous scale and complexity of the issues and challenges raised in this discussion of market resiliency, but it is also mindful of the substantial progress made in these areas after the publication of the CRMPG II Report three years ago. Many observers regard this progress as a classic example of private sector/public sector cooperation. Significant steps were taken in reducing confirmation backlogs, shifting from manual to automated processing, the creation and operation of the DTCC CDS "warehouse," and perhaps most importantly halting the practices of assigning trades without the consent of the original counterparty. In contemplating these and other improvements, it is probably reasonable to conclude that as severe as the crisis of the past 12 months has been, it almost certainly would have been worse if these improvements had not been made. In that spirit, the Policy Group looks forward to a continuation and an intensification of cooperation with the Federal Reserve Bank of New York and other official institutions in a concerted effort to bring about the further enhancement of credit market resiliency as contemplated by the following discussion.

B. Timeliness and Integrity of Transaction Details

Trade matching, confirmation and settlement must be the foundation for any discussion about market resiliency. The rapid confirmation and settlement of a transaction ultimately drives the integrity of market valuations and collateral exchange, ensures common certainty in credit event settlement, and gives the market confidence in the orderly closeout of defaulting counterparties. In short, the standards that market participants apply to the orderly processing of trades must be sufficiently robust to withstand at least the kind of shocks and systemic disruption that the market has experienced over the past 12 months.

That said, a resilient credit derivatives marketplace requires the development of the next generation of efficient, controlled and scalable operational infrastructure, particularly around the population of trades which are eligible for electronic platforms. The industry and its major market participants need to implement tools and practices that achieve a same day (T+0) standard for confirmation and regular ongoing reconciliation of positions, settlements and market-to-market values (MTMs). If this is done, a significant degree of dispute resolution will be avoided.

We urge senior leaders and regulators to take a direct interest in progress on this topic.

Throughout the life cycle of a trade, specific goals must be met to achieve the required standard of resiliency.

Recommendations

V-1. The Policy Group *recommends* trade date (T+0) matching for electronically eligible transactions.
Goal: End 2009.

At the inception of a transaction, an electronic record representing the evidentiary requirements for a legal trade is required to ensure the agreement of all trade and allocation details between counterparties. When achieved on trade date, this record can serve as the binding foundation for all ongoing trade activities – clearing, settlement calculation, and warehouse activities such as credit event processing. Subsequent client trading (*e.g.* novations, partial and full terminations) should likewise follow a T+0 matching standard. These records also serve as an optimal basis for accurate risk management. A T+0 matching standard also supports the goal of implementing a centralized clearing arrangement, the benefits of which are discussed below.

A key point to the success of the above goal is convergence of the affirmation and confirmation processes. The current process of affirmation presumes delays in the legal confirmation process and bifurcates the workflow between the trading desk and operations. As industry participants merge trade date matching with the legal confirmation process, the need for an affirmation workflow is eliminated. To achieve this goal, front office personnel may be required, in coordination with support and control personnel, to communicate systematically and directly with each other to confirm transactions electronically under tight timeframes.

V-2. The Policy Group *recommends* the linkage of confirmation and settlements.
Goal: Dealers early 2009.

The exchange of cash flows on a trade (including but not limited to fees, coupons and credit event settlements) should be based upon the legal electronic trade record. This serves to prevent ongoing disputes around portfolio composition, trade status, economic details, calculations and other common root causes of settlement disputes. Central settlement for credit derivatives was launched in a phased approach within the DTCC's Deriv/SERV Trade Information Warehouse in November 2007. The initial phase has been successfully implemented among a group of 18 dealer firms but has not yet been expanded to include buy-side firms. To strengthen the link between confirmation and settlement, the Policy Group recommends dealers complete development of the central settlement platform. In addition, the Policy Group encourages the broadening of central settlement to buy-side market participants.

V-3. The Policy Group *recommends* a tiered approach to market participation and incentive structure.
Goal: Ongoing.

The increasingly sophisticated market infrastructure will require a two-tiered approach for market participants. High volume participants from both the buy- and sell-sides will be expected to use technology and processes that facilitate adherence to the above same-day submission and matching standards. While it is expected low-volume participants (fewer than four trades per month) will maintain industry guidelines around confirmation and settlement timeliness, it is not expected that this group will necessarily participate electronically. Regulators should impose appropriate incentives on derivatives dealers to adhere to market standards and practices.

V-4. The Policy Group *recommends* incentives to buy-side participants.
Goal: Ongoing.

It is important to recognize that buy-side market participants will operate at different volumes. Moderate to large-volume participants (more than four trades per month) will be expected to adhere to the same standards as dealer-side firms with respect to transmission standards, trade date confirmation, settlement and mark-to-market comparisons. As with adoption of the Novation Protocol, dealers should consider limiting trading activity with firms that do not adhere to industry standards. Adherence to industry standards should be part of a routine dealer operational due diligence (side-by-side with the normal credit due diligence).

C. Implementation Challenges

The marketplace faces challenges on several fronts that must be overcome in order to meet the above next generation goals. These limitations necessitate fundamental changes to industry platforms, standards, processes and participant-specific technology and resources. Most of these changes have not yet been turned into operational implementation plans, which may raise significant practical and cost issues. Senior management should clearly support and set these goals into business plans at each participating firm and review ways to resolve the expected obstacles. Progress made should be reviewed with regulators, as appropriate. These challenges are discussed briefly below and recommendations are made for overcoming them.

1. Segregation of Trade Execution, Affirmation and Confirmation

Presently, credit derivative trades are executed in a variety of methods (for example, voice, broker or vendor platforms). Many participants will separately affirm the trades either via voice, email or a vendor platform. In yet another separate step, legal confirmation is sought via DTCC or a signature on a paper trade. The bifurcation of these processes splits the management and control of a given trade between the trade executors (*i.e.,* sales, trading) and the operations professionals who typically affirm and confirm the trades.

Recommendation

V-5. The Policy Group *recommends* that market participants should seek to streamline their methods for trade execution and confirmation/affirmation, which should facilitate an end-to-end process flow consistent with same-day matching and legal confirmation.

2. Resourcing

To achieve a T+0 standard for matching and legal confirmation, a significant investment will need to be made in human capital for key areas such as legal, technology, operations, controllers and risk management. Senior management should be cognizant of both the cost implications and the lead time required to hire these relatively scarce professionals.

Recommendation

V-6. The Policy Group *recommends* that senior leaders of trading support functions should clearly articulate to senior management the resource requirements necessary to achieve the same-day standards. Recognizing the expense management imperatives driven by recent market conditions, senior management should make every effort to help support functions achieve these standards for the overarching benefit of enhancing market resilience.
Goal: Ongoing.

3. Vendor Readiness and Facilitation

In today's marketplace, vendors provide a variety of solutions to various aspects of the workflow and lifecycle – affirmation, confirmation, prime brokerage give-ups, portfolio reconciliation, *etc.* Often, solutions are not designed to be compatible with one another, with the result that participants must build out and support multiple technology integrations. Furthermore, required time to market on new products and life cycle events often lags market growth and innovation, and vendors face pressure to go live with phased or incremental solutions to remain relevant in the marketplace.

Recommendation

V-7. The Policy Group *strongly urges* that major market participants should deploy a combination of utility and vendor-supplied solutions and should, at a minimum, ensure interoperability of those solutions.
Goal: End of 2009.

4. Speed of Electronic Adoption

Both buy- and sell-side participants have proven to require lengthy ramp-up periods to integrate electronic platforms. Increasingly standardized legal documentation (*e.g.,* standard terms supplement) has provided some benefit, but onboarding negotiations still consume time and resources. As new functionality is rolled out, participants schedule the development and testing according to internal schedules and priorities. These efforts significantly slow the speed to electronic platform usage.

Recommendation

V-8. The Policy Group *recommends* that major market participants on both the sell- and buy-sides should make every reasonable effort to speed up the adoption of electronic platform usage. This should entail revisiting the priorities in development and testing schedules.
Goal: End of 2009.

5. Market Standardization

While tools exist today for standard processing (for example, DTCC pay receive, CLS, RED identifiers, and DTCC new product rollouts), many market participants still lag significantly behind and are inconsistent in the adoption of these tools.

Recommendation

V-9. Consistent with Recommendation V-7 above, the Policy Group further *recommends* that major market participants on both the sell- and buy- sides should hasten their adoption of tools that facilitate standardization in the marketplace. This will in turn facilitate the achievement of the next generation goals for the timeliness and integrity of transaction details.
Goal: End of 2009.

D. Collateral Management Process

Counterparty risk monitoring and risk management are enhanced by robust portfolio reconciliation and collateral management practices. In the sections below, CRMPG III makes recommendations to improve practices in the credit derivatives market. It also addresses collateral management practices in the tri-party repo market, the smooth functioning of which is critical to overall performance of financial markets.

1. Derivatives Market

Recommendation

V-10. The Policy Group further *recommends* frequent portfolio reconciliations and mark-to-market comparisons, including on collateralized instruments.

Goal: eekly end 2008, moving to daily for electronically eligible trades mid 2009.

Along with timely bookings and same-day electronic trade records, frequent portfolio reconciliation standards ensure (1) the ongoing integrity of the trade population versus each trading counterparty and (2) that any material mark-to-market differences are isolated and escalated to the trading desks or higher levels of management for immediate review and resolution. This function serves as a sound basis for accurate margin calculations, a critical component of market resiliency. Ensuring that appropriate fair market valuations are agreed on all product types also will act as a foundation for any close-out situation in the event of a default. In making this recommendation, the Policy Group emphasizes the critical need to maintain the confidentiality of client trade information consistent with applicable internal "wall crossing" restrictions. Dealers should review such processes and enhance them to the extent necessary. To facilitate the implementation of this recommendation, the Policy Group further recommends that the industry develop a common file format for the exchange of portfolio information.

2. Common Collateral Standards

Recommendations

Today's collateral management process, driven in large part by the sell-side, is bespoke in terms of the format, process and resourcing of each major market participant. This bespoke nature strictly limits the industry's capability to quickly diagnose the root causes of disputes. To achieve a best-in-class standard for collateral, the Policy Group recommends:

V-11. ISDA Credit Support Annex documents spell out the bilateral terms of the margin process. While the process is generally standardized, the Policy Group *recommends* that the industry find an effective means to resolve valuations disputes, particularly for illiquid products. Doing so is likely to be a difficult and demanding matter and therefore an industry-wide approach may have to be considered.
Goal: End of 2009.

V-12. The Policy Group *recommends* that, as mark-to-market disputes inevitably surface through the collateral portfolio reconciliation process, the information should be passed to the executing trading desks on a real-time basis to allow for research and resolution. This should, of course, be done with appropriate anonymity for the counterparty's identity, positions and broader portfolio. A close alignment of the collateral team with trading desks – without violating the fire walls and controls that are critically important to the integrity of the financial system – would facilitate such information sharing. As necessary, significant and large value collateral disputes should promptly be escalated to the appropriate senior officers.
Goal: Immediate.

The implementation challenges related to these collateral management goals are similar to those related to the goals for timeliness of transaction details. They should be addressed in a coherent fashion to maximize the opportunity for successful implementation. On a note of caution, as the industry pursues changes needed to bolster the resiliency of the CDS market consistent with these recommendations, *it must do so in a manner that preserves the ability of firms to execute and maintain bespoke transactions which serve legitimate economic interests.*

3. Tri-party Repo Market

The dealer community relies on repurchase agreements (repos) entered into with investors as a principal source of funding. A large percentage of dealer repo financing is arranged in the form of tri-party repos, with Bank of New York and JPMorgan Chase & Co. acting as clearing banks. Tri-party financing originated as an adjunct to the banks' U.S. government securities clearing business, through which the banks, via their accounts at the Federal Reserve Bank of New York, facilitated the settlement of dealer purchase and sale of U.S. Treasury and U.S. government-related entity securities. Tri-party financing evolved as a natural extension of the banks' clearing role and proved to be a highly efficient vehicle for the dealers to finance their securities inventory with the investor community while at the same time offering independent collateral management services to investors, assuring the investors that their collateral would be held by the banks in safekeeping at all times.

In recent years, dealer clearing activity has expanded to include a wider range of less liquid and sometimes harder to value security types, and investors have accepted these securities as collateral for their repo financings. In addition, maturities are often overnight, although investors and dealers also enter into term repos.

While the clearing banks act in the role of agent, on the morning following the repo trade, if the clearing banks are prepared to extend credit to the respective dealers, they will "unwind" the repo, crediting cash to the investors' accounts and holding the dealer's securities to collateralize the intra-day loan.

When clearing tri-party repo transactions, clearing banks extend secured intra-day financing to dealers in two situations:

1. For maturing repo transactions, the clearing bank unwinds the transactions between tri-party investors and dealers between 8 am and 8:30 am. The cash lent by a tri-party investor is returned to the investor in a bailment account held at the clearing bank. The investor may instruct the clearing bank to:
   - wire the cash to another bank (usually from 8:30 am to 10:30 am);
   - use the cash in the bailment account to net payments during the day under a pre-agreed netting program;
   - retain the cash in the bailment account, available to be moved at the investor's instructions; or move the cash to the investor's custody or demand deposit account at the clearing bank.
2. For term repo transactions, the clearing bank also unwinds the transactions between tri-party investors and dealers between 8 am and 8:30 am. The cash lent by a tri-party investor is then moved to a bailment account (per above) in the name of the investor, returning the dealer's securities to its box account. This practice enables the dealer to more easily use its securities for trade settlement and to substitute other eligible collateral.

In both scenarios 1 and 2 above, the clearing bank allows dealers to deliver out of the box securities securing the clearing bank's intra-day financing as long as there is sufficient Net Free Equity (NFE) in the account. The NFE is the current market value of the securities in the box plus the intra-day margin established by the clearing bank *minus* the intra-day financing provided for any particular dealer. The NFE ensures that intra-day secured financing provided by the clearing bank is properly collateralized.

The tri-party repo market could pose systemic risk issues, in particular, if the clearing banks fail to effectuate the "unwind", due to liquidity, collateral or dealer creditworthiness concerns. Another potential source of stress to the financial system emanates from dealer funding risks if the dealer has excessive reliance on overnight financing for less liquid, harder to price securities, or should investors be unwilling to roll their overnight repo arrangements. In light of the manner in which the market has evolved and the risks market participants bear, as described above, the sections below outline actions that can mitigate such risks.

Recommendation

V-13. The Policy Group *recommends* that dealers, investors and the clearing banks agree on "Best Practices" to govern the tri-party repo market. Components of such Best Practices should include the following:

1. Tri-party repo program size.

   Secured financing of dealer inventory plays an important role in the capital structure of the dealer community. However, as with any financing technique, dealers should not be overly reliant on any one type or source of financing, and should establish parameters to assure diversified sources of funding and appropriate term structure. Consideration should be given to the liquidity under stressed conditions of the inventory which is being financed, with sensitivity to avoid excessive overnight funding of illiquid securities. Use of term repos should be encouraged with maturity schedules spread out to avoid concentration of roll-over risk occurring on any single day. The clearing banks should also consider setting specific limits regarding the amount of intra-day unwind exposure that they will take to a given dealer based upon the composition and liquidity of the dealer's collateral and other relevant factors.

2. Margin.

   Margin should be proportional to the risk of the collateral, meaning it should be sufficient to cover the potential price decline of the securities held as collateral during expected liquidation timeframes. To accomplish this, margin should be applied to collateral types at a level granular enough to distinguish their risk, taking into account the price volatility and the liquidity of each security. Investors should regularly review their margin requirements *(investor margin)* in order to assure that they accurately reflect current market conditions, and should also stress test their assumptions for adverse market environments. Clearing banks should determine how much margin is required in order to undertake the intra-day risks associated with the daily unwind and whether to impose concentration and/or notional limits on certain types of securities *(clearing bank margin).* Such clearing bank margin should be set at levels which accurately reflect current market conditions and should be stress tested for adverse market environments. These steps should enable market participants to be well equipped to make the best possible risk assessments. Finally, clearing banks and investors should make individual credit assessments of each dealer to determine margin requirements and the amount of intra-day credit available.

3. Collateral eligibility.

   Collateral eligibility is determined based on negotiations between borrowers and lenders. Clearing banks will establish their own eligibility standards. As a general matter, collateral eligibility should be based on the quality and liquidity of securities being pledged by dealers. Appropriate collateral types should be defined along with concentration and diversification standards. Such standards should be continuously reviewed in light of prevailing market conditions and stress tests. Consideration should be given to publishing aggregate data reflecting market practice indicating collateral mix, by type, ratings and maturities.

4. Collateral valuation.

Collateral valuation methodologies should be transparent and reliable. Clearing banks and investors should understand and be satisfied with the reliability of the sources used to price collateral, whether based on bids or quotes from market participants or pricing models, or sourced by vendors or by multiple or single dealers. Pricing methodology flags should be used to indicate how the price was set and margin should be adjusted to take into account the source and methodology used to derive security prices. Prices used for valuation purposes should reflect the most current market conditions, and stale pricing should not be utilized.

E. Managing Size of Trade Population

Market risk is best measured by net notional exposure. However, gross notional exposure and the number of outstanding line items are relevant to counterparty and operational risk. While considerable progress has been made in enhancing the operational infrastructure of the credit derivatives market since 2005, continued rapid growth in the volume of credit derivatives traded, outstanding gross notional and "warehoused" line items now demand that market participants work together to reduce gross notionals by terminating offsetting trades. Compressing the industry's current outstanding notional would have two immediate and systemic benefits: (1) a reduction in market-wide operational risk and (2) a reduction in counterparty risk, thereby enhancing ease of "close out" going forward.

Recommendation

V-14. The Policy Group *recommends* that market participants actively engage in single name and index CDS trade compression. ISDA has agreed on a mechanism to facilitate single name trade compression with Creditex and Mark-it Partners. Established vendor platforms exist for termination of offsetting index trades, and we urge major market participants to aggressively pursue their use.

The Policy Group notes that the industry has agreed to separate future trade compression and market consistency discussions from the historical portfolio compression. The industry did caveat that the historical compression should not preclude any future consistency or compression solutions and should be supportive of the industry's long-term goal to match and clear CDS on trade date.

Recommendation

V-15. Based on the considerations above, the Policy Group *recommends* that the industry, under the auspices of the current ISDA Portfolio Compression Working Group, commit immediately and with all due speed to achieve consistency of the current product, including potentially:

- utilizing industry preferred Reference Obligations or elimination of Reference Obligations;

- eliminating Restructuring Basis distinctions, recognizing that this needs to be considered in a broader global perspective taking into account regional and national differences; and
- standardizing fee calculations based on a single, common model analytic.

F. Credit Event Settlement

Standard credit derivative documentation currently provides for physical settlement of transactions following the occurrence of a credit event involving the reference entity on the trade. As the volume of outstanding transactions has grown over the last several years so too has the prospect of market disruption due to settlement through disorderly delivery of bonds and loans. In credit events over the last three years for which there were a significant number of affected trades, ISDA has published a protocol to allow parties to amend their outstanding trades to facilitate cash settlement while preserving the option of physical settlement. In each case an ISDA-sponsored auction, managed by Creditex and Mark-it Partners, has been conducted to establish a price for one or more deliverable obligations. Each of these auctions has produced an outcome that has been generally accepted in the market as an appropriate valuation of deliverable obligations.

Participation in the auction by adherence to the protocol is a voluntary process and, while the vast majority of active market participants have participated in the past, there is a concern that, given the voluntary nature of the protocol process, for any given credit event one or more major market participants could choose to stay outside the protocol and auction process. As the protocol and auction process is designed to reduce the need to physically settle a large number of trades, one or more major market participants choosing to stay outside will continue to raise the prospect of a squeeze on deliverable obligations, with resulting volatility and uncertainty around the ability to settle a large number of trades. Though that risk is small and this situation has not occurred in the previous protocols, the uncertainty that could arise would undermine the broad-based acceptance of credit derivative products and justifies expeditious action.

ISDA has anticipated incorporation of the auction mechanism into its standard credit derivative documentation, using the experience of past credit events to make minor modifications to the mechanism. The mechanism has not been utilized for a credit event in Europe or for a credit event involving a very large reference entity with a large number of outstanding obligations. While the mechanism would no doubt benefit from being tested in those circumstances, it is clear now that it is more important to incorporate the mechanism into the standard documentation so that market participants will be committed to follow the process.

Building the settlement auction into the ISDA documentation requires decisions to be made in advance about a number of issues that would otherwise be addressed on the basis of the particular fact situation. There are therefore a number of issues that must be solved before the auction methodology can be built into the ISDA documentation. These include:

- how an auction following a Restructuring Credit Event should be structured, given that the provisions of the ISDA definitions limiting the maturity of deliverable obligations reference the maturity dates of individual contracts (given the difficulties with structuring an auction following a Restructuring Credit Event, it is likely that the process may, initially, move forward focusing solely on Bankruptcy and Failure to Pay Credit Events);

- how the decision as to the deliverable obligations to be included in the auction should be made, and disputes resolved within the timescale of the auction; and
- dispute resolution procedures generally.

In light of this background and the related issues, the Policy Group recommends the following:

Recommendations

V-16. The Policy Group *recommends* that ISDA should update its Credit Derivative Definitions to incorporate the auction mechanism so that counterparties to new credit default swap trades commit to utilize the auction mechanism in connection with future credit events.

V-17. The Policy Group *recommends* that ISDA should run a protocol (a so- called "big bang" protocol) to provide market participants with an operationally efficient means to amend their existing credit default swap trades to utilize the auction mechanism in connection with future credit events. This protocol should not effect any other changes to the bilateral agreements in effect between adopting counterparties.

In making these recommendations, the Policy Group recognizes that some market participants, particularly on the buy-side, might wish to consider the nature and extent of participation in an auction mechanism more selectively than would be afforded through a big bang protocol. As some of these market participants approach the auction issue on a case-by-case basis, the Policy Group strongly encourages them to review the benefits of such an approach as discussed above.

G. Counterparty Close out

The subject of the methodology used to execute close out by a non-defaulting counterparty in the event of a default by one or more counterparties has been a subject of lively discussion in CRMPG III, just as it was in CRMPG II and CRMPG I. While the terms of these discussions are often highly complex, the central issue is the extent to which market participants generally are willing to use the so-called "Close-out Amount" as promulgated by ISDA in 2002 as the methodology for close out of a defaulting counterparty. In this regard, it remains true (as was the case with CRMPG II in 2005) that among many "buy-side" market participants there is a concern that the ISDA Close-out Amount may work to the disadvantage of the defaulting counterparty. For this reason, CRMPG II and CRMPG III were unable to reach agreement calling for the broad application of Close-out Amount as an industry standard. Nevertheless, a clear consensus has emerged around three principles that must be associated with any closeout methodology. These are: (1) commercial reasonableness; (2)

duty of good faith; and (3) fair dealing. The Policy Group believes these principles must guide any future work in this area.

In a simple world in which market prices and/or market inputs for all financial instruments were readily available and systemic financial shocks never occurred, this debate would have been resolved long ago or, perhaps, the debate would have never occurred. However, neither of these conditions has existed for many years. Thus, the risk associated with the close out of a major counterparty in a stressed market environment has risen appreciably. Indeed, one can only speculate as to how much worse things might have been in March 2008 if dozens of counterparties were simultaneously seeking to close out Bear Stearns at the same time.

In these circumstances, the CRMPG III attaches great significance to Recommendation V18 whereby the dealer community is in the process of adopting the Close-out Amount methodology in their relationships with each other. Recognizing that the dealer community as a whole represents a substantial fraction of total transaction volume and the fact that the intra-dealer exposures are very large, this common approach within the dealer community represents a clear and positive step in the direction of containing systemic risk.

Over the course of the deliberations of CRMPG III, the opposition on the part of the buy-side to extending Recommendation V-18 to all market participants surfaced once again. In those circumstances, Recommendation V-19 calls for a further effort to develop a close-out methodology, under the auspices of ISDA, which would apply to all market participants. The Policy Group attaches great importance to the consensus that emerged on the need for prior agreement on valuation parameters as a prerequisite to migrating to a commercially reasonable close-out procedure, described below. At the same time, however, the Policy Group is uneasy about recommending yet another effort to reconcile the differing views with respect to the policy and legal underpinnings of close out in the 2002 ISDA model as this could introduce more uncertainty into a situation that needs more certainty, not less. But given the importance of work on prior agreement on valuation parameters, the Policy Group believes another attempt to come up with a potential industry-wide approach could be worthwhile, provided that such discussions are streamlined in scope and time.

Given the explosive growth and complexity of financial markets in recent years, and with particular emphasis on the CDS market, a further source of potential instability relates to the policies and procedures associated with the close out of defaulted counterparties – especially large counterparties – in a stressed market environment. To achieve orderly close out in such circumstances, the process must meet the following criteria:

- does not add to market instability;
- produces commercially reasonable prices for purposes of close out; and
- is practical to implement for portfolios that are potentially large and contain illiquid positions.

The Policy Group has considered in detail the challenges of closing out a major market participant and reaches the following conclusions:

- The Market Quotation method (1992 ISDA) is impractical for the early termination of a counterparty with a large and/or complex portfolio, particularly one including bespoke transactions.
- At the same time, neither the Loss method (1992 ISDA) nor the Close-out Amount method (2002 ISDA) is acceptable to a large number of counterparties (in particular, buy-side counterparties) due to concerns of potential for unfairly disadvantaging a defaulting counterparty.
- A prerequisite to migrating to a commercially reasonable close-out procedure is for the counterparties to have previously agreed to any necessary valuation parameters and methodologies, to have evidenced these in their relevant agreements (ISDA Master, supplements to the Master or confirmations, as appropriate) and to have established a robust daily process of valuation reconciliation in order to highlight any discrepancies in valuation approach or parameters long before a close out might need to occur.
- There is general agreement that in determining close-out amounts market inputs should be used unless doing so would produce a commercially unreasonable result. However, there remains a significant disagreement as to whether the definition of Close-out Amount in the 2002 ISDA Master Agreement in practice achieves an outcome that is both consistent with that general agreement and commercially reasonable.
- Given this general agreement on the desirable outcome (that market inputs should be used unless doing so would produce a commercially unreasonable result), the Policy Group believes that it should be possible to reconcile the competing views in order that one generally accepted formulation of close-out methodology reflecting that general agreement could be used by the market and that, given the desirability of a consistent industry-wide approach, further efforts should again be made to reconcile these views.

Consistent with these conclusions, the Policy Group recommends the following:

Recommendations

V-18. The Policy Group *recommends* that all large integrated financial intermediaries (*e.g.*, the major dealers) should promptly adopt the Close-out Amount approach for early termination upon default in their counterparty relationships with each other. We note that this can be agreed and suitably documented without making any other changes to the ISDA Master. The Policy Group expects that these arrangements will be in place in the very near term.

V-19. The Policy Group *recommends* that a working group should be formed under the auspices of ISDA, with representatives of both dealer and buy-side firms, to review the methodology for counterparty terminations in order to (1) produce a set of best practices and suggested bilateral templates for the transparency of valuation methodologies and parameters, as noted above, for use by all market participants, (2) consider how contractual provisions could reflect prior reconciliation of valuation parameters and (3) seek to reconcile the differing views on what is necessary to evidence agreement that market inputs will be used unless commercially unreasonable. The Policy Group hopes that the working group will be able to report a recommended approach by December 31, 2008.

V-20. The Policy Group *recommends* that all major market participants should periodically conduct hypothetical simulations of close-out situations, including a comprehensive review of key documentation, identification of legal risks and issues, establishing the speed and accuracy with which comprehensive counterparty exposure data and net cash outflows can be compiled, and ascertaining the sequencing of critical tasks and decision-making responsibilities associated with events leading up to and including the execution of a close-out event.

V-21. The Policy Group *recommends* that all market participants should both promptly and periodically review their existing documentation covering counterparty terminations and ensure that they have in place appropriate and current agreements including the definition of events of default and the termination methodology that will be used. Where such documents are not current, market participants should take immediate steps to update them. Moreover, each market participant should make explicit judgments about the risks of trading with counterparties who are unwilling or unable to maintain appropriate and current documentation and procedures.

V-22. The Policy Group *recommends* that the industry should consider the formation of a "default management group", composed of senior business representatives of major market participants (from the buy- side as well as the sell-side) to work with the regulatory authorities on an ongoing basis to consider and anticipate issues likely to arise in the event of a default of a major market counterparty.

H. Central Clearing

Many of the issues discussed in this section and the related recommendations have a direct bearing on the speed and effectiveness with which the industry can implement a centralized counterparty clearing arrangement (CCP) for classes of transactions starting with CDS. A robust CCP can significantly benefit the stability of the credit derivatives market by creating a shock absorber to lessen the impact of a default by a major participant in the market. A CCP will also fit well into the existing market infrastructure and add to the overall efficiency of risk-reducing efforts within the industry.

A CCP will provide financial resources to absorb the shock of a major participant default through use of initial margin, variation margin and a guarantee fund structure. This effectively mutualizes the counterparty risk of the participants to each other. In addition, a CCP will help to reduce gross amount of trades required to be unwound in the event of a participant default, thereby reducing the operational impact of a participant default. Compression across a given curve point to a position-based notional will be enhanced by a CCP that allows true counterparty indifference in the compression process and centralizes the operational process of multilateral netting.

Moreover, a robust CCP will create an additional layer of risk management across the largest market participants. Unusually large or risky positions may result in additional margin, which can in turn create pressure on participants to maintain high quality risk management practices and appropriate capital.

But there are many challenges in ensuring that a CCP is in fact robust and actually reduces risk, rather than providing merely the appearance of risk reduction. In fact, any CCP will face certain limitations. A CCP cannot, on its own, create additional liquidity that does not naturally exist in the market, though it can facilitate trading which may help increase liquidity in the market. Additionally, the need for frequent and robust trade valuations means that not all asset classes will be eligible for a CCP, which means many of the issues raised above will still need to be addressed on a bilateral basis.

In November 2004 the Bank for International Settlements Committee on Payments and Settlement System and the Technical Committee of IOSCO issued a report titled "Recommendations for Central Counterparties" *(BIS Recommendations).* The report provided 15 headline recommendations which covered the major types of risks CCPs face. The report also included a methodology for assessing implementation of the recommendations, and provides guidance on the assessment of a CCP. Development of any CCP for the clearing of credit derivatives must take these recommendations into account. However, the recommendations leave room on a number of issues for judgment by a CCP, and its regulators, on how to best implement the recommendations.

The sections below set forth some of the key challenges in the development of a CCP for credit default swaps.

1. Participant Criteria

A CCP must control the risks to which it is exposed by dealing only with sound and reliable counterparties. Participation requirements established by a CCP are its primary means to ensure that participants have sufficient financial resources and robust operational capacity to meet obligations arising from participation. To reduce the likelihood of a participant's default and to ensure timely performance by the participant, a CCP should establish rigorous financial requirements for participation. Capital requirements should also take account of the nature of products cleared by a CCP. In addition to capital requirements, some CCPs impose standards such as a minimum credit rating or parental guarantees.

A CCP should establish requirements to ensure that participants have robust operational capacity, including appropriate procedures for managing risks, such that the participants are able to achieve timely performance of obligations owed to the CCP. They should also have arrangements to effect collateral, payment, and delivery obligations to the CCP. Since the nature of the credit markets requires a longer post-default liquidation period than other asset classes, membership criteria should ensure the ability to participate in the unwind process in the event of a participant default.

A secondary participation issue which must be addressed is the extent to which the arrangements for clearing credit derivatives between a CCP and its participants will flow to non-participants. It is important to note that in the context of the credit derivatives market, electronic trade processing, which is often associated with clearing, is and will remain available to the general market within DTCC's Deriv/SERV Transaction Information Warehouse.

2. Availability of Daily Pricing across the Cleared Portfolio

One of the challenges for the clearing of credit defaults swaps will be to ensure sufficiently transparent end-of-day pricing across the entire cleared portfolio. Pricing of cleared trades will be used to measure risk, assess margin and guarantee fund contributions and will be used to unwind the trades of a defaulting participant. This means that before any asset class may be cleared at a central counterparty there must be sufficiently transparent pricing available at the end of each trading day to ensure appropriate margin may be calculated.

One point of concern, even in the liquid parts of the market expected to be cleared by a CCP, is the pricing of "off-the-run" trades. Most trading occurs to the nearest of four quarterly dates that is at least five years from the trade date. For example, most five-year trades executed between June 20 and July 19, 2008 will mature on September 20, 2013. Every three months, the maturity of the "on-the-run" trade is pushed out by three months. Additionally, many investors will unwind trades within six months to a year after they originally put the position in place. As a result, the market sees less activity in trades that have been outstanding for longer than one year and the vast majority of aged credit derivatives exist between major dealers. Any CCP will need to ensure there is appropriate pricing available for cleared products to set acceptable margin and guarantee fund requirements. Participating firms will need to provide higher quality marks than they currently do and must do so for all tenors and names. Margin policies may also require adjustment to reflect any change from "off-the-run" to "on-the-run".

3. Structure of Margin, Guarantee Fund and Assessment Rights

Establishing the appropriate margin and guarantee fund structure presents perhaps one of the greatest challenges a CCP for credit derivatives may face. Agreeing on a structure will require reaching consensus among participants and regulators regarding the risk management models used to measure risk. The BIS Recommendations provide a good deal of qualitative guidance, particularly on the topic of ensuring a CCP's ability to withstand the default of the counterparty to which it has the largest exposure in extreme but plausible market conditions. However, the BIS Recommendations leave the quantitative measurement of the test to be determined by the CCP and its regulators.

A CCP's members will need to agree to an appropriate margin structure which accounts for the following:

- liquidity of each cleared product;
- changes in liquidity of a given cleared product over time ("on-the-run" to "offthe-run");
- potential for increased margin on outsized positions; and
- effort and cost required to unwind a participant's portfolio in the event such participant defaults.

The size of any guarantee fund will reflect the degree of protection provided by the agreed margin structure. Consideration also will have to be given to the inclusion of assessment rights on participants should the margin structure and guarantee fund prove insufficient in the event of participant defaults. As part of the CCP development process, appropriate stress testing of actual and hypothetical portfolios would help provide a solid basis for determining the relative size of these risk management features. A sound risk management program would incorporate ongoing stress testing of portfolios to take account of evolving market and firm-specific conditions.

These issues will need to be addressed in a manner that satisfies the clearing participants, and their regulators, that the CCP is reducing risk across the system and adding to the stability of the market.

4. Regulation

Given the regulatory, media and legislative attention focused on the credit derivatives market, it is important that any CCP ensure appropriate regulatory support. This will require interaction with the various regulatory bodies that regulate not only the CCP itself but also the clearing participants. Any CCP for credit derivatives should engage in a frequent and open dialogue with the various financial markets regulators to ensure it is addressing the BIS Recommendations in a manner that will satisfy the relevant financial markets regulators from inception.

5. Policy Group Views on Development of a CCP

Recommendation

V-23. Recognizing the benefits of a CCP as discussed above, the Policy Group strongly *recommends* that the industry develop a CCP for the credit derivatives market to become operational as soon as possible and that its operations adhere to the BIS Recommendations.

The Policy Group is aware of several CCP initiatives. It is most familiar with The Clearing Corporation effort, which is targeting to begin clearing OTC CDS on indices in the fourth quarter of 2008. In providing its support to any CCP arrangement that can demonstrate it is robust, the Policy Group notes the following, which will be critical to its success:

- senior management support at large market participants will be necessary to ensure the commitment of appropriate financial and operational resources; and
- incorporating non-index CDS trades into the CCP is likely to require agreement of further market conventions for purposes of trade valuation. This may in turn have business impacts, particularly on dealers, that will have to be balanced against the benefits of central clearing.

Ultimately, the Policy Group firmly believes that the challenges of developing a CCP for the CDS market can and will be addressed by the industry in close consultation and cooperation with the official sector, as has been demonstrated in the creation of other CCPs that have served to enhance market resilience.

SECTION VI: EMERGING ISSUES

The July 2005 Report of the CRMPG II contained a section entitled "Emerging Issues". In that section, a number of issues were presented as discussion items that, at the time, were thought to have future implications for emerging financial market practices and supervisory policies and practices. The emerging issues section did not by design include recommendations. The emerging issues discussed by CRMPG II in 2005 were the following:

- sales of complex financial instruments to retail investors;
- managing conflicts of interest;
- risk management for fiduciaries;
- official oversight of hedge funds; and
- supervisory challenges.

Building on the experience of 2005, and with an added sense of urgency, CRMPG III concluded that an open-ended discussion of several emerging issues would represent a further and valuable conclusion to this Report. There are five emerging issues discussed in this section of the Report:

- valuation and price verification;
- asset price bubbles;
- near banks;
- regulatory structure; and
- supervisory policy and practice.

A. Valuation and Price Verification

Over the course of the credit market crisis, one issue that has captured the attention of almost all market participants and public officials is the difficulties of valuation and price verification for complex financial instruments, particularly when the market for such instruments is illiquid. To a considerable extent this issue arises in the context of instruments that are subject to so-called "fair value" (or "mark-to-market") accounting, but valuation and price verification problems also arise for financial instruments that are not subject to mark-to-market accounting.

The debate over fair value accounting for financial instruments has raged for many years. It has been brought into even sharper focus over the past 12 months by the belief in some circles that the application of fair value accounting to certain complex financial instruments in a highly illiquid market has exaggerated market instability and added to downward price pressures. Thus, it is said that the application of fair value introduces artificial elements of volatility into financial statements and results, thereby intensifying the crisis. For some who hold this view, it has been suggested that one or more alternatives to fair value accounting should be permitted in certain market conditions, although even the proponents of such concepts tend to recognize the enormous difficulties in defining how such alternatives would work in practice. Others seem to have real doubts as to whether any such alternative could be sufficiently credible so as to not further damage the credibility of financial institutions whose collective reputation is already under strain.

Those who essentially favor the *status quo* regarding fair value accounting – or even its broader application – argue that the overriding benefit of fair value accounting is the discipline it brings to the risk-taking process. These proponents further stipulate that volatility – by its nature – is a reality, particularly in circumstances in which valuations and price verification, properly performed, can produce reasonable results even in difficult market conditions. Finally, those who advocate fair value accounting would also argue that, even with its limitations, there is no reasonable alternative that would be superior.

It is also noteworthy that both sides of the debate recognize that (1) in certain circumstances – notably financial instruments with easily available "market" prices – fair value is the right answer and (2) an alternative of "historic cost" accounting buttressed with discounted cash flow analysis and impairment tests for sub-par assets is not without its own problems. Finally, both sides of the debate acknowledge that there is an element of asymmetry associated with concerns that apply to the market downside, but not the market upside.

Under any circumstance, the details surrounding the application of either set of standards are frustratingly complex for even the most sophisticated observers and practitioners. In all of these circumstances, fresh attention is being devoted to a systematic review of these accounting standards. For example, on June 3, 2008, the IASB announced the formation of an "Advisory Panel of Experts", drawn from preparers and users of financial statements as well as regulators and auditors, to "discuss the valuation of financial instruments in inactive markets." Similarly, on July 9, 2007, the SEC conducted a "roundtable" on fair value accounting with a similar objective and a similar cross-section of participants.

It is far too early to anticipate what will emerge from these and other deliberations. However, regardless of what may emerge, the Policy Group is strongly of the view that under any and all standards of accounting and under any and all market conditions, individual financial institutions must ensure that wholly adequate resources, insulated by failsafe independent decision-making authority, are at the center of the valuation and price verification process. While the details of approaches and the family of techniques used for these purposes may – and will – differ from time to time and from institution to institution, these efforts should always pass *the two common sense* tests of (1) reasonableness and (2) consistency, both of which apply equally to positions or instruments that have gains and positions or instruments that have losses.

B. Asset Price Bubbles

It is painfully obvious that practitioners and policy makers alike have been less than successful in recognizing the implications of building asset price bubbles even in the advanced stages of their development. In the private sector, this failure reflects the competitive reality that there is a natural aversion against being the last institution in or the first institution out when selective sectors of the economy and financial markets are booming. In the public sector, and especially among monetary authorities, there has been something of an aversion against monetary policy initiatives designed to "target" asset price bubbles on the grounds that (1) such bubbles are difficult to recognize and (2) such policy initiatives may have a disproportionately large impact on the economy as a whole. Even worse, efforts to curtail bubbles may misjudge whether a bubble even exists, such that policy initiatives driven by false signals would have wholly unnecessary adverse consequences for the economy as a whole.

The issue of whether the private sector can do a better job of anticipating asset price bubbles is discussed in the core precepts and in the section on Risk Management. Similarly, public authorities, particularly central banks, are also reconsidering whether monetary authorities might be able – at the margin – to better anticipate asset price bubbles and respond with at least a "tilt" toward a more restrictive monetary policy. Finally, some have also raised the question as to whether the use of contra-cyclical supervisory policies (*i.e.*, selective increases in capital charges) might be contemplated.

The Policy Group believes that active consideration of all of these areas of inquiry is desirable, but in saying so it is also mindful of the "laws of unintended consequences". That is, this subject matter is highly complex and is one where miscalculation or misjudgment can have serious adverse consequences. Finally, and most importantly, there is no substitute for sustained discipline in both public policy and private action, which remains the best recipe to limit the severity of asset price bubbles and contain their damage when inevitably they occur.

C. Near Banks

In the period since the Long Term Capital Management *(LTCM)* episode in 1998, so-called "near banks" or "private pools of capital" have become a major force in the overall financial intermediation and risk-taking process. In the eyes of most informed observers, the term "near bank" applies to hedge funds and private equity funds, although some observers would cast a wider net to include large money managers, pension funds and even endowments. However narrowly or broadly defined, the one common denominator shared by all such institutions is that they are not, for the most part, subject to official prudential supervision.

The subject as to whether hedge funds, and to a lesser extent private equity funds, should be subject to some form of direct prudential supervision has been hotly debated since the LTCM episode in 1998. To some extent, and in some jurisdictions, hedge funds have over the past few years become subject to some limited forms of prudential oversight, but not of the nature and scope that is commonplace for traditional banks and the major investment banks in the United States.

The alternative to direct prudential supervision of near banks has been for the authorities to look to the counterparty relations between major *regulated* institutions and individual hedge funds to provide a meaningful degree of indirect prudential oversight and, when necessary, insights into information on emerging market trends and risks associated with the near banks. As a part of this process of indirect oversight, the major supervisory authorities evaluate, with care and in some detail, the manner in which major regulated financial institutions conduct their counterparty relationships with hedge funds.

During the credit market crisis, a number of hedge funds, including several very large hedge funds, have experienced major difficulties. Some have ceased to exist while others have received substantial financial support from their "owners" or "sponsors". This has, in some cases, added to the already bloated balance sheets of regulated institutions.

On the whole, regulated institutions have done a credible job in managing their exposures to hedge funds even in the midst of the virtually unprecedented turmoil of the past 12 months. We have not, to date, witnessed a re-run of the hedge fund-driven systemic issues raised by the LTCM episode. On the other hand, it cannot be denied that the activities of at least some hedge funds (and some private equity funds) were important contributing factors to the reach and severity of the crisis.

Quite naturally, therefore, the question as to whether hedge funds and other private pools of capital should be subject to some form of direct supervision is receiving fresh attention. The primary downside to direct supervision is, of course, the so-called "moral hazard" risk of extending direct supervision to these institutions. CRMPG I and CRMPG II expressed serious reservations about such direct supervision, primarily on moral hazard grounds, a reservation that remains with CRMPG III.

In the current circumstances, some attention has been given to a modified form of direct, but standby, supervision. Under this approach, the authorities (*i.e.*, the Federal Reserve in the United States) would step in when problems at one or more hedge funds raise systemic concerns. While such an approach will no doubt be debated in public and official circles, CRMPG III believes that this approach too raises moral hazard questions. Moreover, as a practical matter it would be very difficult to administer such an approach, in part, because of the danger that the standby authority might be triggered when it is already too late or, because the triggering of such authority might aggravate the very problem it is seeking to mitigate.

D. Regulatory Structure

Not surprisingly, the credit market crisis has brought into even sharper focus the issue of regulatory structure, particularly in the United States and the United Kingdom. In both of these jurisdictions one of the central questions on the table for discussion relates to the role of the central bank in the conduct of supervisory policy with particular emphasis on seeking to better mitigate concerns about systemic risk.

This sharpened focus on the role of central banks is a natural outgrowth of the observed fact that central banks, for all practical purposes, are the only instrumentalities of public policy that (1) literally have day-to-day operational presence in financial markets and (2) can provide financial markets with large amounts of liquidity on short notice, while retaining the flexibility to also withdraw that liquidity when conditions warrant.

CRMPG III welcomes the initiative of the United States Department of Treasury in setting forth its "blueprint" for regulatory reform in the United States. The Policy Group recognizes that the public and political debate on the particulars of that blueprint will occur over an extended period of time. Regardless of the outcome of that lengthy debate, CRMPG III believes that the issue of the role of the central bank in the arena of prudential supervision and financial market oversight requires expedited consideration and resolution. Needless to say, and in the aftermath of recent developments, including but not limited to the Bear Stearns case, the resolution of this issue will have to carefully weigh and balance the implications of such resolution for the moral hazard dilemma while recognizing the unique role that central banks play in helping to promote financial stability. In weighing and balancing these factors, the Policy Group would note the following: (1) if the supervisory reach of the Federal Reserve, for example, is to be extended, it must have the direct and ongoing authority to discharge those responsibilities; and (2) legitimate moral hazard concerns notwithstanding, there will always be extreme circumstances in which extraordinary interventions by central banks or governments are necessary. However, as witnessed in recent months, extraordinary intervention by the authorities clearly *does not* mean that financial institutions and their shareholders will be protected from substantial losses.

E. Supervisory Policy and Practice

As noted throughout CRMPG II and CRMPG III, supervisory practice and policy as applied to large integrated financial intermediaries constitute a sizeable challenge for the international community of prudential supervisors. On the whole, however, the supervisory process works reasonably well, especially as the emphasis of supervisory practices has shifted, in recent years, toward a principles-based approach. As noted earlier in this Report, nowhere are the benefits of such a shift in emphasis more apparent than in the March 6, 2008 Report of the Senior Supervisors Group. Thus, the Policy Group believes that there are clear opportunities to apply the philosophy of that effort to other aspects of supervisory practice. Moreover, because the effort of the Senior Supervisory Group included officials from a number of national jurisdictions, the effort was an obvious plus in terms of enhanced international communication and coordination. Needless to say, the follow-up to such efforts as related to individual institutions must largely be conducted by national level primary supervisors on a case-by-case basis. Even allowing for that fact, the cross-border benefits of the approach of the Senior Supervisors Group are a large and positive step in the direction of more effective supervisory practice.

While acknowledging the gains that have been made in supervisory practice, the Policy Group believes that the case for devoting greater resources to the supervisory effort is clear and compelling. The case for greater resources starts with attracting and retaining more, and more highly skilled, personnel and compensating such personnel in ways that will not fully match private sector practices, but will at least narrow the so-called "public service discount" in compensation.

There are, obviously, direct and indirect fiscal costs associated with devoting more resources to the supervisory process that are quite real in the current setting of pressing fiscal problems in virtually all countries. However, in weighing and balancing fiscal priorities, recent experience reminds us that the fiscal costs of enhancements to the resources applied to the supervisory process must be evaluated relative to the costs of failing to move in that direction.

In the arena of supervisory policy, one particular subject that is in need of further progress is implementing Basel II capital adequacy standards. The Policy Group and virtually all observers agree that a risk-based framework for capital standards is the optimal available approach to such standards, especially across borders, individual institutions and classes of institutions.

However, for understandable reasons, the design and implementation of Basel II has consumed almost a decade. Even now, implementation schedules differ among countries, reflecting in part differing views of individual regulatory bodies (especially in the United States). In addition, further refinements in the methodology for calculating the Basel II capital requirements have been recommended by the Financial Stability Forum and are now on the drawing boards. Finally, some observers have long-standing concerns about the potential for a pro-cyclical bias in the application of Basel II. This concern, in part, grows out of the important role of credit ratings in the Basel II methodology; a concern that, if anything, has probably been magnified by the recent issues that have arisen regarding credit ratings.

The Policy Group is under no illusion that there is a quick and easy solution to any of these issues regarding Basel II. Having said that, the Policy Group wishes to urge all deliberate speed on the part of the international community of supervisory authorities in (1) seeking to stabilize, at least for a reasonable period of time, the methodology associated with Basel II, (2) moving toward a common implementation date across major jurisdictions and (3) ensuring a competitive and supervisory level playing field in the application of Basel II across classes of institutions and across national boundaries.

APPENDIX A: TERM SHEETS FOR HIGH-RISK COMPLEX FINANCIAL INSTRUMENTS

Financial institutions must use term sheets when marketing high-risk complex financial instruments. As this is often the first document reviewed by an investor/counterparty, it is essential that a term sheet convey significant terms and critical information clearly. The Policy Group recommends that term sheets be used when marketing high-risk complex financial instruments, *whether in the form of a security, a derivative or other instrument,* and that any such term sheets include the following categories of information, where applicable:

- A brief overview of the issuer and its capital structure, including a description of all liabilities to be offered. For each liability, the term sheet should include at least the expected notional, coupon, rating, relative seniority, average life (with underlying assumptions noted) and final legal maturity. For derivatives, the term sheet should identify the swap counterparty and credit support provider, if there is one.
- Identity of the collateral or asset manager, if any.
- Significant characteristics of the expected portfolio, including information regarding expected spread, ratings, geography, industry, asset class, correlation and any minimum or maximum parameters, as well as the significant terms of any hedges (*e.g.*, interest rate, currency), expected to be purchased by the issuer.
- Significant terms, including major service providers (*e.g.*, trustees, swap counterparties, guarantors), denominations, currency, exchange listing (if any), call periods, payment dates, pricing and closing dates, reinvestment periods, call periods, PIK provisions, defaulted asset provisions, termination provisions, make-whole payments, quality and coverage tests, the ramifications of failing applicable tests, substitution/reinvestment/management parameters, payment events (*e.g.*, credit events, floating amount events), voting rights and payment waterfall terms. Where possible, information should be displayed graphically (*e.g.*, the waterfall may be displayed as a flow chart, rating diversity may be displayed in a pie chart, *etc.*). Expected or current levels of quality and/or coverage tests should also be displayed against trigger levels.

- Scenario analysis that includes a breakeven analysis for debt and an IRR (or similar) analysis for equity tranches. The analysis should be done over a range of assumptions, including severe downside stress scenarios. Scenario analysis should also include an analysis of what assumptions would result in a significant percentage loss (*e.g.*, 50%) of principal or notional. All implicit and explicit assumptions should be clearly indicated and calculation methodologies should be explained. Significant assumptions should be stress-tested with the results plainly disclosed.
- Investor eligibility requirements (*e.g.*, QIB/QP, Reg. S, ERISA) and expected tax treatment.
- Appropriate risk factors, including risks associated with the instrument structure, leverage, market (interest rate, currency, credit) risks, hedging (if any) effectiveness, counterparty risks, and conflicts of interests with service providers (*e.g.*, multiple roles).
- Appropriate disclaimers.

Appendix B: CDO Risk Characteristics (Excerpted from CRMPG II)

The following material originally appeared in the July 2005 CRMPG II Report. While some of the references to spread levels, as well as market size, composition and practices reflect structured credit products in the years up to and including 2005, the discussion of CDO products in the corporate and asset-backed markets is still quite relevant.

C. Structured Credit

1. Instrument Description and Market Developments

The structured credit market has existed since 1988, and issuance began in earnest in 1997. The last two years, however, has seen the transformation of the market from a niche sector to a core asset class within fixed income. In some ways, this transformation can be attributed to a maturing market with improved liquidity and transparency, established analytic platforms, increased standardization, increased acceptance of credit derivatives technology and a growing track record. But what has truly pushed structured credit into the mainstream is a growing understanding by investors motivated to increase yields in the current low-spread environment. Structured credit still offers a spread pickup versus nearly all other like-rated credit products, although that premium is diminishing.

The structured credit market can be broadly separated into synthetic and cash instruments.

- *Synthetics:* Each vehicle sources exposure to a pool of pure credit risk using credit default swaps (CDS) on 100 or more single-names. Risk is tranched into distinct attachment and detachment points, meaning that investors can customize any number of loss exposures. Most pools are referenced to single-A/BBB corporate credits, although asset-backed securities (ABS) may also be referenced. Equity leverage is typically 20-30x, and deals generally have maturities of five to ten years, depending on the maturity of the underlying CDS. In most synthetics, like the one depicted in Chart 4 below, the motivation for issuance has shifted from issuer balance sheet risk management (early deals) to investor desire to take on a customized risk profile (current deals).

- *Cash:* Cash CDOs gain exposure to credit risk via a bankruptcy remote special purpose vehicle that purchases a diversified pool of cash assets (100+ names). The portfolio is generally managed by a third party but may be static in some cases. Risk is tranched into various loss exposures with customized structures. Each structure contains extensive rules that restrict asset exposures and triggers that that help protect the notes if the collateral deteriorates. Weighted average lives are typically 7 to 12 years.

Synthetic issuance can be measured either by the amount of risk actually distributed to investors (approximately $700 billion globally), or the amount of single-name CDS sold to support this issuance (approximately $1.6 trillion globally). The latter number is more often cited in the market and can be thought of as the delta equivalent of the former, thereby illustrating the leverage in the transactions. In the cash market, outstanding risk is approximately $550 billion globally.

The synthetic market is composed of several types of transactions.

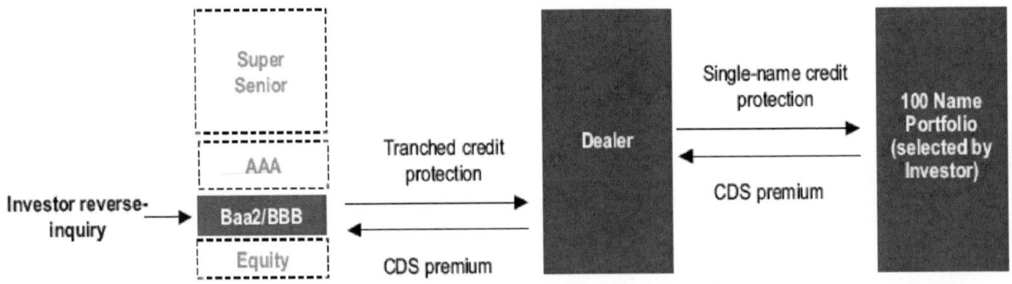

Chart 4. Indicative Synthetic CDO (Baa2/BBB Tranche).

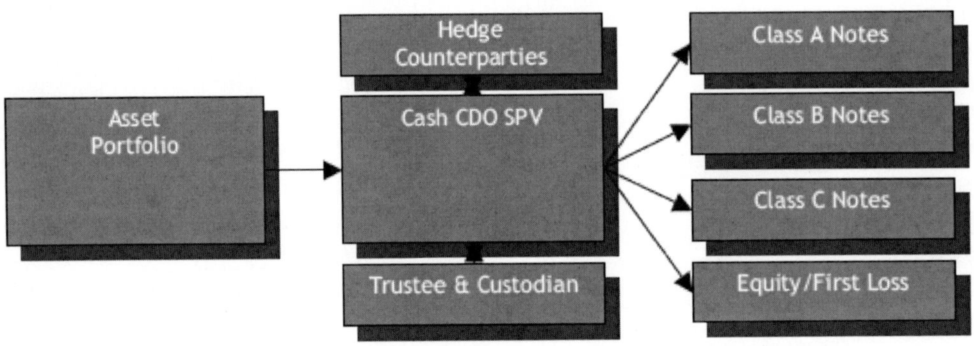

Chart 5. Indicative Cash CDO.

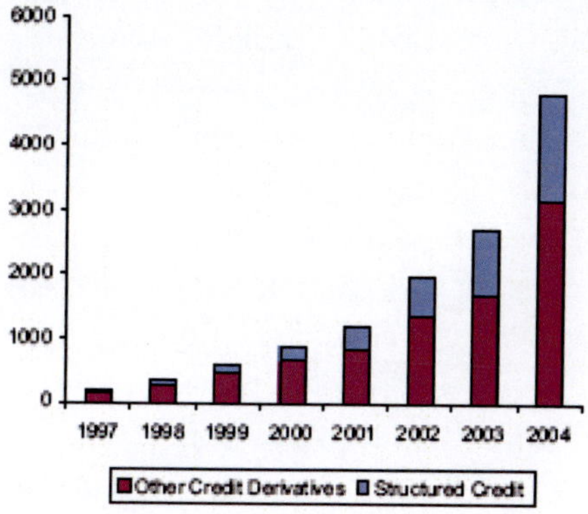

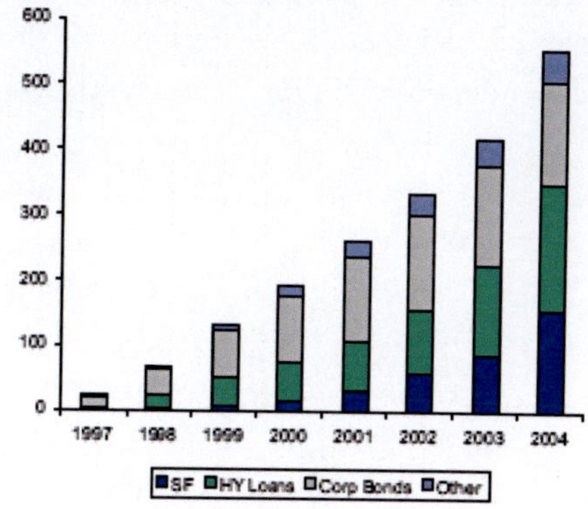

Source: JPMorgan.

Chart 6. Total Outstanding Global Credit Derivatives Volume ($bn).

- *Tranched Index Trades:* One of the most standardized and easy to understand products in the structured credit market, the portfolio is linked to an index such as DJ TRAC-X. It references a static portfolio with standardized attachment points. Market inception was 2003.
- *Bespoke:* The portfolio is chosen by the investor, and is generally static but may have limited substitution rights. There may be customized or standardized attachment points. Market inception was 2002.
- *First to Default Swaps*: These tend to be based on smaller portfolios than other structured credit trades (five names). The investor receives periodic spread until the first credit event occurs. Market inception was 2003.
- *Managed:* These transactions are somewhat more complex than other synthetics due to additional portfolio tests, triggers and limitations. The portfolio is selected and managed by a third-party asset manager. The structure is based on rating agency requirements and investor demand. In older deals, risk was generally fully distributed, but since 2004 most deals have hedged part of the risk on financial intermediaries' balance sheets. Market inception was 1997, but volume grew significantly in 2000.
- *CDO-squared:* CDO-squared or CDO-of-CDOs are probably the most complex transactions in the structured credit market. They are effectively a synthetic CDO tranche referencing other CDO tranches. Subordination in "inner CDOs" protects against initial corporate credit events, and subordination in the "master CDO" protects against credit events in the inner CDOs to a threshold, beyond which losses accumulate quickly. There has been huge growth in the last year due to tight spreads in other credit markets.
- *EDS:* Equity default swaps may be used as collateral for CDOs, but only a few deals have referenced EDS exclusively. More often, there is a 10% – 15% bucket for EDS in a CDO that mostly references CDS (although many investors have been wary of even including a bucket this size).

The cash market is composed of several types of transactions. Most outstanding deals are "Cashflow" CDOs, where cash flows sequentially through the interest and principal waterfall to equity unless certain triggers are violated. These triggers deteriorate only when the par value of collateral decreases due to defaults or trading losses (i.e., cash flows are largely independent of collateral market value fluctuations).

- *Cashflow HY CLOs:* Collateral is typically BB/B leveraged loans (8x – 1 2x levered). Market inception was 1996 with steady growth since (35% of outstanding issuance).
- *Cashflow SF CDOs:* Collateral is usually either AAA/AA ABS (100x levered) or BBB ABS (20x levered). Current deals have high home equity loan exposure. Market inception was 1998 with rapid growth in 2003 – 2004 (27% of outstanding issuance).
- *Cashflow HY CBOs:* Collateral is typically BB/B high yield bonds (8x – 12x levered). Market inception was 1990 with little issuance after 2001 due to problems in older deals (14% of outstanding issuance).
- *Cashflow Other:* Collateral may include emerging markets, trust preferred securities, municipals, project finance or other assets (5% of outstanding issuance.)

The remaining deals are "Market Value" CDOs, where de-leveraging can be triggered by market value changes. Collateral sometimes includes hedge funds and private equity, which must be liquidated to make coupon payments (3x – 5x levered). Collateral may also include liquid securities. Interest in these deals has increased in 2005 (5% of outstanding issuance).

2. Forces Driving Market Activity (Both Cash and Synthetic)

(a) *Balance sheet*

Early "Balance Sheet" CDOs were initiated by holders of securitizable assets, such as commercial banks, which desired to sell assets or transfer the risk of assets. The motivation of these deals was typically to shrink the balance sheet, or reduce required regulatory or economic capital. Today, fewer Balance Sheet CDOs exist, although they are still common in Asia.

(b) *Arbitrage*

The motivation for most CDOs is arbitrage. These deals are inspired by asset managers, dealers and equity tranche investors, who use the CDO structure to fund collateral purchases. Asset managers gain stable management fees, grow assets under management and often achieve upside through incentive fees and retained equity risk. Financial intermediaries gain underwriting fees. Equity tranche investors hope to achieve a leveraged return between the yield on the assets and the financing cost of the debt. This potential spread is the "arbitrage" of the arbitrage CDO.

(c) *Spread pick up*

For rated debt investors, the key motivation is a spread pick-up versus like-rated investments in the corporate or ABS market. In addition, CDOs are a means to customize exposures that cannot be achieved any other way, gain access to a diversified pool of assets and gain access to markets such as leveraged loans.

3. Long and Short Users

Cash CDOs are sold to institutional investors and are registered as 144A or Reg S securities. Cash CDOs are overwhelmingly a long-only market. Shorts are more common in the synthetic space, although approximately 75% that market is still long only. Approximately 70% of cash transactions are originated out of the United States with US assets, although the investor base for these transactions is global. Thus far, more synthetic risk is distributed in Europe versus the United States due primarily to MTM issues for US investors.

(a) *CDO Equity*

The arbitrage CDO market originated as a way for CDO equity investors to obtain non-recourse leverage as an alternative to repo financing. CDO equity coupons are targeted to have internal rates of return in the 10 – 20% area, and are seen as an attractive addition to alternative asset allocations, a bucket that may also include private equity and hedge funds. Unlike private equity, CDO equity coupons tend to be front-loaded (later in the deal life defaults or de- leveraging typically cause cashflows to decline). Coupons are sensitive to defaults/recoveries/prepayments, but have limited exposure to market prices.

Insurers and reinsurers (largely buy-and-hold investors located in Europe) were the earliest participants in the CDO equity market and are still large participants today. More recently, hedge funds and other total return investors have also become involved. Other buyers include pension plans and endowments, who can often avoid mark-to-market requirements that other investors face. Banks are also involved, especially in Asia. Banks often desire CDO equity in the form of combination notes, where equity is combined with another bond from the CDO structure or a treasury strip to achieve a desired rating, principal-protection or some form or regulatory arbitrage. Some CDO equity has been sold to asset managers running CDO equity funds, and to private clients in Europe via brokers and investment consultants. The fact that asset mangers often hold 20 – 30% of the equity in deals that they manage is seen by many as a positive.

(b) *CDO debt*

Investors in rated notes desire yield enhancement versus like-rated credits in the ABS or corporate market. In addition, investors are choosing systematic risk over idiosyncratic. For example, strategies such as long mezzanine tranches can decrease event risk by cushioning against initial losses in a pool. Mezzanine investors include hedge funds, banks, insurance companies and asset managers. Long senior strategies provide constant return with catastrophic-only risk. Banks are key investors, as are reinsurers, monolines and insurance companies. Today, most cash senior tranches are sold as part of negative basis trades, where a bank goes long the senior tranche and simultaneously buys protection from a monoline on the same tranche. Older AAA risk often has a monoline guarantee.

CDO-squared have historically been buyers of cash CDO mezzanine tranches, which are then re-securitized into CDO-squared vehicles. More recently synthetic CDO-squared have been creating synthetic mezzanine CDO tranches for inclusion in CDO-squared, or Senior CDO tranches as a 20% bucket in a High Grade SF CDOs.

(c) *Short positions*

Most short positions are synthetic, as there is no shorting of cash bonds other than with total return swaps, which are limited in use. Synthetic short positions have been increasing, especially in more liquid index trades, but they are still a small portion of the overall market. Shorts may be used by investors with assets on balance sheet to hedge at a reduced cost versus hedging an entire portfolio (short mezzanine), or to hedge idiosyncratic risk (short equity). However, shorts are more often used by total return investors as part of carry trades (e.g., long equity, short mezzanine), or long correlation trades (e.g., sell equity protection with delta hedges).

4. Risk Management Issues

Participants in the structured credit market are subject to a number of risks, including exposure to market moves, counterparty risk, model risk, valuation and liquidity issues, legal risk and operational risk.

(a) *Exposure to market moves*

The chart below provides a synopsis of the key risks faced by different structured credit products. A more detailed discussion on related issues follows below.

	Instruments			
Risks	*CDS*	*Cash CDO*	*Synth CDO*	*CDO-Squared*
Credit Spreads	•	•	•	•
Recovery Rates	•	•	•	•
Correction		•	•	•
Overlap (within a single deal)				•
Serial Dependence				•
Warehousing		•		

Chart 7.

(i) Credit spreads

A position's sensitivity to credit spreads depends on its seniority in the structure (degree of leverage). Equity tranches or first loss pieces, for example, can be highly sensitive to credit spread moves, as illustrated in Chart 8 below.

(ii) Recovery rates

There are potentially low or zero recoveries on junior tranches, especially if risk is systemic and tranches are thin. The downside to single-name risk is the recovery rate, and the downside on a tranche is zero. Depending on tranche width, CDO-squared starts to look like being short a digital option.

(iii) Correlation

The value of a tranche within a structure is determined in part by assumptions regarding correlation. The relationship of the tranche value to the correlation assumptions is not always intuitive. As illustrated in Chart 10 below, first loss tranches increase in value under high correlation assumptions while senior tranches decrease in value under such assumptions.

(iv) Overlap

Risk is increased to the extent that a limited investment universe for reference pools leads to high overlap across pools. CDO-squared often have the same names in multiple portfolios. These issues may be exacerbated by the fact that structured credit remains largely long only, which means that investors have similar risk exposure.

Although CDO-squared get the most attention, overlap is an issue for all CDOs. One large financial intermediary has estimated that the overlap between two CLOs from the same manager can be 50 – 70%. CLOs from different managers still have name overlap in the neighborhood of 25%.

(v) Serial dependence

For CDO-squared, risk is serial dependent (i.e., the exact sequence of credit events matters).

(vi) Warehouse risk

The ramp-up period for new cash deals can be over six months, leaving dealers and asset managers exposed to market moves during this period if the deal cannot close. This is less of a risk for synthetics, which can ramp up quickly.

(b) Counterparty risk

(i) Exposure measurement

Properly measuring the exposure of these transactions can be challenging due to, among other things, the large number of underlying risk factors, the non-linearity associated with a potential change in value of positions and the relatedness of reference entities in multi-name structures.

(ii) Risk mitigation

As much of this activity is in derivative form, counterparty risk is usually mitigated by upfront payments for risky tranches, minimum counterparty ratings for more senior tranches and collateral arrangements. Treating collateral consistently with the supporting agreements is yet another challenge for counterparty exposure measurement.

(c) Model risk

(i) Dealer hedging

Dealers run a balanced rather than perfectly hedged book. The entire capital structure is not always distributed and residual risk (delta, gamma, recovery rate, correlation) must be hedged.

(ii) Ratings arbitrage

Many CDO investors buy tranches based on ratings, with the implied assumption that CDO performance should at least approximate other like-rated fixed income securities. To the extent that CDO defaults or recoveries are worse than the rating indicates, investors may have more risk than they realize (some CDO sectors have clearly performed worse than single-name CDS with equivalent rating/risk). Other investors buy CDO tranches as a form of ratings arbitrage, which could lead to less required economic and regulatory capital than would otherwise be the case.

(d) Valuation and liquidity

(i) Mark-to-market

Derivatives accounting rules result in high MTM sensitivity for synthetic tranches, which may lead to forced selling in a downturn, especially given a "youthful" market. Europe has been moving more to MTM accounting, and it may be a challenge for banks to buy as this progresses. Although cash CDOs have less MTM sensitivity than synthetics, buyers are not immune to this risk and may also have to sell based on ratings triggers.

(ii) Valuation and liquidity

Valuation for Cash CDOs and managed synthetics is generally market based with daily pricing on Bloomberg for recent large synthetic deals. Market liquidity has improved greatly in the last two years. Cash CLOs and widely distributed managed synthetics are the most liquid, with the best liquidity at the top of the capital structure (largest and easiest to analyze tranches). SF CDOs (complex underlying ABS) and CDO equity (sensitive cash flows) are less liquid.

Valuation for non-managed trades is generally model based, with strongest liquidity for index tranches, including pricing for standardized tranches on Bloomberg. Model risk (valuations, risk represented to investors, hedging) is highly relevant for synthetics. There have been examples where investors/asset managers have experienced serious valuation issues where fraud may have been involved.

(e) Legal risk

(i) Understanding transactions

Recent lawsuits including HSH vs. Barclays and Banca Popolare vs. BofA have sought damages for securities allegedly mis-sold (higher risk than declared), mismanaged (substitutions not in best interest of investors) and misreported (inaccurate price evaluations). Issues of whether investors understand the risk are especially relevant for complex structures such as CDO-squared. Ultimately, these disputes suggest that the intermediaries may have thought that they have sold risk when, in fact, they have not.

(ii) CDS legal risk

As many structured credit transactions involve CDS, they will tend to be exposed to the other legal risk discussed in Section B: Credit Derivatives above.

(f) Operational risk

(i) Confirmations

Faced with the complexity of transactions and technology platforms that are often incompatible, firms can experience delays in confirming transaction details.

(ii) Performance tracking

The complexity of transactions also puts strain on back office operations due to the potential need to track and modify the composition of asset pools, monitor tranche performance and book multiple legs of transactions in the appropriate finance and risk systems.

The charts below illustrate the sensitivities of a sample structured credit position to key input variables.

5. CDX and Tranched CDX Sensitivities

The charts below outline the sensitivity of the CDX and Tranched CDX to spreads, correlation and number of defaults *from a long-protection perspective.* It is assumed that the long-protection positions were taken on April 6, 2005.

Below is a brief description of the terminology used throughout this section:

- *CDX:* 5 yr CDX .NA.IG.4. Throughout this section, it will also be called "plain-vanilla CDX". As of 04/06/05, the 5yr CDX.NA.IG.4 spread was 47 bps.
- *Tranched CDX:* Synthetic CDO with the same portfolio of reference entities as that defined for the 5yr CDX.NA.IG.4. The collateral is split into tranches, where each tranche bears losses at a different level of subordination. The most junior tranche may experience the first 3% of losses. The next tranche will bear any loss over 3% up to 7%, and so on.

  0 – 3 → Equity Tranche or First loss Tranche
  3 – 7% → 4Mezzanine Tranche
  7 – 10% ↓
  10 – 15% ↓
  15 – 30% ↓
  30 – 100% → Senior Tranche
  0 – 100% → CDX (plain-vanilla CDX)

- *MTM:* Expressed as % of tranche notional.
- *Spread Multiple:* Makes reference to multiples of the index spread. 100% refers to the index spread as of 04/06/05 (47bps). 50% refers to a spread of 23.5bps.
- *Correlation:* Refers to the correlation of probabilities of default. It tells us how likely the portfolio is to experience its expected loss.
- Low Correlation:
  - Defaults occur independently.
  - Most likely outcome is a few number of names defaulting.
  - xpected loss is likely to be reached (as of 04/06/05, the CDX expected loss was 2.43%).
- High Correlation:
  - Defaults occur in groups.
  - Most likely outcome is many defaults at the same time. In a hypothetical extreme case (correlation = 100%) either 0 names default or 100% of the names default.

– Expected loss is not likely to be reached.

MTM vs. Spread Multiple – all tranches

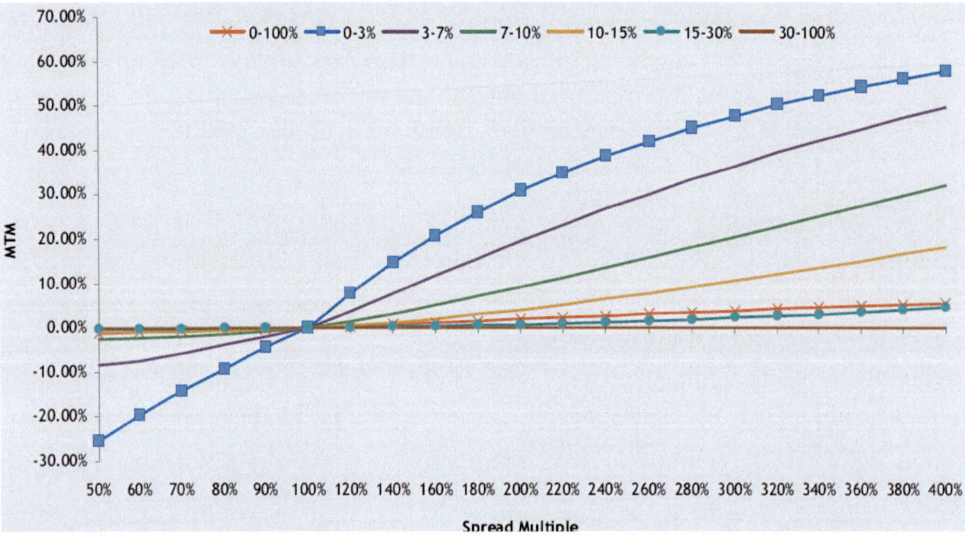

Note: 0 - 3% assumes no upfront.

CDX (0-100%) and Junior Tranches

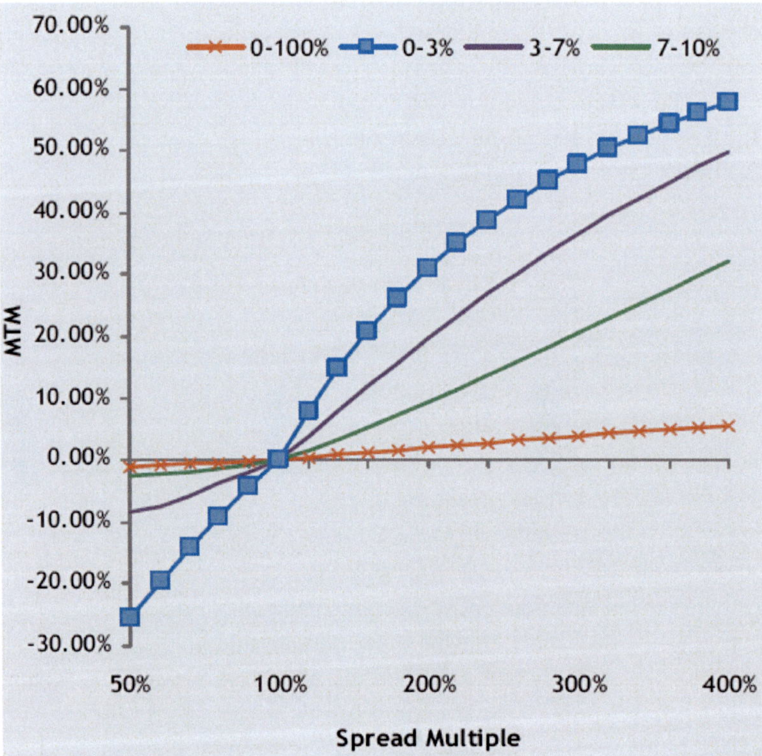

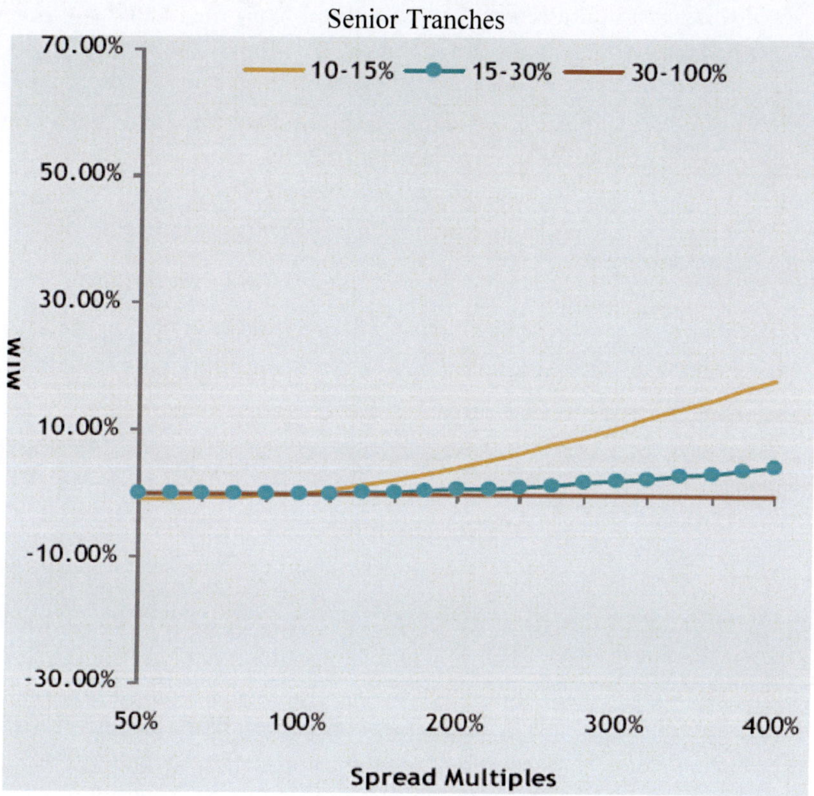

Chart 8.

(a) *Chart 8: Sensitivity to Spreads*

The chart below describes the sensitivity of the CDX (0 – 100%) and the CDX tranches to changes in the CDX Index Spread (in this example, a spread multiple of 100% makes reference to 47bps). The positive slope of both the plain-vanilla CDX and the CDX tranches confirms that a spread widening increases the value of a long protection position. Intuitively, if an investor bought protection and then spreads widen, the value of that trade increases.

The sensitivity is larger in the junior tranches than in both the plain-vanilla CDX and the senior tranches because the most junior tranches (in particular 0 – 3%) are those affected for sure with the first defaults. The likelihood of names defaulting increases as spreads widen.

Chart 9 quantifies the impact that a 100% widening in the index spread (from 47 bps to 94 bps) will have on the MTM of a protection buyer with contracts of $1 million on each tranche.

Were the investor a protection seller, the MTM would be negative, and the investor would report losses equivalent to the gains in the table with the signinverted.

The MTMs in this table make reference to a Spread Multiple of 200% in the previous graphs (equivalent to an Index Spread of 94bps= 200% x 47bps)

Tranche	MTM	**IF the CDX index spread goes up to 94bps AND a protection buyer has a $1mm contract on....**
0-100%	2.02%	...the gain will be 2.02% x $1MM = $20K
0-3%	30.84%	... the gain will be 30.84% x $1MM = $308K
3-7%	19.58%	... the gain will be 19.58% x $1MM = $196K
7-10%	9.27%	... the gain will be 9.27% x $1MM = $93K
10-15%	4.22%	... the gain will be 4.22% x $1MM = $42K
15-30%	0.74%	... the gain will be 0.74% x $1MM = $7K
30-100%	0.00%	... the gain will be 0.00% x $1MM = $0K

Chart 9.

(b) *Chart 10: Sensitivity to Correlation*

Chart 10 below describes the MTM sensitivity of the CDX (0 – 100%) and the CDX tranches to changes in correlation. Correlation is only relevant to the tranches because the impact of defaults over a specific tranche will depend onthe level of tranche subordination. Few defaults (low correlation) will only affect junior tranches whereas many defaults at the same time (high correlation) willimpact the more senior tranches as well. The MTM of the plain-vanilla CDX (0 – 100%) is not sensitive to different levels of correlation because any number of defaults (few or many) will affect it anyway.

When correlation is low (extreme hypothetical case: 0%), few defaults are expected and therefore the expected loss (2.43%) is likely to be reached. Being long, the equity tranche (0 – 3%) becomes riskier and as a result being long protection on equity gains value. This explains the negative slope of the first loss tranche.

When correlation is high (extreme hypothetical case: 100%), either 0% or 100% defaults are expected, and therefore the expected loss (2.43%) is not likely to be reached. Being long senior tranches becomes riskier than when correlation was low and therefore being *long protection on senior tranches gains value.* This explains the positive slope in the non-equity tranches.

(c) *Chart 11: Sensitivity to Number of Defaults*

Chart 11 below describes the sensitivity of the CDX (0 – 100%) and the CDX tranches to the number of defaults. The recovery rate assumption used is 40%. Since the index has 125 equally weighted names, one default will generate a loss of 0.48% of the portfolio (1 /125 * 0.6). In the same fashion, six defaults will generate a loss of approximately 3% of the portfolio (6 / 125 * 0.6).

The positive slope of both the plain-vanilla CDX and the CDX tranches confirms that defaults increase the value of a long-protection position. Intuitively, if an investor bought protection and then credits default, the value of that trade increases.

MTM (y axis) vs. Correlation (x axis)

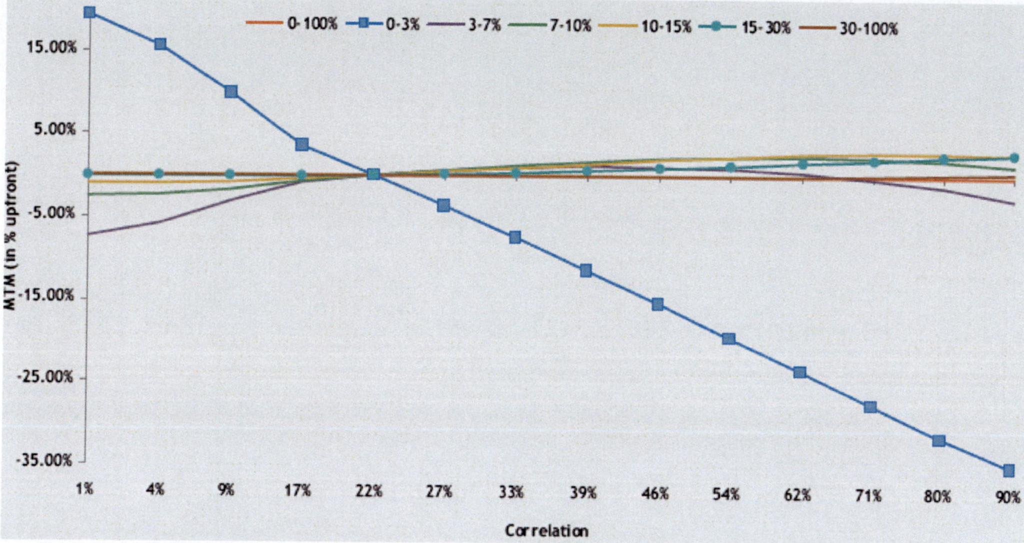

CDX (0-100%) and Junior TrancheCDX (0-100%) and Junior Tranches

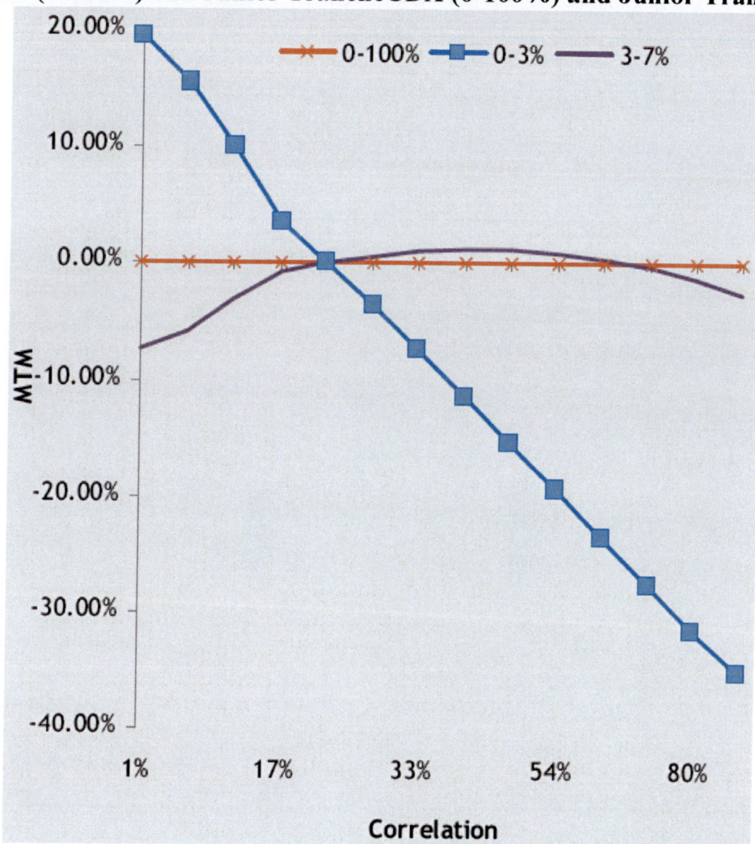

Chart 10. (Continued)

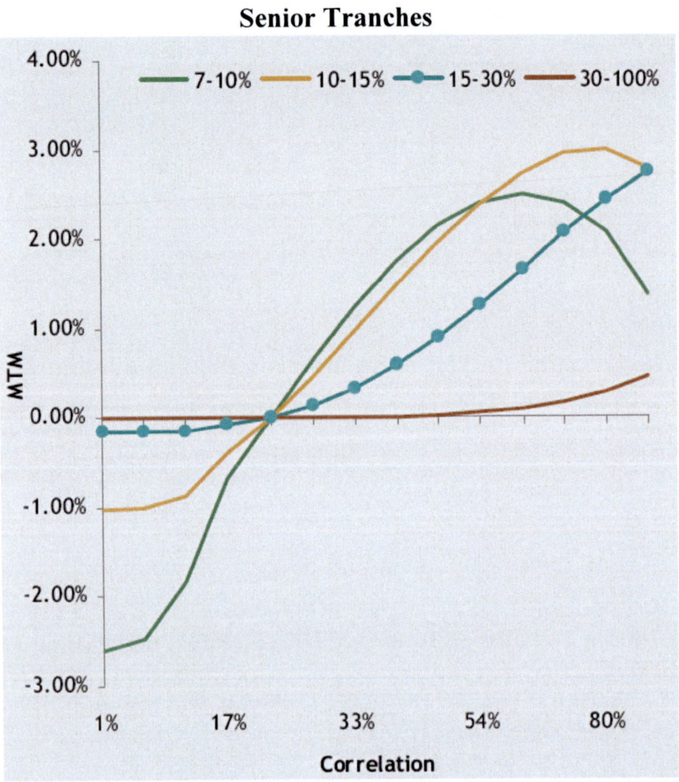

Chart 10.

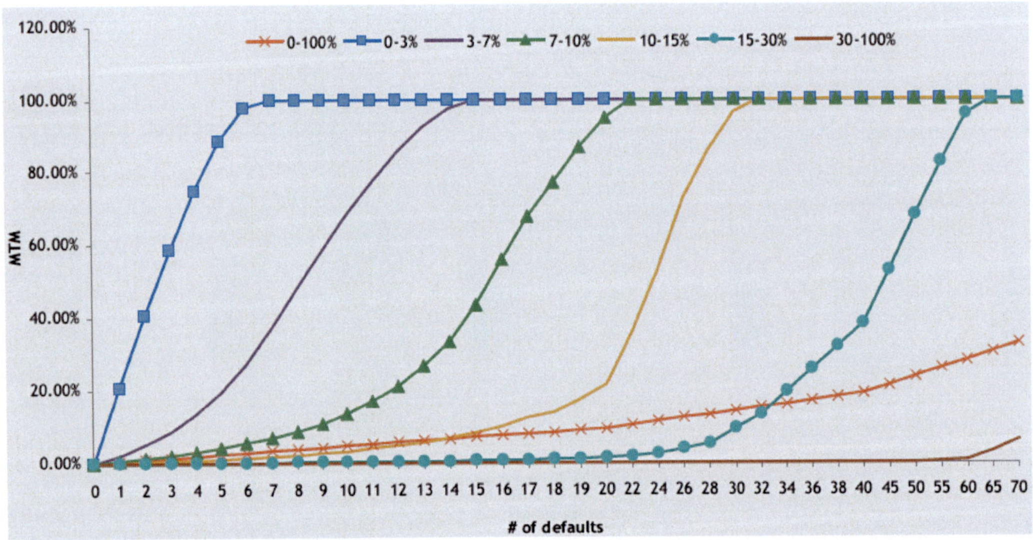

Recovery rate=40%.
Index has 125 equally weighted names.
1 default= 0.48% 6 defaults = approx. 3%.

Chart 11.

Notice that each tranche reaches 100% of its notional at the number of defaults that produce a loss equivalent to the upper bound of the tranche. For instance, the equity tranche reaches a MTM of 100% at six defaults, which is equivalent to a loss of 3% of the portfolio. Also notice that the slope of each non-equity tranche becomes steeper exactly at the max level of defaults that the immediate junior tranche can bare. For example the 3 – 7% tranche becomes steeper at six defaults.

Defaults impact each tranche very differently. The impact over the plain-vanilla CDX is linear because the index is equally weighted. The impact over the 0 – 3% tranche is the largest (the curve is the steepest) because all the burden of the first defaults will only impact this tranche.

In: Reforming Risk in Financial Markets
Editor: Melvin R. Turley, pp. 117-149
ISBN 978-1-60692-445-7

Chapter 2

OBSERVATIONS ON RISK MANAGEMENT PRACTICES DURING THE RECENT MARKET TURBULENCE*

Mario Draghi
Financial Stability Forum, Bank for International Settlements, Basel, Switzerland

March 6, 2008

TRANSMITTAL LETTER

Mr. Mario Draghi, Chairman
Financial Stability Forum
Bank for International Settlements
Centralbahnplatz 2
CH-4002 Basel
Switzerland

Dear Mr. Draghi:

On behalf of the Senior Supervisors Group, I am writing to convey a report that assesses which risk management practices worked well, and which did not, at a sample of major global financial services organizations during the recent period of market turmoil. This report, *Observations on Risk Management Practices during the Recent Market Turbulence*, summarizes the results of a review that we undertook this past autumn of firms' practices. It also reflects the results of a roundtable discussion that participating supervisory agencies held with industry representatives on February 19 at the Federal Reserve Bank of New York.

A few caveats are necessary when reviewing this report. First, while the analysis covered eleven of the largest banking and securities firms (and the roundtable included representatives of five additional firms), it did not cover the universe of all major firms active in the relevant

* This is an edited, excerpted and augmented edition of a Senior Supervisors Group publication, dated March 6, 2008.

markets. Second, the observations reflect supervisory judgments based primarily on detailed discussions with these firms, supplemented with information drawn from ongoing supervisory work. Finally and most importantly, the analysis was completed *prior to the conclusion* of the period of market turmoil.

Subject to these caveats, the report identifies a number of risk management practices that may be associated with negative or positive performance to date.

The predominant source of losses for firms in the survey through year-end 2007 was the firms' concentrated exposure to securitizations of U.S. subprime mortgage-related credit. In particular, some firms made strategic decisions to retain large exposures to super-senior tranches of collateralized debt obligations that far exceeded the firms' understanding of the risks inherent in such instruments, and failed to take appropriate steps to control or mitigate those risks. Such firms have taken major losses on these holdings, with substantial implications for their earnings performance and capital positions.

Another risk management challenge concerned firms' understanding and control over their potential balance sheet growth and liquidity needs. For example, some firms failed to price properly the risk that exposures to certain off-balance-sheet vehicles might need to be funded on the balance sheet precisely when it became difficult or expensive to raise such funds externally. Likewise, some firms found that they could not syndicate their holdings of leveraged loans because of reduced investor appetite for those assets and that they could not cancel their commitments to fund those loans. The resulting effects on the balance sheets of major firms from these sources have been substantial, although the impact on capital ratios has been significantly less than the effect from the write-downs on their exposures to securitizations of subprime mortgage-related credit.

Firms that avoided such problems demonstrated a comprehensive approach to viewing firm-wide exposures and risk, sharing quantitative and qualitative information more effectively across the firm and engaging in more effective dialogue across the management team. Senior managers in such firms also exercised critical judgment and discipline in how they valued its holdings of complex or potentially illiquid securities both before and after the onset of the market turmoil. They had more adaptive (rather than static) risk measurement processes and systems that could rapidly alter underlying assumptions to reflect current circumstances; management also relied on a wide range of risk measures to gather more information and different perspectives on the same risk exposures and employed more effective stress testing with more use of scenario analysis.

In addition, management of better performing firms typically enforced more active controls over the consolidated organization's balance sheet, liquidity, and capital, often aligning treasury functions more closely with risk management processes, incorporating information from all businesses into global liquidity planning, including actual and contingent liquidity risk.

Using the observations of the report to set expectations, primary supervisors are critically evaluating the efforts of the individual firms they supervise to address weaknesses in risk management practices that emerged during the period of market turmoil. Each supervisor is ensuring that its firms are making appropriate changes in risk management practices, including addressing deficiencies in senior management oversight, in the use of risk measurement techniques, in stress testing, and in contingency funding planning.

Finally, our observations help to define an agenda for strengthening supervisory oversight of relevant areas. In particular, we have identified the following areas relevant to this agenda.

First, we will use the results of our review to support the efforts of the Basel Committee on Banking Supervision to strengthen the efficacy and robustness of the Basel II capital framework by:

- reviewing the framework to enhance the incentives for firms to develop more forward-looking approaches to risk measures (beyond capital measures) that fully incorporate expert judgment on exposures, limits, reserves, and capital; and
- ensuring that the framework sets sufficiently high standards for what constitutes risk transfer, increases capital charges for certain securitized assets and asset-backed commercial paper liquidity facilities, and provides sufficient scope for addressing implicit support and reputational risks.

Second, our observations support the need to strengthen the management of liquidity risk, and we will continue to work directly through the appropriate international forums (for example, the Basel Committee, International Organization of Securities Commissions, and the Joint Forum) on both planned and ongoing work in this regard.

Third, based on our shared observations from this review, individual national supervisors will review and strengthen, as appropriate, existing guidance on risk management practices, valuation practices, and the controls over both.

Fourth and finally, we will support efforts in the appropriate forums to address issues that may benefit from discussion among market participants, supervisors, and other key players (such as accountants). One such issue relates to the quality and timeliness of public disclosures made by financial services firms and the question whether improving disclosure practices would reduce uncertainty about the scale of potential losses associated with problematic exposures. Another may be to discuss the appropriate accounting and disclosure treatments of exposures to off-balance-sheet vehicles. A third may be to consider the challenges in managing incentive problems created by compensation practices.

We are simultaneously releasing the report publicly to inform the broader industry of the results of our review and to identify areas of practice where industry attention is necessary.

Sincerely,

William L. Rutledge
Chairman

I. Introduction

After an extended period of ample financial market liquidity and generally low credit spreads in many economies, the sharp loss in the value of subprime mortgages and related mortgagebacked securities and the deterioration in investor appetite during the summer of 2007 led to broad and deep market distress. Because these and other innovative products had been created during the prior period of more benign market conditions, banks and securities firms had not observed how such products would behave during a significant market downturn and found their risk management practices tested to various degrees.

Asset-backed securities (ABS[1]) in general and mortgagebacked securities (MBS) in particular experienced the greatest degree of stress in 2007. The loss in the value of subprime mortgages throughout the year led to growing uncertainty about the valuations of credit instruments such as collateralized debt obligations (CDOs) that often included such subprime mortgages in what investors and rating agencies had previously considered high-quality assets. Consequently, investors sought clarity about the quality of specific assets supporting investment securities and shunned those whose risk they could not easily assess. Their willingness to purchase similar securitized assets backed by mortgages waned as they realized the difficulties of assessing the quality of the underlying assets, as did their willingness to purchase other complex credit products, such as collateralized loan obligations (CLOs). Consequently, many types of credit instruments, such as MBS and other ABS, CDOs, CLOs, and asset-backed commercial paper (ABCP), became illiquid during this time, causing steep decreases in many secondary market prices and requiring corresponding markdowns in the valuations of firms' holdings of affected assets.

Early on in this period of market turbulence, our group— senior supervisors of such major financial services firms from France, Germany, Switzerland, the United Kingdom, and the United States[2]—convened to assess whether shortcomings in risk management may have contributed to the losses. More specifically, we sought to identify risk management practices that may have tended to work well, and those that may no have, so that we could better evaluate whether changes in supervisory guidance and expectations are necessary.

To this end, we developed an extensive questionnaire covering senior management oversight and risk management performance across key dimensions. We shared the questionnaire with a sample of eleven global banking organizations and securities firms that are significant competitors in affected markets and that experienced a range of outcomes through the early months of the market turmoil. In November 2007, we met with senior management at the selected organizations to elicit their perspectives on how well or how poorly key elements of their corporate governance, business strategy, and risk management practices had worked up to that point in time. By analyzing the results of these systematic discussions and by using information otherwise available to principal supervisors, our senior supervisory group sought to determine the effectiveness of different risk management practices over the period of stress through the end of calendar year 2007. We then met with industry representatives on February 19, 2008, in New York to share our observations and seek comments on them.

This report outlines supervisors' observations on the risk management practices that may have enabled some firms to weather the financial market turmoil better than others through year-end 2007. Specifically, supervisors focused on practices related to the following:

- the role of senior management oversight in assessing and responding to the changing risk landscape; the effectiveness of market and credit risk management practices in

[1] A list of abbreviations used in this report appears in Appendix A.

[2] The seven supervisory agencies participating in this project are the French Banking Commission, the German Federal Financial Supervisory Authority, the Swiss Federal Banking Commission, the U.K. Financial Services Authority, and, in the United States, the Office of the Comptroller of the Currency, the Securities and Exchange Commission, and the Federal Reserve. The list of working group members appears in Appendix B.

understanding and managing the risks in retained or traded exposures as well as in counterparty exposures, in valuing complex and increasingly illiquid products, and in limiting or hedging exposures to credit and market risk, and
- the effectiveness of each firm's liquidity risk management practices in assessing its vulnerability to that risk in a stressed environment and taking appropriate action.

It should be emphasized that the observations in this report reflect our understanding of risk management practices at eleven major firms through our year-end 2007 review period. Our work does not represent a comprehensive review of the turmoil and all firms' experiences. As market events progress, other weaknesses may emerge, and our observations may not prove to be definitive or complete. Consequently, this report should be viewed as an interim assessment of the key risk management practices that have affected major firms' ability to weather the current market turbulence.

II. Summary of Key Observations and Conclusions

The market distress that began in the second half of 2007 occurred after an extended period of ample financial market liquidity and generally low credit spreads. The banking organizations and securities firms in our sample entered the turmoil in relatively sound financial condition and generally with capital well above regulatory requirements. However, as a result of these events, many firms absorbed significant losses, and the prolonged disruption in market liquidity stressed most firms' liquidity and capital

The widespread retraction of interest among investors in purchasing various kinds of assets caused many major financial services firms to experience substantial write-downs and unexpected losses in their portfolios; some firms have subsequently had to raise new capital. Financial businesses such as those involved in the syndication to external investors of leveraged loans to corporate borrowers faced dwindling demand for their products and consequently losses as positions had to be marked down.

But the primary source of losses came from concentrated exposures that some major financial services organizations had to U.S. subprime mortgage-related credit, particularly in businesses involved in the warehousing, structuring, and trading of CDOs backed by such credits. Several firms found that their aggregate exposure to this risk was larger than they initially recognized. What drove most directly the absolute and relative dimensions of loss were the strategic decisions that some firms made to retain large exposures in super-senior tranches of CDOs that far exceeded the firms' appreciation of the risks inherent in such instruments. Firms did not recognize the possibility that losses on the underlying MBS could reach levels that could impair the value of even the super-senior tranches of collateralized debt obligations of asset-backed securities (ABS CDOs).

Many firms were more vulnerable to a prolonged disruption in market liquidity than they expected. Firms were surprised by the nature and length of the market disruption and were forced to fund exposures that they had not anticipated in their contingency funding plans. This included retaining exposures in warehouse portfolios for significantly longer periods of time than expected when firms realized they were unable to find buyers for securities such as residential mortgage-backed securities (RMBS), ABS CDOs, and highyield bond exposures.

Firms likewise found that they could neither syndicate to external investors their leveraged loan commitments to corporate borrowers nor cancel their commitments to fund those loans despite material and adverse changes in the availability of funding from other investors in the market. Moreover, some firms were required to fund contractual commitments backstopping a range of offbalance- sheet financing vehicles that they had not anticipated they would have to fund themselves, such as ABCP conduits. In other cases, firms under no contractual obligations still provided voluntary support to these and other off-balancesheet financing vehicles, including structured investment vehicles (SIVs), because of concerns about the potential damage to their reputations and to their future ability to sell investments in such vehicles if they failed to provide support during the period of market distress.

Nevertheless, during the turmoil, all firms were able to obtain adequate liquidity to fund their operations and, in certain cases, to bring additional assets onto their balance sheets that they had not planned to fund. However, all firms faced higher funding costs and, in most cases, did not have as much contingent funding liquidity as they would have liked.

While firms were neither universally effective nor ineffective across all relevant dimensions, our supervisory group identified actions and decisions that have tended to differentiate firms' performance during the period of market turbulence through year-end 2007. Some firms recognized the emerging additional risks and took deliberate actions to limit or mitigate them. Others recognized the additional risks but accepted them. Still other firms did not fully recognize the risks in time to mitigate them adequately. Many of our observations on risk management practices relate to the decisions that firms made to take, manage, measure, aggregate, and hedge (or not hedge) such exposures. In particular, we found important differences in firms' approaches to four firm-wide risk management practices and to three specific business lines.

A. Four Firm-Wide Risk Management Practices that Differentiated Performance

Firms that tended to deal more successfully with the ongoing market turmoil through year-end 2007 adopted a comprehensive view of their exposures. They used information developed across the firm to adjust their business strategy, risk management practices, and exposures promptly and proactively in response to changing market conditions.

1. Effective Firm-wide Risk Identification and Analysis

Through robust dialogue among members of the senior management team (including the chief executive officer, the chief risk officer, and others at that level), business line risk owners, and control functions, firms that performed well through year-end 2007 generally shared quantitative and qualitative information more effectively across the organization. Some firms were consequently able to identify the sources of significant risk as early as mid-2006; they had as much as a year to evaluate the magnitude of those risks and to implement plans to reduce exposures or hedge risks while it was still practical and not prohibitively expensive. Senior managers developed a firm-wide plan to reduce or hedge those exposures and did not rely on the hope that business lines would make decisions individually that would benefit the firm's exposures collectively.

In firms that experienced greater difficulties, business line and senior managers did not discuss promptly among themselves and with senior executives the firm's risks in light of evolving conditions in the marketplace. This left business areas to make some decisions in isolation regarding business growth and hedging, and some of those decisions increased, rather than mitigated, the exposure to risks.

2. Consistent Application of Independent and Rigorous Valuation Practices across the Firm

At firms that performed better in late 2007, management had established, before the turmoil began, rigorous internal processes requiring critical judgment and discipline in the valuation of holdings of complex or potentially illiquid securities. These firms were skeptical of rating agencies' assessments of complex structured credit securities and consequently had developed in-house expertise to conduct independent assessments of the credit quality of assets underlying the complex securities to help value their exposures appropriately. Finally, when they reached decisions on values, they sought to use those values consistently across the firm, including for their own and their counterparties' positions. Subsequent to the onset of the turmoil, these firms were also more likely to test their valuation estimates by selling a small percentage of relevant assets to observe a price or by looking for other clues, such as disputes over the value of collateral, to assess the accuracy of their valuations of the same or similar assets.

In contrast, firms that faced more significant challenges in late 2007 generally had not established or made rigorous use of internal processes to challenge valuations. They continued to price the super-senior tranches of CDOs at or close to par despite observable deterioration in the performance of the underlying RMBS collateral and declining market liquidity. Management did not exercise sufficient discipline over the valuation process: those firms generally lacked relevant internal valuation models and sometimes relied too passively on external views of credit risk from rating agencies and pricing services to determine values for their exposures. Given that the firms surveyed for this review are major participants in credit markets, some firms' dependence on external assessments such as rating agencies' views of the risk inherent in these securities contrasts with more sophisticated internal processes they already maintain to assess credit risk in other business lines. Furthermore, when considering how the value of their exposures would behave in the future, they often continued to rely on estimates of asset correlation that reflected more favorable market conditions.

3. Effective Management of Funding Liquidity, Capital, and the Balance Sheet

The importance of maintaining a firm-wide perspective is similarly evident in differences in the enforcement of more active controls over the consolidated organization's balance sheet, liquidity, and capital positions. Those firms that avoided more significant problems through our year-end review period aligned treasury functions more closely with risk management processes, incorporating information from all businesses in global liquidity planning, including actual and contingent liquidity risk. These firms had created internal pricing mechanisms that provided incentives for individual business lines to control activities that might otherwise lead to significant balance sheet growth or unexpected reductions in capital. In particular, these firms had charged business lines appropriately for building contingent liquidity exposures to reflect the cost of obtaining liquidity in a more difficult market environment.

Moreover, better performing firms actively managed their contingent liquidity needs. For example, some firms avoided business lines such as CDO warehousing or SIVs because the perceived contingent liquidity risk outweighed the potential returns. When implementing their plans, these firms exhibited greater discipline in adhering to limits in the face of changing market conditions.

Firms that experienced greater problems tended to have weaker controls over their potential balance sheet growth and liquidity. Their treasury functions were not closely aligned with risk management processes and lacked complete access to flows of information across all businesses in the firm and an understanding of the changing contingent liquidity risk of new and existing businesses. In some cases, contingency funding plans were based on incomplete information because the firm did not consider properly the risk of certain exposures being added to the balance sheet or failed to price appropriately the usage of the balance sheet or of contingent liquidity needs such as those liquidity needs for SIVs and for syndicated leveraged loan deals. Accordingly, these firms failed to create incentives for business lines to manage such potential scenarios prudently.

4. Informative and Responsive Risk Measurement and Management Reporting and Practices

Firms that tended to avoid significant challenges through year-end 2007 typically had management information systems that assess risk positions using a number of tools that draw on differing underlying assumptions. Generally, management at the better performing firms had more adaptive (rather than static) risk measurement processes and systems that could rapidly alter underlying assumptions in risk measures to reflect current circumstances. They could quickly vary assumptions regarding characteristics such as asset correlations in risk measures and could customize forward-looking scenario analyses to incorporate management's best sense of changing market conditions.

Most importantly, managers at better performing firms relied on a wide range of measures of risk, sometimes including notional amounts of gross and net positions as well as profit and loss reporting, to gather more information and different perspectives on the same exposures. Many were able to integrate their measures of market risk and counterparty risk positions across businesses. Moreover, they effectively balanced the use of quantitative rigor with qualitative assessments. This blend of qualitative and quantitative analysis provided a high level of insight and consistent communications to management about evolving conditions, enabling the firm to pursue opportunities as they emerged and, more importantly, to reduce exposures when risks outweighed expected rewards.

Firms that encountered more substantial challenges seemed more dependent on specific risk measures incorporating outdated (or inflexible) assumptions that management did not probe or challenge and that proved to be wrong. Some firms that lacked alternative perspectives on risk positions lost sight of how risk was evolving or could change in the future and what that might mean for the aggregate size of their gross versus net exposures. Some could not easily integrate market and counterparty risk positions across businesses, making it difficult to identify consolidated, firm-wide sensitivities and concentrations.

What follows is a review of firms' use of two particular sets of risk management tools during the period of market turbulence, namely value-at-risk (VaR) measures and stress testing.

First, VaR measures formed a key barometer for most firms in understanding their sensitivity to changes in market conditions. In the course of market events, most firms indicated that their VaR measures performed as expected, but many identified weaknesses in the assumptions and specifications underpinning their VaR measures. Some firms identified shortcomings in their assumptions about the scale of shocks or degree of market volatility they may face; how their holdings of (relatively new forms of) instruments may behave in comparison with more established debt products when shocks strike markets; or how the accuracy of their VaR measure is affected by the accuracy of price estimates for less liquid or illiquid securities. Nonetheless, some firms emphasized that the dependence on historical data makes it unlikely that a VaR-based measure could ever capture severe market shocks that exceed recent or historical experience, highlighting the importance of supplementing VaR with other views on risk.

Second, with regard to stress testing and related scenario analyses, the firms surveyed experienced more divergent results. Some found that their stress tests or scenario analyses generally matched the movements in market prices, but others found that the actual shocks to credit spreads tended to be wider and longer lasting than their prior analyses had suggested. Many firms plan to refine their stress tests to alter, for example, their estimates about the economic benefits of diversification in stressed markets. While it should be emphasized that the goal of stress testing cannot be to anticipate the scale of every future shock, which would be an unachievable expectation, some firms found it challenging before the recent turmoil to persuade senior management and business line management to help develop and pay sufficient attention to the results of forward-looking stress scenarios that assumed large price movements.

A common shortcoming in the implementation of both VaR measures and stress tests at some firms, and especially at those that experienced greater challenges, related to the failure to treat appropriately the basis risk between cash bonds and derivative instruments such as credit default swaps. Another issue was the use of proxy volatility data as a substitute for risk assessments of instruments that did not have a long price history of their own. For example, some firms that encountered more substantial challenges tended to assume that they could apply the low historical return volatility of corporate credits rated Aaa[3] to super-senior tranches of CDOs, a more novel instrument that rating agencies had likewise rated Aaa.. That assumption turned out to be wrong and increased those firms' exposure to basis risk. Furthermore, some firms placed too much reliance on the external credit ratings of structured products and did not challenge the resulting calculations of VaR (or static stress shocks calibrated from historical data series) that their risk measurement engines generated based on these ratings and related optimistic assumptions. As mentioned earlier, the dependence of these firms on rating agencies' assessments stands in marked contrast to the sophistication of their existing internal credit assessment processes in other business lines. Such firms failed to assess properly both correlation risks generally and basis risks and correlation risks specifically within particular asset classes.

---

[3] The credit ratings notations used in this report reflect the scale used by Moody's Investors Service, a credit rating agency. The use of this scale is for illustrative purposes only.

B. Three Business Lines where Varying Practices Differentiated Performance

In addition to noting differences in outcomes attributable to varying risk management practices that firms applied across their businesses, our supervisory group found that differences in risk appetite, business strategy, and risk management approaches in three particular business lines have led to considerable variability in firms' performance.

1. CDO Structuring, Warehousing, and Trading Businesses

The losses resulting from write-downs of positions in supersenior tranches of CDOs backed by subprime mortgages have accounted for a majority of the overall losses for major financial services firms active in this business during the second half of 2007. Affected firms sought to expand this business rapidly, generally with poor risk management practices.

In particular, the firms did not consider that the positions might be of poorer credit quality than the external credit rating indicated and that even senior tranches could lose considerable market value if the underlying collateral suffered losses (or was downgraded) or if market liquidity receded for these products. Such firms typically sustained significant losses because they retained the super-senior position of CDOs backed by subprime mortgages or other similar assets and treated them as "par" assets.

In addition, internal incentives were missing or inadequately calibrated to the true risk of the exposures to the super-senior tranches of CDOs. Poor internal controls for balance sheet usage, such as weaknesses in the application of internal pricing or limits, did not create adequate incentives to restrict or hedge the risks related to these positions in a timely fashion. Likewise, internal risk capital measures that relied too much on agency ratings underestimated the true price of the risk of such positions. Furthermore, we believe that traditional credit risk management disciplines such as conducting analyses of industry sectors and using limits were not in place in several cases.

2. Syndication of Leveraged Financing Loans

Some firms worked aggressively to defend or expand market share in the syndication of leveraged financing loans, and many of those that later faced challenges in this business did not properly account for the price risk inherent in the syndicated leveraged lending pipelines. This oversight resulted in inadequate aggregate risk measures. Some firms did not consider the importance of marking pipeline positions to market, but rather treated them more like loans and valued them at or close to par. Given changes in the financial markets, some firms had to fund deals and postpone others. In contrast, several firms that scaled back activities in this business line as they saw underwriting standards deteriorate were able to avoid significant challenges.

3. Conduit and SIV Business

Several firms did not properly recognize or control for the contingent liquidity risk in their conduit businesses or recognize the reputational risks associated with the SIV business. Many firms did not properly price for the correlated contingent liquidity risk in asset-backed conduits, an error that led to unexpected claims on the firms' own liquidity resources. In some cases, firms concerned about risks to their reputations felt compelled to bring SIV assets on their balance sheets or to finance assets that they had expected to sell. Such decisions imposed substantial costs on the organizations and led to some further expansion of the firms' liquidity and capital needs. In addition, certain non-recourse financing products (such as leveraged total return swaps) created issues for certain firms because of the deterioration in the price and market liquidity of the assets underlying some of these products.

C. Supervisory Response

Our observations on risk management practices during the recent market turbulence have relevance both to the supervision of individual firms and to the agenda for strengthening supervisory oversight.

Using the observations of the report to set expectations, primary supervisors are critically evaluating the efforts of the individual firms they supervise to address weaknesses in risk management practices that emerged during the period of market turmoil. Each supervisor is ensuring that its firms are making appropriate changes in risk management practices, including addressing deficiencies in senior management oversight, in the use of risk measurement techniques, in stress testing, and in contingency funding planning.

Moreover, our observations help to define an agenda for strengthening supervisory oversight of relevant areas. In particular, we have identified the following areas relevant to this agenda.

First, we will use the results of our review to support the efforts of the Basel Committee on Banking Supervision to strengthen the efficacy and robustness of the Basel II capital framework by:

- reviewing the framework to enhance the incentives for firms to develop more forward-looking approaches to risk measures (beyond capital measures) that fully incorporate expert judgment on exposures, limits, reserves, and capital; and
- ensuring that the framework sets sufficiently high standards for what constitutes risk transfer, increases capital charges for certain securitized assets and ABCP liquidity facilities, and provides sufficient scope for addressing implicit support and reputational risks.

Second, our observations support the need to strengthen the management of liquidity risk, and we will continue to work directly through the appropriate international forums (for example, the Basel Committee, International Organization of Securities Commissions, and the Joint Forum) on both planned and ongoing initiatives in this regard.

Third, based on our shared observations from this review, individual national supervisors will review and strengthen, as appropriate, existing guidance on risk management practices, valuation practices, and the controls over both.

Fourth and finally, we will support efforts in the appropriate forums to address issues that may benefit from discussion among market participants, supervisors, and other key players (such as accountants). One such issue relates to the quality and timeliness of public disclosures made by financial services firms and the question whether improving disclosure practices would reduce uncertainty about the scale of potential losses associated with problematic exposures. Another may be to discuss the appropriate accounting and disclosure treatments of exposures to off-balance-sheet vehicles. A third may be to consider the challenges in managing incentive problems created by compensation practices.

We offer below our detailed observations on the risk management practices—relating to senior management oversight, liquidity risk management, and credit and market risk management—that tended to differentiate firms' performance through year-end 2007.

III. SENIOR MANAGEMENT OVERSIGHT

Well-managed organizations rely on their leadership to articulate strategy, the range of outcomes that are acceptable to maintain and increase franchise value, and the structure through which organizations pursue their strategy and increase the firm's value as a going concern. Imbedded within these responsibilities is the task of determining in which businesses to engage and to what degree, and hence the kinds and levels of risks the firm will accept. The responsibilities necessarily include the task of creating an infrastructure to take on appropriate exposures that will achieve targeted returns and simultaneously to identify, measure, and manage the associated risks.

A firm's business/risk mix, the level of risk it accepts, and the management and control structure through which it operates reflect senior management's view of, and willingness to do business in, the market environment. During the recent market turbulence, the senior management of the firms in our review differed both in their outlook for the broader business environment and in their willingness to accept the risks emerging in particular markets. In addition, some senior managers missed or underestimated the risks in products and markets that they exploited as sources of growth; these products and markets later became sources of weakness and material losses in the turmoil. But the outcomes varied, even among those firms that had leaders who understood and accepted the risks in products or markets that later proved to be problematic.

How senior management at various firms approached the current market turmoil appears to have differed in a number of important ways that help to explain firms' outcomes through year-end 2007. Four such differences in approaches included the following:

- the balance that each firm's senior management in general achieved between its desire to do business and its appetite for risk as reflected in the tone set for developing or enforcing controls on the resulting risks;
- the role that senior management in particular played in identifying and understanding material risks and acting on that understanding to mitigate excessive risks;
- the efforts that senior management undertook to surmount organizational structures that tended to delay, divert, or distort the flow of information up the management chain of the firm; and
- the breadth and depth of cross-disciplinary discussions and communication of insight into relevant risks across the firm.

A. The Balance between Risk Appetite and Risk Controls

An overarching difference is apparent in the balance that senior management achieved between expanding the firms' exposures in what turned out to be high-risk activities and fostering an appropriate risk management culture to administer those activities. Senior management at nearly all firms surveyed had allowed the businesses to increase their exposure to market risk, but some firms' senior management was far more assertive than others' in encouraging the increased risk taking. For example, firms that experienced material unexpected losses in relevant business lines typically appeared to have been under pressure over the short term either to expand the business aggressively, to a point beyond the capacity of the relevant control infrastructure, or to defend a market leadership position. In some cases, concerns about the firm's reputation in the marketplace may have motivated aggressive managerial decisions in the months prior to the turmoil.

A further distinction among the firms was the degree to which senior management encouraged a firm-wide approach to risk management and the enhancement of control structures to keep pace with the growth of risk taking. In addition, it was critical for firms to have risk management functions that are not only independent, but also have sufficient authority within the organization.

An issue for a number of firms is whether compensation and other incentives have been sufficiently well designed to achieve an appropriate balance between risk appetite and risk controls, between short-run and longer run performance, and between individual or local business unit goals and firm-wide objectives. Many firms are assessing their overall financial performance for 2007 and, in light of their results, reevaluating their approaches to performance-driven compensation and other incentives going forward.

In addition, in some of the firms that felt most confident in their risk identification practices during the market turmoil and that avoided material unexpected losses through year-end 2007, senior managers promoted a continuous dialogue between business areas and risk management functions at the top of the firm on whether the firm was achieving an appropriate balance between its risk appetite and risk controls. These discussions became more active as the market turmoil intensified.

In contrast, senior management at some other firms that recorded relatively larger unexpected losses tended to champion the expansion of risk without commensurate focus on controls across the organization or at the business-line level. At these firms, senior management's drive to generate earnings was not accompanied by clear guidance on the tolerance for expanding exposures to risk. For example, balance sheet limits may have been freely exceeded rather than serving as a constraint to business lines. The focus on growth without an appropriate focus on controls resulted in a substantial accumulation of assets and contingent liquidity risk that was not well recognized. This pattern was particularly apparent in several significant business lines.

- For example, some firms did not fully appreciate the market risk of *CDO warehouse and packaging businesses* even as these businesses were expanding substantially. Some management teams believed that they would be able to sell at a favorable price whatever credit instrument they structured. Consequently, as explained in more detail below, senior management and risk management at these firms did not challenge business lines' assumptions regarding the risks associated with the exposures retained on the firms' balance sheets, nor did they require that steps be taken to test the accuracy of valuations. Management did not anticipate the duration of the warehouse pipeline or require hedging of those exposures. They did not seek to limit these risks by reducing or hedging retained positions on a timely basis; some firms continued to underwrite or increase their exposures until the summer of 2007 despite an array of data indicating rising stress in the subprime mortgage market and worsening credit market conditions.

- In the *syndicated loan business,* some firms ignored limits on syndicated loans as covenants and market material adverse change (MAC) clauses increasingly fell away. Other firms, faced with the same information about evolving market conventions and weakening lender protections, reduced the volume and nature of transactions they were willing to finance. A number of firms in effect provided financial sponsors with out-ofthe- money options as commitments made without market MAC clauses and with thin market flex terms[4] were taken up in substantial volumes. The size of assets that were potentially being added to dealer firms' balance sheets challenged their prospective liquidity, capital, and balance sheet capacity and adversely affected asset quality. Effective firms were more likely to use prudent transfer pricing to account for contingent liquidity and balance sheet usage.
- Similarly, regarding *liquidity support for conduits*, a number of firms belatedly recognized that the out-ofthe- money liquidity support options were being taken up in substantial numbers and the associated risks were not fully priced. Additionally, concerns about reputational damage drove some firms to provide unanticipated support to vehicles, including consolidating these positions onto their balance sheet, when no contractual support was required.

B. Senior Management's Role in Understanding and Acting on Emerging Risks

A second difference noted by our supervisory group concerns the role that the firms' senior managers (including its chief executive officer, chief risk officer, and others) played in understanding the emerging risks and acting on that understanding to mitigate excessive risks.

The senior management teams at some of the firms that felt most comfortable with the risks they faced and that generally avoided significant unexpected losses had prior experience in capital markets. Consequently, the nature of market-related events over the summer of 2007 played to their experience and strength in assessing and responding to rapidly changing market developments and issues such as uncertainty in valuations. As risk issues were identified and brought to the attention of senior managers, executives in many of the firms that avoided significant losses championed robust and timely risk mitigation efforts, including executing hedges, deciding to write down exposures, and enhancing management information systems.

[4] Market flex terms are the prices and other terms that syndicators set for borrowers to sell the loans to outside investors.

In contrast, some of the executive leaders at firms that recorded larger losses did not have the same degree of experience in capital markets and did not advocate quick, strong, and disciplined responses.

This observation does not imply that firms should select executive leaders on the basis of their experience in managing risk in trading businesses. Instead, it emphasizes the need for senior management teams as a whole to include people with expertise in a range of risks since the source of the next disruption is impossible to predict. Recent events suggest that firms are more likely to maintain a risk profile consistent with the board and senior management's tolerance for risk if they establish risk management committees that discuss all significant risk exposures across the firm, meet on a frequent basis, and include executive and senior leaders from key business lines and independent risk management and control functions—for example, the chief financial officer and senior managers from the legal function and operations areas—as equal partners.

The third and fourth areas where the varying approaches of firms' senior managers may help to explain differences in the firms' experiences relate to efforts to ensure that organizational structures did not delay, divert, or distort the flow of information upward or across the firm.

C. Timing and Quality of Information Flow up to Senior Management

In a period of quickly shifting market developments, the timely provision of accurate information to senior management was critical to a firm's ability to respond rapidly. Certainly difficult or complex issues must be analyzed and discussed vigorously at all levels of the institution. However, the highest level of management should be involved in decisions that may have significant implications, such as altering materially a consolidated organization's overarching strategy or balance sheet.

As for timing, senior managers at virtually all firms understood and were discussing changes in markets and risks by the first half of 2007. At some firms, however, managers escalated their concerns about emerging risks to senior managers in business and risk management functions (including the chief executive officer, chief risk officer, and others) as early as the summer of 2006. Accordingly, some firms gained up to a year to consider ways to investigate the risks and reduce or hedge their exposure to the highest risk assets while it was still practical and inexpensive to do so. Others lagged in discussing the emerging risks at the senior management level until 2007, when it was already becoming too difficult to address them.

The quality of information shared with senior management varied as well. In some cases, hierarchical structures tended to serve as filters when information was sent up the management chain, leading to delays or distortions in sharing important data with senior management. In contrast, some firms effectively removed organizational layers as events unfolded to provide senior managers with more direct channels of communication.

D. Breadth and Depth of Internal Communication across the Firm

Firms that understood quickly the kinds and scale of risks they faced and that generally avoided significant losses through year-end 2007 relied on information from many parts of their businesses and communicated that information both up to senior management and across businesses.

In contrast, the existence of organizational "silos" in the structures of some firms appeared to be detrimental to the firms' performance during the turmoil. Silos tended to compartmentalize information: in some cases, information gathered by one business line was not shared with other business lines where the information would have been useful. This inadvertent diversion or withholding of key information left different business areas to make decisions in isolation and in ignorance of other areas' insights. For example, although some business line managers recognized that underwriting standards for some products were loosening, other business line managers did not; instead, they continued to add to the firms' warehouses assets whose credit quality was likely deteriorating.

In some other firms, however, the treasury function served as a central point between silos and was integrated more closely in the firm-wide risk management process. This structure improved decision making, with positive implications for a firm's consolidated balance sheet, capital position, and liquidity needs. In particular, some firms had well-developed linkages between the control functions (as well as treasury) and the businesses. At firms that avoided significant losses, risk management had independence and authority but also considerable direct interaction with senior business managers and was not viewed as remote from the businesses. While the independence of risk management functions was not cited as an issue at the firms visited for this review, the degree to which risk management functions interacted with business line management was lower at firms that experienced greater difficulties during the turmoil.

Some firms defined and discussed risk broadly across business lines. Those firms ensured that relevant insights from one business were used to scale the firm's strategy and risk appetite in other businesses. For example, some firms that avoided significant losses sought insights from consumer and financing businesses and used their understanding of changes in default rates on the underlying assets to scale the risk in the CDO warehouse businesses. Similarly, some firms that avoided significant losses cited a degree of integration among the liquidity, credit, market, and finance control structures that was lacking at other firms.

Senior managers at firms that experienced more significant unexpected losses tolerated a more segregated approach to internal communications about risk management. This behavior may have contributed to the lack of awareness among managers of the risks they faced and the resulting losses. Several firms that were challenged by market events acknowledged the need to improve their integration of credit and market risk management with accounting and financial control functions. Some firms lacked an effective forum in which senior business managers and risk managers could meet to discuss emerging issues frequently; some lacked even the commitment to open such dialogue.

How firms approached particular categories of risk— especially liquidity, market, and credit risk—provides further insight into practices that differentiated firms' experiences through year-end 2007.

IV. LIQUIDITY RISK MANAGEMENT

While most firms entered the period of turmoil in relatively sound financial condition with apparently sufficient liquidity, the nature, depth, and duration of the market's loss of liquidity were so severe that strains developed. As investors' interest in purchasing some classes of assets fell sharply, firms' willingness to extend credit and liquidity to others softened because they wished to retain liquidity for their own needs and because they became more uncertain about their counterparties' possible exposure to losses.

The level of contingent liquidity reserves held by individual institutions varies as a function of a range of factors, including business model, degree of centralization, geographic dispersion, local market structure, regulatory jurisdiction, and relevant deposit insurance scheme. For example, securities firms may choose to hold more excess liquidity than banks because they lack the stable funding source of insured retail deposits. In addition, firms use a variety of processes and measures to establish the minimum level of liquidity reserves they believe they must hold. These processes could include behavioral models with complex inputs and underlying calculations, spreadsheets listing sources and uses of funds, or simple measures and ratios. While initially capital and liquidity positions were relatively strong, certain firms' resources were somewhat strained by previously planned acquisitions at the time that, or just before, the turmoil unfolded.

However, many institutions found that during the turmoil their liquidity reserves were not as large as they would have liked. Most experienced higher borrowing rates and were unable to obtain funding in amounts or maturities at or close to historical norms. Moreover, the market turmoil has lasted longer than most firms anticipated in their contingency plans.

Finally, some firms faced unexpected challenges obtaining U.S. dollar funding. The reduction in the availability of dollar-denominated funding reflected an increase in counterparty credit risk. Firms faced uncertainty about the scale of positions held and losses taken by counterparties seeking dollar funding, and some firms felt that significant demand for dollar funding was indicative of increased risk. Regarding cross-border intra-group funding needs, most firms were not of the view that local regulatory restrictions trapping liquidity in specific affiliates presented significant problems. Some firms did cite limitations in the United States attributable to Section 23A of the Federal Reserve Act, which limits certain transactions with affiliates. Others indicated that long positions in some legal entities denominated in certain major currencies could not be used to cover U.S. dollar funding needs at other legal entities during the turmoil.

Firms that managed their funding liquidity needs more successfully through year-end 2007 encouraged individual business lines to assess and communicate their likely needs for funding to the treasury function and to price those internal claims on liquidity appropriately in light of actual market conditions.

A. Planning and Managing Internal Pricing for Contingent Events

Those treasurers that were *ex ante* more effective in identifying and managing funding liquidity risk had been in close and regular contact with business lines and understood the potential contingent liquidity risk of existing and new products across their firms. However, other firms' assessments of, and planning for, contingent liquidity risk were not sufficient or comprehensive.

Of particular importance, it emerged that firms that experienced the most significant challenges in meeting their funding liquidity needs were those that, before the turmoil began, had not priced contingent liquidity internally or externally to reflect the *ex post* assessment of the nature and risk profile of these liabilities. For example, some firms' internal transfer pricing systems did not assess business lines for building contingent liquidity exposure. During the interviews, several firms noted that going forward they plan to increase internal and external pricing for liquidity, including contingent liquidity.

Furthermore, prior to the events of the summer of 2007, many firms had not included assumptions about the need to fund certain off-balance-sheet obligations in their contingency funding planning. Some of these liquidity obligations were contractual, but treasurers were neither monitoring the risks nor incorporating them into their processes for managing liquidity risk. Other liquidity obligations were not contractual but were nevertheless fulfilled in order to protect the reputation of the businesses. Firms' liquidity management plans generally did not account for the increased absence of market MAC clauses and narrower flex pricing in their syndicated lending business—changes in business practice that materially altered the contingent funding risk of these positions.

B. Funding Liquidity Management during the Stress Event

During the crisis, effective funding managers were able to monitor and manage their funding liquidity positions using quantitative and qualitative information and to make decisions quickly based on rapidly changing market information. Experienced judgment to deal with the unexpected nature of the crisis was critical to the adequate management of liquidity risk. For example, early in the market turmoil, senior management at some firms decided to build up liquidity reserves in anticipation of increased funding needs.

The flexibility of firms' funding liquidity management tools in responding to unanticipated and evolving market conditions was also critical. Some firms employ behavioral tools to model their contingent liquidity risk; these models build in assumptions based on preselected stress scenarios that were not appropriate for recent market conditions. During the crisis, several firms that employ these types of tools switched to more flexible tools that lack built-in assumptions and that could help firms more easily understand the impact of current market conditions on their liquidity positions.

C. Contingency Funding Plans

Many of the observations our supervisory group has made regarding firms' contingency funding plans are common to all firms. Although the processes and analyses that firms used in their contingency funding plans varied somewhat in effectiveness, nearly all firms' plans failed to anticipate fully the severity and nature of recent market stresses in a number of ways. Indeed, almost all firms mentioned that they intend to make improvements to their contingency plans based on their recent experiences. In many cases, the challenges that firms have faced demonstrate the limits on the types of events addressed in their contingency plans.

In late 2007, firms faced stresses that were not anticipated or prepared for in their contingency funding plans. Many firms had assumed that the most stressful scenario they would face would be a firm-specific credit event. Even those that used market-wide stress scenarios in their contingency funding plans did not fully foresee the nature or extent of the market disruption. Four ways in which firms' plans did not anticipate the depth of the market turmoil are described below.

- Many firms had not expected that asset market liquidity would be impaired and had assumed that secured funding would always be available during a stress event; in fact, many secured funding markets such as assetbacked commercial paper (ABCP) and the U.S. mortgage dollar roll market[5] were unavailable in late 2007.
- Most firms had not assumed that the size of their balance sheet would increase during a stress event. In fact, many firms have recently been faced with growing balance sheets: some needed to hold underwriting commitments on their balance sheets longer than anticipated; others purchased assets to support sponsored ABCP conduits or affiliated asset management funds.
- Most firms had not expected difficulty in obtaining funding in major currencies. Some firms in Europe found it more difficult to obtain dollar funding, particularly in term maturities, due to the strain in the foreign exchange swap market. At the height of the uncertainty surrounding the extent of firms' structured credit exposures, participants in the foreign exchange swap market began to differentiate firms based on the perceived exposure, on peer groupings or jurisdictions, as well as on specific "names" of firms. This affected the cost and availability of liquidity in adverse market conditions, and some firms that were dependent on cross-currency funding may not have sufficiently factored the potential change in market liquidity into their contingency plans.
- Firms had not planned for a funding disruption lasting as long as the current one.

Furthermore, many of the stresses that had been outlined in firms' contingency funding plans have not been relevant for recent events. For example, many major banking organizations expected that some retail deposit run-off would occur during a stress event; however, retail deposits generally have been stable or slightly higher over recent months in the major banks surveyed for this exercise.

Because many firms used the stress scenarios in their contingency funding plans to determine the size and composition of their contingent liquidity reserves, these reserves may not have been as robust as anticipated in some firms. For example, reserves held in the form of mortgagebacked securities were not easily monetized to obtain liquidity. Moreover, several of the firms surveyed cited the need to hold more liquidity in the holding company in the future.

Regardless of whether firms had employed firm-specific or market-wide scenarios, their contingency funding plans generally assumed severe stress events and were not designed to address conditions in which they would need to make business decisions to maintain their

[5] In the dollar roll market, an institution sells a security (usually a mortgagebacked pass-through security) for immediate delivery and agrees to repurchase a substantially identical security (but not the same security) on a future date at a specified price.

reputation and position in the market. For example, firms did not anticipate the need to support entities for which they were not contractually obligated to do so, such as money market funds or SIVs. Firms had also not anticipated the need to deal with intense media coverage or to incorporate reputation risk considerations into funding decisions. Furthermore, firms had not fully anticipated the need to balance funding liquidity management needs with the desire to maintain business relationships with customers. For example, one firm noted that it needed to continue providing funding for certain customers in order to protect the business relationship.

V. Credit and Market Risk Management

In addition to managing difficulties arising from receding market liquidity, firms have faced significant additional challenges in actively managing credit and market risk as liquidity in many instruments diminished sharply. Those firms that were the most successful through year-end 2007 in dealing with the turmoil challenged their internal assumptions about the valuation and the behavior of products and markets by applying a wide range of credit and market risk measures and tools; equally important, they used judgment as well as these more quantitative techniques in deciding how to respond to market developments.

A. Valuation Practices Relevant to Risk Management

In our discussions with firms, we identified major shortcomings in the valuation practices of some firms that bear directly on risk management. The valuation process is central to risk management, particularly for over-the-counter derivatives. In this report, we use the term "valuation" to refer to the efforts a firm undertakes to verify the prices it has assigned to certain holdings for its books and records. The goal of verifying prices is to estimate the price at which the firm could sell or transfer a financial instrument in a normal market transaction today. This price may reflect either an outright sale of the position to a buyer or the cost of hedging the position. Firms use a variety of techniques for estimating this price, including, for example, relying on prices obtained in observed trades; interpolating or extrapolating a price from observed trades of similar products; modeling cash flows; or relying on risk-neutral pricing models.

Actions prior to the Market Turmoil

Our supervisory group noted that some firms had established robust price verification processes prior to the onset of the turmoil, and, using those tools, were more sensitive to the potential for their exposures to certain complex assets to fall in value. They adopted a more active approach to verifying their sense of valuations using internal resources, often in a coordinated, centralized fashion. The few firms that used valuation models for exposures to super-senior tranches related to subprime mortgages prior to the third quarter of 2007 were able to begin to consider at an early enough stage countermeasures such as the sale of positions or the purchase of hedges. Such firms were thus generally successful in avoiding significant unexpected write-downs in those portfolios.

Firms that adopted more active approaches to valuation typically devoted considerable resources to establishing specialized product financial control staff able to perform a fundamental analysis of the underlying positions. Some firms also enforced discipline internally in marking their assets to their estimated prices. This discipline was evident, for example, in the use of consistent marks across both proprietary positions and financed counterparty positions. Such firms furthermore factored position size (to account for the market impact of immediate sales of such size) and the dispersion of observed prices into their valuation marks.

Other firms, however, had not created robust internal processes prior to the turmoil to verify or challenge their business units' own estimates of the value of their holdings. For example, some firms that retained super-senior tranches of ABS CDOs, which rarely traded, benchmarked those instruments to spreads realized on primary market transactions. The use of information from primary market transactions may have given false comfort about the true value of retained positions in the absence of secondary market trading. In addition, some firms tended to rely too heavily on rating agencies' assessments that complex securities such as CDOs were equivalent to the highest quality assets and consequently continued to value them at par for too long into the period of market turmoil.

Actions during the Market Turmoil

Once the turmoil began, taking action to avoid losses from a write-down of CDO positions had, as noted above, become prohibitively expensive. Instead, firms faced the challenge of understanding at an early stage what the scale of loss would be.

Those firms that had active valuation approaches sought clues about the accuracy of their valuations through various actions, such as the following:

- When faced with a difficulty in establishing valuations, some of these firms would require the trading desk to sell a sufficient portion of the exposure to observe an actual market price. These sales served to establish marks that were often conservative, but the firm still needed to judge whether market activity was sufficient to obtain a reliable price quotation for marking an entire book of that exposure.
- Similarly, some of these firms monitored disputes over the market value of collateral posted by counterparties to help mark their own holdings of the same or similar securities. Business management brought valuation disputes from the back office to the attention of senior managers, often at an early stage.

Other firms discounted these techniques and, in some cases, used valuations biased toward par values that they did not actively challenge, even in the latter half of 2007; these valuations may have been questionable and may not have fully reflected the downside risk.

Shortcomings in valuation practices were exacerbated by several market realities.

1. Market Liquidity Premia Embedded within Pricing

Driven by an abundance of liquidity from 2002 to mid-2007, spreads on credit products and structured finance products tightened to historically low levels. The events of the second half of 2007 might suggest that these tight spread levels reflected technical factors and did not adequately reflect the market, credit, and liquidity risk characteristics of those assets. Market liquidity for certain products dried up, notably for certain types of ABS, CDOs, ABCP, and leveraged loans. In the absence of any trading, price discovery proved virtually impossible. In the primary and secondary markets for other products, liquidity did not dry up but did recede substantially, even in instances when there was no prima facie evidence that the asset quality had deteriorated (for example, highly rated short-dated ABS backed by student-loan receivables). It became clear that market participants were demanding a liquidity premium for buying assets. In previous stress events, there was evidence that liquidity premia had emerged for certain types of assets, but in the current turmoil, the premia seem to have been more significant, more broadly based, and more persistent. This change in the nature and duration of the premia contributes to the valuation challenge.

2. Ongoing Refinements to Models

Many firms are constantly developing and refining their models, which often results in a large increase in write-downs when an updated model is used for pricing. As the complexity of a model is tied to the size and nature of exposure (for example, CDOs), the models tend to be complex and dissimilar across the firms. However, the industry appears to be converging on the use of common loss estimates for the underlying mortgages; some firms have begun using information drawn from indices such as the ABX series, which comprises credit default swaps on subprime mortgages, to help estimate losses in the underlying mortgages.

3. Uncertainty in the Performance of Subprime Assets

Finally, uncertainty about the ultimate performance of the underlying mortgage pools — and the need to incorporate new information about the performance of these pools as it becomes available—means that valuations will continue to be subject to considerable volatility for the foreseeable future. While major valuation problems clearly existed for several other important classes of exposure, firms did not report difficulty in marking the value of the leveraged finance pipeline. Several firms did state that their past practice had been to recognize valuation changes only after closing. However, those firms indicated that they had recently altered their practices to recognize changes in the value of the pipeline beginning upon commitment.

B. Use of a Range of Risk Measures

Most firms that avoided significant unexpected losses used a wide range of risk measures to discuss and challenge views on credit and market risk broadly across different business lines in a disciplined fashion. Some firms gave particularly thorough consideration to the interplay of the market sensitivities of derivative exposures (the "greeks"), notional limits, value-atrisk, static single-factor stress tests, and historical and forwardlooking scenario analysis in a way that the other firms did not. These firms tended to use processes and measures that could be adjusted to reflect new circumstances, and they understood the limitations of individual risk measures. We note below eight key differences in the use and specification of risk measures through year-end 2007.

1. Use of Multiple Tools

Firms that avoided significant unexpected losses tended to use many or all of these tools cited above, and at least some of the tools were meant to provide different views of risk. In contrast, firms that experienced more significant problems were too dependent on a single methodology, or a limited set of tools, or they relied on inflexible applications that could not be adjusted to crisis conditions or that were flawed. This second group of firms tended to apply a "mechanical" risk management approach, accepting the estimates of their primary risk systems without challenges based on other tools and expert judgment.

2. Consideration of Notional Measures

In light of some firms' uncertainty about the accuracy of assumptions underlying their risk measures during the current period of turbulence, several firms cited the usefulness of revisiting simple notional limits to highlight potential concentrations of risk. These measures are devoid of assumptions and give management a simpler perspective on the potential scale of the risks.

In contrast, other firms cited difficulties that arose from their dependency on net measures of risk or measures of risk that rely on certain assumptions about correlation, market liquidity, and other factors that may not be true in a given event. Some, but not all, firms that recorded more significant unexpected losses lost sight of the aggregate size of their exposures. For example, several firms said that their risk measures assigned zero net risk to negative basis trades. In this type of trade, an investor holds a long position in a corporate bond combined with purchased credit protection on the bond in the form of a credit default swap (CDS). The investor engaging in a negative basis trade earns the spread between the two when the CDS cost is lower than the yield received on the bond. The assessment of zero risk was based on an assumption that the correlation between bond prices and CDS prices would follow historical relationships. Such an assumption, however, ignores the fact that the market liquidity risk in unwinding the position can cause a historical price relationship to break down when the volume of trades made on that position is large.

3. Use of Value-at-Risk

VaR measures were a key indicator for most firms seeking to understand their sensitivity to changes in market conditions. While most firms reported that their VaR systems generally worked as expected across all businesses, many firms identified weaknesses in their particular implementation of VaR and cited plans to change their VaR methodology. Nevertheless, firms indicated that VaR, as a backward-looking measure of risk dependent on historical data, may never fully capture severe shocks that exceed recent or historical norms.

For example, some firms' initial assessment of the true potential losses they faced were likely skewed downward by their VaR measures' underlying assumptions and a dependence on historical data from more benign periods. Firms suggested that VaR calculations based on new market data were anywhere from about 10 percent to at least 200 percent higher compared with VaR calculations conducted using data sets reflecting earlier, and more favorable, market conditions. The increase in most firms' VaR calculations ranged from 30 percent to 80 percent.

Firms reported between two and sixteen back-testing exceptions during the third quarter of 2007 alone. Most of these exceptions were generated by much higher market volatility and realized asset price correlation than the historical data series implied.

As a consequence, many firms are planning to change the volatility estimates in their VaR methodologies to make them more sensitive to volatility spikes. To this end, firms may use shorter horizon price histories or give greater weight to more recent observations, and they may update the volatility estimates more frequently (for example, on a daily basis). Some firms used VaR systems calibrated to minimum regulatory guidelines or standards. This design made the VaR estimates less meaningful to the firms' actual businesses. One firm underscored the value of a low VaR threshold (95 percent instead of 99 percent) coupled with a dynamic volatility model as an early warning tool. The low threshold would be crossed more often and thus could serve as a signal to prompt management queries and efforts to uncover anomalies that could reveal unrecognized risks.

Firms that plan to update volatility parameters in their VaR systems more frequently believe that this change will provide management with timely signals of the altered risk of a position. These firms see the change in the VaR as an indicator that senior management can use to probe the firm's risk profile. One firm, however, found that the most recent data for one risk class had lower volatility and expressed the view that judgment was required in the choice of historical window for capturing the relevant volatility input. A number of firms described the value of using multiple measures of risk to make use of all available information, such as using volatility estimates from the very recent past as well as estimates drawn from a long historical interval. The former would provide early warning signals of changes in current market conditions while the latter would provide the perspective of stressful episodes in the past.

In addition, in some instances firms did not get clear signals about the effectiveness of risk measurement from their VaR back-testing processes. Most firms attributed profit- and lossrelated VaR exceptions to the sharp increases in realized volatility, a result that was to be expected in light of the severity of the market turmoil and the optimistic volatility assumptions in many firms' VaR models. As discussed below, valuation issues caused some back-test VaR exceptions, such as the "lumpy" recognition of losses as positions migrated from market-price-based to model-based valuations. At some firms, this problem may have been exacerbated by a failure to test the valuation of illiquid or rarely traded products with actual trade prices; this allowed stale prices to impair valuations and risk assessments and led to large all-at-once revaluations when the market liquidity risk discount in the product was discovered.

4. Quality of Price Data Sets and Volatility Estimates

Difficulties in marking-to-market complex or illiquid assets like CDO tranches had cascading effects on the accuracy of VaR measures. Firms that avoided significant losses generally had a disciplined approach for marking exposures to market values and used these marks more consistently in the time series data that fed into the volatility estimates in their VaR calculations. This, in turn, made their VaR calculations much more sensitive to evolving risks than those of institutions that marked illiquid positions at par and failed to test their valuations against trade prices. The ability to capture evolving market conditions in risk measures can provide early warning indicators that prompt management to review a firm's risk profile. Perhaps as important, and separate from estimating volatility, the practice of testing valuations of illiquid products against actual trade prices revealed valuation anomalies that were an early warning signal to risk managers about valuation model errors and changing market conditions.

5. Basis Risk

Among the risks that were missed or misestimated was basis risk or correlation risk within an asset class, as well as correlation risk more broadly. Most firms' VaR measures did not properly capture the basis risk between cash bonds and credit default swaps (or the basis risk that exists between bonds and loans). This weakness, in which the behavior of derivative instruments was assumed incorrectly to be closely related to the behavior of bonds, led to inconsistencies in the risk measures but was not a direct cause of material observed losses to date. Some profit and loss volatility not predicted by VaR models and some losses were attributable to the basis risk in hedge positions that was not captured in VaR models. Consequently, some firms are reconsidering what should be treated as a true hedge for risk management objectives, as discussed below.

For example, several firms misestimated basis risk in their approaches to managing the CDO warehousing and packaging business and significantly underestimated the risk of the super-senior positions they retained as a result. The practice at some firms of valuing super-senior tranches of subprime CDOs at or close to par value and assuming that their risk profile could be approximated using the historical corporate Aaa spread volatility as a proxy failed to recognize these instruments' asymmetric sensitivity to underlying risk (in contrast to an unstructured corporate bond of the same rating). The first loss protection built into the securitization structure created an asymmetric exposure to losses in the underlying assets, so that the senior tranche became more sensitive to default rates as credit quality deteriorated. As volatility spiked up and credit spreads widened, the increasing sensitivity of the instrument to underlying risk led to accelerating mark-to-market losses. In general, the construction of CDOs tends to make them more sensitive to systematic shocks. In contrast, highly rated corporate debt issuances tend to be more sensitive to "idiosyncratic" risk, or risks associated with characteristics specific to the corporation that issued the debt.

6. Design and Integration of Market Risk Measurement Tools

With regard to market risk measurement tools, some firms that avoided significant losses appear to use both "conditional" and "unconditional" measures of market risk to provide information and limit risk. Dynamic volatility models for VaR are examples of conditional measures, which are more sensitive than unconditional measures to short-term changes in market risk; scenario analysis is an example of an unconditional measure. Firms that avoided significant losses have additional risk measures that reflect differences in assumed levels of correlations between market variables in benign versus stressed market conditions. Still, most firms surveyed expressed a desire to increase the sensitivity of their VaR models and other measures of risk to shorter term changes in the market environment.

7. Integration of Exposures across Risk Types

Firms that avoided significant losses appear to have a better ability to integrate exposures across businesses for both market and counterparty risk management. Other firms did not appear to have sufficient abilities to identify consolidated, firm-wide, single-factor stress sensitivities and concentrations.

8. Use of Profit and Loss Reporting as a Signal of Emerging Stress

Successful firms had in place granular profit and loss reporting systems, which were often used in conjunction with risk management tools subject to regular senior management review, and those systems may have provided additional insight into signs of stress. One firm noted the need to implement more granular reporting. An additional feature of a successful firm's approach to VaR was the active use of the VaR process to alert management to the need to uncover and probe anomalies in profit and loss and VaR that could provide early warnings of stress or other unrecognized risks.

C. Stress Testing and Scenario Analysis

In recent years, the industry as a whole has acknowledged the importance of developing and using forward-looking scenarios and stress tests to explore known and unknown risks, including how exposures may change in light of unexpected changes or shocks to the business environment. Most firms in the survey have indeed sought to supplement measures of current exposure with more forward-looking measures of their risk; the firms surveyed used a wide variety of techniques. These included static single-factor changes to market variables calibrated to extreme moves in historical data series, historically based scenarios, and forward-looking scenarios (collectively, "stress tests").

Some firms found that the size of price movements in their static shock simulations and/or credit scenarios generally matched the observed market movements, while others found the actual widening of credit spreads to be larger and of longer duration than assumed. At some firms, a particular challenge to risk managers was obtaining senior management and business line acceptance of stress tests—in particular, the hypothetical forward-looking scenarios—which seemed extreme to some senior managers. Many managers recognize that stress tests themselves should be dynamic—such that they consider new scenarios as business conditions evolve—yet still be stable enough to provide firms with a useful gauge for monitoring the evolution of their risk profile over time. In light of recent events, most firms in the survey found problems in certain features of their stress tests or with the stress tests of particular products, and many firms indicated that they planned to make specific changes in the design and implementation of stress tests.

1. Risk Identification and Modeling Issues

Many firms expressed a desire to build a higher level of detail into their stress test models and systems. Some firms are revising their stress tests to reduce correlation benefits among exposures and to impose larger credit spread shocks. To help risk managers discover exposures overlooked by high-level aggregated risk measures, some firms mentioned the value of exposure measures based on both gross and net positions.

Many modeling issues that affected firms' VaR measures also affected their stress tests and, in particular, tests involving static single-factor shocks. As in their VaR tests, some firms used price histories associated with corporate issuers rated Aaa as proxies for stress price movements in those new products that did not have sufficiently long data histories of their own. Firms that used single-factor stress tests calibrated to historical data significantly underestimated the risk of super-senior subprime CDO positions. Several firms that experienced losses used VaR and static single-factor stress tests calibrated using the same historical data series. As a result, the stress tests provided no new information.

One firm observed that the level of detail necessary to model the risks in securitization properly is considerable. Simple measures of the sensitivity of super-senior subprime CDO tranches to the Aaa spread were not sufficient to capture the credit risk in the product without detailed knowledge of the CDO's composition. Two problems in the rating and treatment of these products became apparent. First, the senior tranches were rated at or equivalent to an Aaa credit risk despite the deteriorating credit standards at origination. Second, on the basis of this Aaa rating, some firms used the historical returns volatility of other securities rated Aaa as a proxy for the price risk of senior subprime exposure, even though these super-senior tranches represented new securities for which firms had little historical performance data.

Many firms' stress measures did not properly capture the basis risk between cash bond and credit default swaps, although, as noted earlier, this shortcoming does not seem to have led to significant losses. Some firms failed to capture syndicated loan pipelines and unfunded loan commitments in their firm-wide stress tests. Some firms used single-factor shocks calibrated to shorter holding periods than were revealed to be appropriate in light of the loss of market liquidity. At one firm, the relatively short duration of the stress shock was based on an unrealistic assumption that positions could be reduced within that interval.

2. Senior Management Involvement in Stress Testing and Scenario Analysis

Senior management involvement was important to the effective use of stress tests, especially macro scenarios, as risk management tools. Senior management's endorsement of stress testing as a guide in decision-making was seen as particularly valuable when the tests revealed vulnerabilities that firms found costly to address (in terms of hedging costs or forgone business). Less successful firms had difficulty getting senior management and business-line management to embrace the use of forward-looking scenarios with large underlying price movements and to participate in the development and use of such tools. According to some risk managers, the larger the shock imposed, the less plausible the stress tests or scenarios in the eyes of business area and senior management.

3. Links between Scenarios and Business Practices

Several firms emphasized the need to improve the applicability of forward-looking scenario analysis to the business practices of the firm. Knowledge of how business areas made money helped risk managers identify relevant stress scenarios or provide warning when the assumptions underlying singlefactor stress tests were inaccurate measures of risk. Similarly, some managers have stressed the importance of considering how market shocks appear to counterparties. A number of firms mentioned the constant need to review scenarios and to develop new ones at both the firm and desk levels. System flexibility was cited as crucial, although some firms may not haave had sufficiently flexible systems to handle customized scenarios and stress tests.

D. Hedging of Market and Credit Risks

Firms that avoided significant losses reduced risk through active and early decisions to reduce or exit businesses that were likely to be affected by the changing environment. Such decisions were generally made well before the events started to unfold. As an additional tool to reduce risk, all firms sought to hedge their exposures to market risk and counterparty credit risk.

While all firms surveyed used some form of hedging as a means to reduce exposure to market risk, they experienced varying degrees of success in using them. Some firms hedged the risk of a decline in the market value of their holdings of subprime-related assets (for example, RMBS, ABS, CDOs) or leveraged loans by selling short credit indices and associated tranches. Firms faced the following key challenges in adopting an effective market risk hedge:

- For a hedge to produce the desired effect, it had to be put in place well in advance of the adverse market reactions, at a time when pricing was still relatively advantageous; this window closed in the second quarter of 2007. Firms that tried to hedge their exposure too late found the price of the protection prohibitive.
- The available credit index instruments introduced significant basis risk. This basis risk—that is, the risk inherent in the imperfect correlation between the underlying cash position and the hedge instrument (derivative)—weakened the effectiveness of the hedging strategy. In some instances, this led to losses on both the cash position and hedge, particularly for firms that sought to hedge relatively late.
- Because limited numbers of hedging instruments existed, many market participants relied on the same credit indices as hedges. The resulting strong demand for short positions, coinciding with the erosion of asset market liquidity, led to a further widening in price differences between cash and derivative positions for technical reasons. These developments amplified the basis risk and further diminished the effectiveness of the hedge (by creating a "crowded hedge").

Other firms entered into credit derivative contracts with monoline financial guarantors to hedge a portion of their retained super-senior CDO positions.

- Firms that sought to offset the risk of these positions by purchasing protection from financial guarantors were subject to a "wrong-way" counterparty credit exposure because the financial capacity of these counterparties to perform on their contracts is correlated with the value of the underlying positions being hedged.

Firms that avoided substantial losses made the decision to implement hedges based on their consolidated risk positions across businesses and in light of a wide range of available qualitative and quantitative risk information. Some of these firms coordinated the short positions through active "macro overlay" positions approved by senior management in dialogue with the business owners and risk control staff. By contrast, firms that did not maintain a consolidated perspective on risk and instead left hedging decisions to the business lines generally found their hedging strategies to be less effective, as different traders or business lines relied on the same hedge in an uncoordinated manner.

It should be noted that the use of a "macro" overlay hedge represents a step away from the view that a firm consists of a set of decentralized business lines and a step toward a view that senior management has a responsibility to orchestrate efforts to offset consolidated risks at the top of the firm. However, some managers cautioned against drawing too strong of a conclusion from the success of some of the macro hedges in use in this one recent period. Others noted that implementing a macro overlay hedge at the top of the firm introduces an element of moral hazard, lessening the accountability of individual business lines for the risks they create.

One final observation regarding hedging practices is that firms that hedged their exposures effectively also insisted that warehouse businesses capture the implicit cost of hedging market risk in their performance measures or required warehouse sponsors to assume a greater portion of the market risk. These stipulations raised the level of discipline in the business of warehousing assets.

As a result of the lessons learned during the recent financial turmoil, risk managers at several firms are rethinking their market risk hedging practices. Among the issues under consideration are the degree of acceptable basis risk and its measurement, the absolute notional size of hedges and underlying positions, and the likely performance of hedges during severe market movements.

E. Credit Underwriting and Reporting

While risk measures and hedging techniques address exposures that firms have already assumed, firms also stressed the importance of understanding the quality of new credits that their businesses originated or purchased from others. Competition in underwriting new credits weakened the standards that some firms applied. This was evident in both the underwriting of residential mortgages and leveraged loans.

With regard to the leveraged loan market, several firms commented on the absence of covenants and market MAC clauses. These firms felt that they had knowingly given financial sponsors an option without appropriate compensation. In addition, firms acknowledged that leverage levels had increased and that structural features beneficial to weaker borrowers, such as payment-in-kind/toggle features that permit borrowers to delay cash payment on coupons, had become more prevalent.This weakening of lending terms caused some firms to curtail their activity; subsequently, some managers recommended the reintroduction of stricter limits on the use of facilities that lack covenants related to material changes in market conditions.

Firms also noted that mortgage underwriting standards had deteriorated. An increasing portion of mortgages was being underwritten without verifying the borrower's source of income for repayment ("stated income" loans). In addition, mortgages were often underwritten based upon initial "teaser" rates rather than a rate consistent with bearing the obligation to maturity. Undeclared and undocumented second liens also served to increase borrowers' payments relative to their income and decreased borrowers' equity position in the home.

With regard to the CDO warehousing business, some firms cited the need for better controls over indirectly sourced credits. Some firms relied too heavily on agency ratings in the CDO warehousing and packaging business and did not pay sufficient attention to internal assessment and the quality of the underlying assets. Some firms acknowledged that investors were likewise too dependent on rating agencies for assessments of the risk inherent in certain exposures or relied too heavily on assumptions regarding diversification benefits that turned out to be inaccurate.

When firms conducted their own due diligence for lending businesses, they were generally comfortable with the credit risk. However, they did not anticipate the price risk.

F. Counterparty Risk Measurement and Management

Most firms indicated few problems in reporting and understanding counterparty risk as a result of the recent market events. In general, firms reported satisfaction with their estimates of potential exposure and the modeling of events through stress tests related to counterparty credit risk, though they cited some of the same weaknesses they noted in market risk measurement. Managers stated that their firms' risk management systems and personnel were generally able to produce complete and accurate accounts of firm-wide risk exposures to particular counterparties daily with a lag of one business day. Many firms emphasized the importance of constantly reviewing and improving credit risk and counterparty credit risk reporting and measurement systems and the need to avoid concentrations.

With regard to daily risk management decisions, firms differed in their response to increased market volatility: several firms noted the need to raise initial margins, while others appeared to have been comfortable with levels established before market events. Overall, the number of counterparties closed out of positions because of their inability to meet variation margin payments appears to have been relatively small. All firms emphasized the importance of valuation to margining processes. Generally, management teams indicated that the number of disputes with counterparties was not material through year-end 2007. Several firms cited the signaling value of disputes in assessing the conservatism of their own and their counterparties' marks.

Monoline Insurers

While most managers indicated during their conversations with our supervisory group in late 2007 that their firms' exposures to counterparty credit risk were less problematic than their exposures to market risk, some cited concerns about material direct and indirect exposures to financial guarantors and, in particular, monoline insurers—firms that underwrite a single form of insurance (credit protection in this instance). A direct exposure arises when an investor purchases derivatives (including credit default swaps) from a financial guarantor against the default of an underlying issuer, makes loans to the guarantor, or makes an equity investment in the guarantor. An indirect exposure to a financial guarantor arises from an investor's purchase of securities whose performance is guaranteed by a financial guarantor. Subsequent to our meetings, these concerns have become more widespread and pronounced across the industry, with many firms' exposures continuing to grow through year-end 2007.

Traditionally, financial guarantors had insured the performance of high-quality municipal bonds. Firms often have indirect exposures to financial guarantors through their tender-option bond and variable-rate demand note programs and through holdings of wrapped securities. In recent years, financial guarantors have become more active in insuring exposures to structured credits; most recently, they have begun selling credit default protection through credit derivatives on CDOs, including insuring securities that incorporate subprime mortgages. Dealer firms often bought protection against retained senior and super-senior tranches of CDOs. Purchasing this protection added a direct exposure on top of the existing indirect exposures to the financial guarantor. Additionally, since the financial guarantor was often more vulnerable to securities that included subprime mortgages than the firm seeking protection, the creditworthiness of the financial guarantor was correlated with the valuation of the exposures on which protection was purchased (an example of "wrong-way" counterparty risk).

Many firms take into consideration the credit quality of a financial counterparty when valuing derivative transactions. Firms make fair value adjustments to the carrying value of derivative contracts to adjust for the counterparty's creditworthiness. Some firms have relied on their internal or external agency credit ratings of the counterparty to calculate these credit valuation adjustments, while other firms adjust valuations on the basis of market factors. As the markets' perception of the creditworthiness of certain financial guarantors has diverged from the assigned agency rating, several firms have adjusted their valuation practice for these counterparties by basing their reserves on changes in market prices of credit default swap contracts to the counterparty. As a result, some firms have written down the value of purchased protection from these counterparties.

The rapid growth of current exposures, in excess of prior estimates of potential future exposure, highlights the reliance of measures of potential future exposure on historical volatility measures and illustrates the need to augment these measures with other approaches, such as scenario analysis or stress testing. In turn, such scenarios or stress tests should be designed to consider the vulnerabilities of hedges (that is, the credit quality of counterparties providing them), as in the case of hedges purchased from, or referencing, financial guarantors. Many firms drew comfort from having monitored their net exposures to CDOs and similar products by purchasing credit protection from financial guarantors. However, the growth in concentrations of financial guarantor counterparty risk highlights the need for firms to monitor gross counterparty risks, as well as net market risks. Moreover, the prevailing materiality of firms' exposures to financial guarantors at present indicates that firms should carefully monitor and stress-test the build up of "wrong-way" counterparty risk, especially when the counterparty, such as a monoline insurer, has not posted collateral.

Concluding Comments

The almost unprecedented nature, depth, and duration of the current market turmoil have raised major challenges for nearly all significant participants in financial markets. In this environment, participants face increasing pressure to understand the risks they face, to measure and assess such risks appropriately, and to take the necessary steps to reduce, hedge, or otherwise manage such risk exposures. This report has examined the risk management practices that tended to differentiate outcomes of several global banking organizations and securities firms—all active competitors in the financial markets currently experiencing stress—with a view toward identifying the practices that tended to work well and those that did not through the end of 2007.

Our work has consequently proved useful in clarifying for principal supervisors the areas in need of improvement in the infrastructure, processes, and practices of some firms. As acknowledged throughout this report, a number of firms had already identified, or were beginning to identify, at least some of the deficiencies we cite in their own assessments, and many were already developing plans to address those weaknesses. The relevant supervisors are monitoring and assessing these and other remedial efforts to improve the quality of individual firms' risk management in light of the recent turmoil. Moreover, we will support continued collaboration on related efforts to revise relevant supervisory guidance, expectations, and policy through the appropriate coordinating bodies, such as the Basel Committee on Banking Supervision, the International Organization of Securities Commissions, and the Joint Forum. Finally, we note that efforts to address some of the most complex topics ahead may benefit in due course from broader discussions among supervisors, market participants, and others.

While we have sought to highlight examples of risk measurement and management practices that have tended to be associated with better or weaker performance during the current market turmoil, we recognize the contributions of other factors to business outcomes as well. A host of other considerations specific to each firm, such as its business strategy and risk appetite, influences the balance a firm seeks between risks and rewards. We recognize, moreover, that the turmoil continues in some markets at the time of this writing and that new areas of weakness may emerge in the near future not identified or anticipated in our review. As market events continue to unfold, supervisors and the financial industry may identify other issues that deserve broader investigation. We welcome continued dialogue with industry representatives, market observers, and other public authorities on these and other shared concerns.

Appendix A: Abbreviations Used in this Report

ABCP	Asset-backed commercial paper
ABS	Asset-backed securities
ABS	CDO Collateralized debt obligation of asset-backed securities
CDO	Collateralized debt obligation
CDS	Credit default swap
CLO	Collateralized loan obligation
MAC	Material adverse change
MBS	Mortgage-backed securities
RMBS	Residential mortgage-backed securities
SIV	Structured investment vehicle
VaR	Value-at-risk

APPENDIX B: MEMBERS OF THE SENIOR SUPERVISORS GROUP

FRANCE *Banking Commission* Didier Elbaum Alain Laurin Guy Levy-Rueff Frederick Visnovsky GERMANY *Federal Financial Supervisory Authority* Sabine Lautenschläger-Peiter Peter Lutz SWITZERLAND *Swiss Federal Banking Commission* Tim Frech Roland Goetschmann Thomas Hirschi Daniel Sigrist UNITED KINGDOM *Financial Services Authority* Stan Bereza Nicholas Newland Andrea Pack	UNITED STATES *Board of Governors of the Federal Reserve System* Deborah P. Bailey Roger T. Cole Jon D. Greenlee Steven M. Roberts *Federal Reserve Bank of New York* Arthur G. Angulo Brian L. Peters William L. Rutledge (*Chairman*) *Office of the Comptroller of the Currency* Kathryn E. Dick Douglas W. Roeder Scott N. Waterhouse *Securities and Exchange Commission* Matthew J. Eichner Denise Landers Michael A. Macchiaroli Erik R. Sirri

Secretariat

F. Christopher Calabia, Kathryn B. Chen, John E. Kambhu, Wilma Sabado, and Til Schuermann, all of the Federal Reserve Bank of New York.

In: Reforming Risk in Financial Markets
Editor: Melvin R. Turley, pp. 151-170
ISBN 978-1-60692-445-7

Chapter 3

POLICY STATEMENT ON FINANCIAL MARKET DEVELOPMENTS: THE PRESIDENT'S WORKING GROUP ON FINANCIAL MARKETS[*]

Department of Treasury, Board of Governors of the Federal Reserve System, Securities and Exchange Commission, Commodity Futures Trading Commission

Department of the Treasury
Washington, D.C.

Secretary of the Treasury

March 13, 2008

[*] This is an edited, excerpted and augmented edition of a Department of Treasury publication, dated March 2008

MEMORANDUM FOR THE PRESIDENT

From: Henry M. Paulson, Jr.
Subject: President's Working Group on Financial Markets Policy Statement

Last August, you called on the President's Working Group on Financial Markets (PWG) to review the underlying causes of developing financial market turmoil. I am pleased to transmit to you the policy statement of the PWG, which is led by me as the Secretary of the Treasury and includes the chairmen of the Federal Reserve Board, the Securities and Exchange Commission, and the Commodity Futures Trading Commission.

The PWG, working with the Office of the Comptroller of the Currency and the Federal Reserve Bank of New York, issued the statement to present the Group's findings on the causes of recent market turmoil and recommend changes to help avoid a repeat of recent events.

Obviously, market turmoil is still playing out, and all market participants and policy makers are deeply engaged in addressing the current situation. We must implement these recommendations with an eye toward not creating a burden that exacerbates today's market stresses.

We will monitor and report back to you on the implementation of these recommendations. In addition, we will make further recommendations later this year if we do not see the progress we are seeking.

Our objectives — which we believe these recommendations will achieve — are improved transparency and disclosure, better risk awareness and management, and stronger oversight. Collectively, these recommendations will mitigate systemic risk, help restore investor confidence, and facilitate economic growth.

Since mid-2007, financial markets have been in turmoil. Soaring delinquencies on U.S. subprime mortgages were the primary trigger of recent events. However, that initial shock both uncovered and exacerbated other weaknesses in the global financial system. Because financial markets are interconnected, both across asset classes and countries, the impact has been widespread. Global capital markets must function smoothly and effectively for economies to achieve sustainable growth. It is therefore in the interests of both policy makers and market participants to identify the causes of the market turmoil and to take the steps necessary to mitigate systemic risk, restore investor confidence, and facilitate stable economic growth.

The President's Working Group on Financial Markets (PWG) has undertaken a thorough analysis of the underlying factors contributing to the recent and on-going market stress. This analysis has been conducted to identify the weaknesses in global markets, institutions, and regulatory policies that triggered, amplified, or failed to mitigate the stress. On the basis of this analysis, the PWG has developed a comprehensive set of recommendations to address those weaknesses. This statement summarizes that analysis and sets out recommendations. It is comprised of three sections: a diagnosis and summary of recommendations; a review of factors contributing to the market turmoil; and a fuller discussion of policy issues and recommendations.

I. DIAGNOSIS AND SUMMARY OF RECOMMENDATIONS

Diagnosis

The global market turmoil has not yet abated, so any diagnosis is necessarily incomplete. Nonetheless, it seems clear from experience to date that the principal underlying causes of the turmoil in financial markets were:

- a breakdown in underwriting standards for subprime mortgages;
- a significant erosion of market discipline by those involved in the securitization process, including originators, underwriters, credit rating agencies, and global investors, related in part to failures to provide or obtain adequate risk disclosures; flaws in credit rating agencies' assessments of subprime residential mortgage- backed securities (RMBS) and other complex structured credit products, especially collateralized debt obligations (CDOs) that held RMBS and other asset- backed securities (CDOs of ABS);
- risk management weaknesses at some large U.S. and European financial institutions; and
- regulatory policies, including capital and disclosure[1] requirements, that failed to mitigate risk management weaknesses.

The turmoil in financial markets clearly was triggered by a *dramatic weakening of underwriting standards for U.S. subprime mortgages, beginning* in late 2004 and extending into early 2007. But the loosening of credit standards and terms in the subprime market was symptomatic of a much broader erosion of market discipline on the standards and terms of loans to households and businesses. Following many years of benign economic conditions and plentiful market liquidity, global investors had become quite complacent about risks, even in the case of new and increasingly complex financial instruments.

Competition and the desire to maintain higher returns created significant demand for structured credit products by investors. Originators, underwriters, asset managers, credit rating agencies, and investors failed to obtain sufficient information or to conduct comprehensive risk assessments on instruments that often were quite complex. Investors relied excessively on credit ratings, which contributed to their complacency about the risks they were assuming in pursuit of higher returns. *Although market participants had economic incentives to conduct due diligence and evaluate risk-adjusted returns, the steps they took were insufficient, resulting in a significant erosion of market discipline.*

Faulty assumptions underlying rating methodologies and the subsequent re-evaluations by the credit rating agencies (CRAB) led to a significant number of downgrades of subprime RMBS, even of recently issued securities. Downgrades were even more frequent and severe for CDOs of ABS with subprime mortgage loans as the underlying collateral. The number and severity of negative ratings actions caused investors to lose confidence in the accuracy of the ratings of a wide range of structured credit products. This loss of investor confidence

[1] In this document disclosure requirements refer to the requirements of prudential regulators of financial institutions rather than to the Securities and Exchange Commission's (SEC) disclosure regulations and requirements applicable to U.S. public companies.

caused many structured finance markets to seize up and caused markets for asset-backed commercial paper (ABCP), some of which was backed by RMBS and CDOs of ABS, to contract substantially.

These developments revealed *serious weaknesses in risk management practices at several large U.S. and European financial institutions,* especially with respect to the concentration of risks, the valuation of illiquid instruments, the pricing of contingent liquidity facilities, and the management of liquidity risk. Common themes were the failure of stress testing procedures to identify institutions' vulnerabilities to system-wide shocks to markets and market participants, and difficulties aggregating exposures across business lines and valuing instruments when markets became illiquid. These weaknesses were particularly evident with respect to the management of risks of holding CDOs of ABS, sponsoring or supporting off- balance sheet conduits that issued ABCP, and syndicating leveraged loans. As a result, some institutions suffered significant losses and many experienced significant balance sheet pressures. Balance sheet pressures contributed to a tightening of firms' lending standards and terms for a wide range of borrowers, which in turn has contributed to the slowing of U.S. economic growth.

In some cases, *regulatory policies failed to mitigate those risk management weaknesses.* For example, existing capital requirements encouraged the securitization of assets through facilities with very low capital requirements and failed to provide adequate incentives for firms to maintain capital and liquidity buffers sufficient to absorb extreme system-wide shocks without taking actions that tended to amplify shocks. Further, supervisory authorities did not insist on appropriate disclosures of firms' potential exposure to off-balance sheet vehicles.

Summary of Recommendations

The PWG has carefully reviewed the weaknesses in markets, institutions, and regulatory and supervisory practices that have contributed to financial turmoil and has developed recommendations to address those weaknesses. In developing its recommendations, the PWG has sought to avoid exacerbating the current strains on markets and institutions or risking unintended consequences. As noted above, the market turmoil has not yet abated. Thus, the PWG or its member agencies may put forward additional recommendations as events unfold and new insights are gained. Although no single measure can be expected to place financial markets on a sound footing, the PWG believes that implementation of its comprehensive and complementary set of recommendations would constitute an effective response to the identified weaknesses. In general, the recommendations include measures to be implemented by government authorities or market participants that will:

- reform key parts of the mortgage origination process in the United States; enhance disclosure and improve the practices of sponsors, underwriters, and investors with respect to securitized credits, thereby imposing more effective market discipline;
- reform the credit rating agencies' processes for and practices regarding rating structured credit products to ensure integrity and transparency;

- ensure that global financial institutions take appropriate steps to address the weaknesses in risk management and reporting practices that the market turmoil has exposed; and
- ensure that prudential regulatory policies applicable to banks and securities firms, including capital and disclosure requirements, provide strong incentives for effective risk management practices.

Recommendations for *reforming key parts of the mortgage origination process* include:

- All states should implement strong nationwide licensing standards for mortgage brokers;
- Federal and state regulators should strengthen and make consistent government oversight of entities that originate and fund mortgages and otherwise interface with customers in the mortgage origination process. All states should work towards adopting the principles set forth in the guidance developed by the federal regulators for nontraditional and subprime mortgage lending and ensure that effective enforcement mechanisms are in place to deal with noncompliance with such standards; and
- The Federal Reserve should issue stronger consumer protection rules and mandate enhanced consumer protection disclosures, including disclosures that would make affordability over the life of the mortgage more transparent and that would facilitate comparison of the terms with those of alternative products. State and federal authorities should coordinate to enforce the rules evenly across all types of mortgage originators.

Recommendations for *improving investors' contributions to market discipline* include:

- Overseers of institutional investors (for example, the Department of Labor for private pension funds; state treasurers for public pension funds; and the SEC for money market funds) should require investors (and their asset managers) to obtain from sponsors and underwriters of securitized credits access to better information about the risk characteristics of such credits, including information about the underlying asset pools, on an initial and ongoing basis;
- Overseers should ensure that these investors (and their asset managers) develop an independent view of the risk characteristics of the instruments in their portfolios, rather than rely solely on credit ratings; and
- The PWG will engage the private sector to create a committee to develop best practices regarding disclosure to investors in securitized credits, including ABS and CDOs of ABS.

Recommendations for *reforming the ratings processes for and practices regarding structured credit and other securitized credit products* include:

- Credit rating agencies should disclose what qualitative reviews they perform on originators of assets that collateralize ABS rated by the CRA and should require underwriters of ABS to represent the level and scope of due diligence performed on the underlying assets;

- The CRAs should reform their ratings processes for structured credit products to ensure integrity and transparency. The PWG welcomes the steps already taken by the CRAs, and particularly encourages the CRAs to:
  - enforce policies and procedures that manage conflicts of interest, including implementing changes suggested by the SEC's broad review of conflict of interest issues;
  - publish sufficient information about the assumptions underlying their credit rating methodologies, so that users of credit ratings can understand how a particular credit rating was determined;
  - make changes to the credit rating process that would clearly differentiate ratings for structured products from ratings for corporate and municipal securities;
  - make ratings performance measures for structured credit products and other ABS readily available to the public in a manner that facilitates comparisons across products and credit ratings;
  - work with investors to provide the information investors need to make informed decisions about risk, including measures of the uncertainty associated with ratings and of potential ratings volatility; and
  - ensure that adequate personnel and financial resources are allocated to monitoring and updating ratings.
- The PWG will facilitate formation of a private-sector group (with representatives of investors, issuers, underwriters, and CRAs) to develop recommendations for further steps that the issuers, underwriters, CRAs, and policymakers could take to ensure the integrity and transparency of ratings, and to foster appropriate use of ratings in risk assessment;
- PWG member agencies will reinforce steps taken by the CRAs through revisions to supervisory policy and regulation, including regulatory capital requirements that use ratings; and
- The PWG will revisit the need for changes to CRA oversight if the reforms adopted by the CRAs are not sufficient to ensure the integrity and transparency of ratings.

Recommendations to *strengthen global financial institutions' risk management practices* include:

- Global financial institutions should promptly identify and address any weaknesses in risk management practices that the turmoil has revealed;
- The PWG will support formation of a private-sector group to reassess implementation of the Counterparty Risk Management Policy Group II's (CRMPG II) existing guiding principles and recommendations regarding risk management, risk monitoring, and transparency, and to modify or develop new principles and recommendations as necessary to incorporate lessons from the recent turmoil, including lessons regarding valuation practices;

- Supervisors of global financial institutions should closely monitor the firms' efforts to address risk management weaknesses, taking action if necessary to ensure that weaknesses are addressed;
- U.S. banking regulators and the SEC should promptly assess current guidance and develop common guidance to address the risk management weaknesses revealed by the recent market turmoil, including improvements to:
  - management information systems, including procedures that ensure aggregation of exposures across all business lines and ensure rigorous valuations of instruments and exposures;
  - concentration risk management, liquidity risk management, stress testing and other risk management practices that are necessary to ensure that liquidity and capital cushions are sufficiently robust to absorb extreme system-wide shocks; and
  - governance of the risk management and control framework, including the development of, and adherence to, practices that address incentive problems in compensation policies.
- U.S. authorities should encourage other supervisors of global firms to make complementary efforts to develop guidance along the same lines.

Recommendations to *enhance prudential regulatory policies* include:

- Regulators should adopt policies that provide incentives for financial institutions to hold capital and liquidity cushions commensurate with firm-wide exposure (both on and off-balance sheet) to severe adverse market events. These cushions should be forward looking and adjust appropriately through peaks and valleys of the credit cycle;
- Regulators should enhance guidance related to pipeline risk management for firms that use an originate-to-distribute model;
- The Basel Committee on Banking Supervision (BCBS) should promptly complete the work it has initiated to update the Committee's 2000 guidance on liquidity management, including the sound practice guidelines to be followed by regulated financial institutions as well as the oversight principles for supervisors.
- The BCBS and IOSCO should review capital requirements for ABS CDOs and other re-securitizations and for off-balance sheet commitments, with a view toward increasing requirements on exposures that have been the source of recent losses to firms;
- Regulators should require financial institutions to make more detailed and comprehensive disclosures of off-balance sheet commitments, including commitments to support ABCP conduits and other off-balance sheet vehicles; Regulators should encourage financial institutions to improve the quality
- of disclosures about fair value estimates for complex and other illiquid instruments, including descriptions of valuation methodologies and information regarding the degree of uncertainty associated with such estimates;
- Regulators should review the current use of ratings in regulation and supervisory rules. At a minimum, regulators should distinguish, as appropriate, between ratings

of structured credit products and ratings of corporate and municipal bonds in regulatory and supervisory policies; and
- Authorities should encourage FASB to evaluate the role of accounting standards in the current market turmoil. This evaluation should include an assessment of the need for further modifications to accounting standards related to consolidation and securitization, with the goal of improving transparency and the operation of U.S. standards in the short-term. Additionally, authorities should encourage FASB and IASB to achieve more rapid convergence of accounting standards for consolidation of ABCP conduits and other off-balance sheet vehicles.

Additionally, while the infrastructure of the financial markets thus far has coped quite well with heightened price volatility and surging trading volumes, the PWG believes that the supervisors of OTC derivatives dealers, who have been working together under the leadership of the Federal Reserve Bank of New York, should insist on further enhancements to the infrastructure for the rapidly growing OTC derivatives markets.

Recommendations to *enhance the OTC derivative market infrastructure* include:

- Supervisors should insist that the industry promptly set ambitious standards for the accuracy and timeliness of trade data submission and the timeliness of resolutions of trade matching errors for OTC derivatives;
- Supervisors should urge the industry to amend standard credit derivative trade documentation to provide for cash settlement of obligations stemming from a credit event in accordance with the terms of the cash settlement protocol that has been developed but not yet incorporated into standard documentation; and Supervisors should ask the industry to develop a longer-term plan for an integrated operational infrastructure supporting OTC derivatives that:
  - captures all significant processing events over the entire lifecycle of trades;
  - delivers operational reliability and scalability;
  - maximizes the efficiencies obtainable from automation and electronic processing platforms by promoting standardization and interoperability of infrastructure components;
  - enhances participants' ability to manage counterparty risk through netting
  - and collateral agreements by promoting portfolio reconciliation and accurate valuation of trades;
  - addresses all major asset classes and product types; and
  - encompasses the buy side as well as the dealer community.

II. Comprehensive Review of Contributing Factors

1. Underwriting standards for U.S. adjustable-rate subprime mortgages weakened dramatically between late 2004 and early 2007. As housing prices subsequently

softened, the delinquency rate for such mortgages soared, exceeding 20 percent of the entire outstanding stock of adjustable-rate subprime mortgages in late 2007.[2]

2. Nearly all of these mortgages were packaged in residential mortgage-backed securities (RMBS) and a large share of the subprime RMBS were purchased by managers of CDOs of asset-backed securities (ABS), so-called ABS CDOs. The subprime RMBS and the ABS CDOs were structured in tranches and a very large share of the total value of the securities issued was rated AA or AAA by the credit rating agencies.
3. Both U.S. and international investors were eager purchasers of these securities. Indeed, the loosening of credit standards and terms in the subprirne market was symptomatic of a broader erosion of market discipline on the standards and terms of loans to households and businesses. Following many years of benign economic and financial conditions, global investors had become quite complacent about risks, even in the case of new and increasingly complex financial instruments.
4. Many of the global investors in the AA and AAA tranches relied heavily on the ratings in making investment decisions or in communicating risk appetites to their investment managers, rather than undertaking their own independent credit analysis on instruments that often were quite complex. When it became apparent that even AAA tranches of some ABS CDOs could face large writedowns, investors lost faith in the ratings of complex structured products more broadly.
5. No longer willing to rely on ratings and unable to perform their own credit analyses, investors pulled back from a wide range of structured product markets. Issuance of all types of non- agency RMBS declined substantially. In addition, issuance of collateralized loan obligations (CLOs) became more difficult, at a time when a huge overhang of leveraged loan commitments ($225 billion in the U.S. alone) had already made investors reluctant to buy such loans at committed spreads and terms.
6. From 2004 to 2007, ABCP markets in the U.S. and abroad had grown very rapidly. Much of the growth was accounted for by conduits, including structured investment vehicles (SIVs) and CDOs, which purchased securities, including non-agency RMBS and CDOs, rather than by more traditional conduits that purchased short-term corporate and consumer receivables. As in the case of structured finance products, investors in ABCP, including money market funds, seem to have relied heavily on credit ratings rather than making their own assessments of the structure of these programs and the underlying collateral. As investors became aware that some of the underlying collateral was RMBS and CDOs, they pulled back from the ABCP market generally, and even, to some extent, from more traditional programs. In the United States alone, ABCP outstanding declined by about one-third, or $370 billion, between early August 2007 and late December 2007. Since that time the amount of U.S. ABCP outstanding has changed little on balance.
7. The seizing up of structured credit markets and the contraction of ABCP markets imposed significant liquidity pressures on many of the largest U.S. and European financial institutions. These firms were the leading underwriters of non-agency RMBS and of ABS CDOs. When the structured credit markets shut down, the firms

[2] By contrast, the delinquency rate on the stock of outstanding fixed-rate subprime mortgages increased by only three percentage points over the same period, to around 8 percent.

were left holding mortgages and RMBS that could not be sold off Firms also were left holding exposures to leveraged loans that were in the process of being syndicated. Still more exposures were created when, in order to protect their reputations, some firms elected to purchase assets from, or extend credit to, off-balance sheet vehicles that they had organized and money market and other investment funds that they managed.

8. Many of these same firms were revealed to have concentrated exposures to subprime credit risk. While the business model of these firms with respect to subprime mortgages had been described as "originate to distribute," it gradually became apparent that some had retained significant credit exposures to the subprime market by retaining super-senior CDO tranches and by providing credit and liquidity enhancements to ABCP programs that invested in super-senior tranches of RMBS and CDOs. As a result, some firms suffered significant losses.
9. Firms themselves struggled to determine the size of these exposures and the resulting losses. As the structured credit markets seized up, reliable market-based price discovery became much more difficult for an increasing share of firms' portfolios; in many cases, models that were used for valuation in the absence of reliable market prices had not been adequately developed, or were not appropriate for the complex securities being evaluated. In addition, some firms had difficulty identifying and aggregating their exposures to subprime mortgage assets. As a result, they became concerned about the adequacy of their capital and the size of their balance sheets. They also became less confident of their assessments of the credit risk of other market participants that were known or suspected of holding such securities. In addition to concerns about counterparties' valuation practices, information about their holdings of such securities generally was not publicly available.
10. The combination of liquidity and balance sheet pressures and heightened credit concerns made banks reluctant to provide others with term funding. Term premiums embodied in LIBOR rates increased, at times to more than 100 basis points, and some other types of term funding became more difficult and costly. Traditional central bank liquidity tools were unable to bring term premiums in the interbank markets down. Changes to the primary credit program that the Federal Reserve announced in August 2007 — the narrowing of the spread of the primary credit rate relative to the target funds rate and increased scope to borrow at term — had little success, perhaps because they did not eliminate the stigma associated with borrowing from the central bank. Moreover, discount window facilities likely do not substantially reduce banks' concerns about balance sheet pressures or counterparty risk. With creditors skittish and banks' balance sheets increasing, conditions in term funding markets remained strained through year-end 2007.
11. More generally, uncertainty about asset valuations in illiquid markets and about financial institutions' exposures to asset price changes left investors and markets jittery. Of particular concern were the exposures of financial guarantors to protection they had provided on super- senior CDO tranches. Downgrades of these institutions' credit ratings could disrupt financial markets in which investors rely heavily on their guarantees, notably the U.S. municipal bond market. In addition, failure of one of the guarantors would impose additional losses on financial institutions that had purchased CDO protection from the guarantor.

12. Prior to year-end 2007, a new tool, the Term Auction Facility (TAF), was deployed by the Federal Reserve. It appears not to have been hindered by concerns about stigma and appears to have helped reduce term premiums. However, it is uncertain how much of the reduction in term premiums just after year-end 2007 resulted from the availability of the TAF and how much was the result of relieved concern following year-end.
13. By early 2008, the financial disorder had not abated. Issuance of RMBS remained very weak, issuance of commercial mortgage-backed securities (CMBS) was off substantially from the first half of 2007, and CLO issuance was running well below its levels of spring 2007. Term premiums declined with the turn of the year but subsequently have widened, reportedly on renewed concerns about bank balance sheet pressures and heightened uncertainty about the economic outlook. More recently, liquidity in the agency RMBS market has deteriorated, yields on municipal bonds have risen substantially relative to those on comparable-maturity Treasuries, and issuance of municipal bonds has declined noticeably. Costs of residential mortgage and business credit were up significantly compared to the summer of 2007, and survey evidence pointed to tighter standards for a broad range of loans. In part, the higher costs and tighter standards appeared to reflect concerns about the effects of the contraction in the housing sector and the developments in financial markets on the broader economy.
14. Losses from hedge fund defaults through year-end 2007 were negligible, but preliminary data indicate that hedge fund performance was poor in January, and in the last few weeks, a growing number of hedge funds have missed margin calls. Counterparties continue to monitor their exposures to hedge funds closely.
15. The infrastructure of the financial markets generally has coped quite well with the heightened price volatility and surging trading volumes. Backlogs of unconfirmed trades in credit derivatives increased substantially in July and August 2007 but subsequently receded. Although liquidity in the credit derivatives markets has declined noticeably by some measures, those markets have continued to perform important price discovery and risk management functions.

III. Policy Issues and Recommendations

A. Reforming the Mortgage Origination Process

Issues

1. State-licensed mortgage brokers, who take loan applications and shop them to depository institutions or other lenders, had similarly weak incentives. Weak government oversight of these entities also contributed to the rise in unsound underwriting practices.
2. Originators had weak incentives to maintain strong underwriting standards, particularly at a time when securitizers, credit rating agencies, and mortgage investors did not conduct due diligence sufficient to align originator incentives with

the underlying risks. Against this backdrop, limited government oversight of mortgage companies not affiliated with regulated depositories, which made about half of higher-priced mortgages in 2006, contributed to a rise in unsound underwriting practices in the subprime sector, including, in some cases, fraudulent and abusive practices.

3. Consumer protection rules and disclosure requirements did not sufficiently protect consumers against improper lending.

Recommendations to Address Issues

1. State financial regulators should implement strong nationwide licensing standards for mortgage brokers. As a first step, the CSBS and the American Association of Residential Mortgage Regulators (AARMR) have already created a nationwide licensing system and database for mortgage professionals; seven states began participating when the system was initially started, and dozens more committed to participate over time.
2. Federal and state regulators should strengthen and make consistent government oversight of all entities that originate and fund mortgages and otherwise interface with customers in the mortgage origination process. All states should work towards adopting the principles set forth in the guidance developed by the federal regulators for nontraditional and subprime mortgage lending and ensure that effective enforcement mechanisms are in place to deal with noncompliance with such standards. One key step that already has been taken is that the Conference of State Bank Supervisors (CSBS) issued principles-based underwriting guidance on subprime mortgages in July 2007 that was nearly identical to guidance issued earlier by federal supervisory agencies. In addition, a group of supervisors has launched a pilot program to review the underwriting standards and senior management oversight of risk management strategies for ensuring compliance with consumer protection laws and regulations at selected nondepository lenders with significant subprime mortgage operations.[3] The results of these reviews should be analyzed in order to determine whether to continue the project and, if so, how to focus future reviews.
3. The Federal Reserve should issue stronger consumer protection rules and mandate enhanced consumer protection disclosures that would make affordability over the life of the mortgage more transparent and that would facilitate comparison of the terms with those of alternative products. To this end, the Federal Reserve is currently engaged in a review of the Truth in Lending Act (TILA) rules for mortgage loans, including consumer testing, and plans to propose new mortgage disclosures based on the results. The Federal Reserve has already proposed changes to the TILA rules to address concerns about incomplete or misleading mortgage loan advertisements and solicitations and to require lenders to provide mortgage disclosures more quickly. Those changes should be enacted once appropriate account has been taken of feedback received over the 90-day comment period. In December 2007, the Federal Reserve used its authority under the Home Ownership and Equity Protection Act (HOEPA) to propose new rules that address abuses related to prepayment penalties,

[3] The Federal Reserve, the Office of Thrift Supervision, the Federal Trade Commission, the CSBS, and the American Association of Residential Mortgage Regulators (AARMR) are participating in the pilot program.

failure to escrow for taxes and insurance, stated-income and low-documentation lending, and failure to give adequate consideration to borrowers' ability to repay. These rules should be enacted once appropriate account has been taken of feedback received over the 90-day comment period.

4. State and federal authorities should coordinate to enforce consumer protection and disclosure rules evenly across all types of mortgage originators.
5. Federal and state authorities should pursue mortgage market participants who engaged in fraudulent transactions and any parties undertaking fraudulent schemes to take advantage of households facing foreclosure.

B. Improving Investors' Contributions to Market Discipline

Issues

1. Investors and asset managers failed to obtain sufficient information or to conduct comprehensive risk assessments. For many investors, the use of credit ratings in risk management systems has fallen behind innovation in financial markets. In particular, many investors seem to treat a credit rating as a "sufficient statistic" for the full range of risks associated with an instrument, when, in fact, credit ratings are assessments of creditworthiness, and not of liquidity, market, or other risks. Some investors also relied exclusively on ratings for valuation purposes.
2. In turn, originators, underwriters, and sponsors did not always supply investors with sufficient information related to assets they were selling, securitizing, or using as collateral for structured credit products.
3. Separately, firms that sponsor ABCP programs or provide liquidity or credit enhancements to such programs disclose to their own shareholders and creditors considerably less information about the nature and composition of risk characteristics of the underlying assets than they would if the assets were on their own balance sheets.
4. Although market participants had economic incentives to conduct due diligence and evaluate risk-adjusted returns, the steps they took were insufficient, resulting in a significant erosion of market discipline.

Recommendations to Address Issues

1. Overseers of institutional investors (for example, the Department of Labor for private pension funds; state treasurers for public pension funds; and the SEC for money market funds) should require investors (and their asset managers) to obtain from sponsors and underwriters of securitized credits access to better information about the risk characteristics of such credits, including information about the underlying asset pools, on an initial and ongoing basis.
2. Overseers should ensure that these investors (and their asset managers) develop an independent view of the risk characteristics of the instruments in their portfolios, rather than rely solely on credit ratings.
3. To limit rating shopping, underwriters and sponsors of structured finance products should publicly disclose whether, after submitting final data and information about a

proposed structure to one or more CRAs and receiving preliminary ratings from the CRA(s) based on the information, they choose to publish some but not all of the preliminary rating(s) as final ratings. The disclosure should include the reason for not having any such preliminary ratings published as final ratings.

4. To enable investors to improve their due diligence for structured finance products, underwriters and sponsors should provide improved disclosures for RMBS, ABS CDOs, and other structured products. Asset managers and financial institutions, including those running conduits, should provide improved disclosures.
5. Investors should take account of differences in risk between different classes of instruments, rather than relying on generic credit ratings when making investment decisions, communicating investment mandates to investment managers, and evaluating investment managers.
6. Where investors utilize investment consultants, they should insist that the consultants develop an independent view of the broad range of risk characteristics of the types of instruments in the investor's portfolio, rather than solely relying on the credit ratings.
7. Building on its existing templates for disclosures by multi-seller ABCP conduits, the American Securitization Forum (ASF) should develop templates for disclosures to investors for other types of securitizations. Supervisors should encourage banks and other regulated entities that sponsor ABCP conduits to make disclosures consistent with the templates.
8. The PWG will engage the private sector to create a committee to develop best practices regarding disclosure to investors in securitized credits, including ABS and CDOs of ABS.
9. Consistent with their disclosures of on-balance sheet risk, public companies that sponsor or provide credit or liquidity enhancements to ABCP programs should disclose the distribution of assets underlying the programs by type, industry, and credit risk to the extent material to the company.

C. Reforming the Ratings Agencies' Process for and Practices regarding Structured Credit and other Securitized Credit Products

Issues

1. Credit rating agencies contributed significantly to the recent market turmoil by underestimating the credit risk of subprime RMBS and other structured credit products, notably ABS CDOs.
2. With respect to subprime RMBS, in part the rating agencies underestimated the credit risk because they underestimated the severity and breadth of the softening in housing prices and the potential for fraud.
3. The rating agencies' models for rating ABS CDOs relied on assumptions about correlations between ABS that underestimated the degree of linkages between underlying securities.
4. As acknowledged by the rating agencies, structured products have quite different risk characteristics from corporate bonds. Nonetheless, they used the same rating

categories for both types of instruments and many investors seem to have acted as if they did not understand or appreciate that the risk characteristics differed.

5. The methodologies that the rating agencies used to rate structured products are reasonably transparent. Nonetheless, greater transparency is both possible and desirable.

Recommendations to Address Issues

1. Credit rating agencies should disclose what qualitative reviews they perform on originators of assets that collateralize ABS rated by the CRA and should require underwriters of ABS to represent the level and scope of due diligence performed on the underlying assets.
2. The CRAs should reform their ratings processes for structured credit products to ensure integrity and transparency. The PWG welcomes the steps already taken by the CRAs, and particularly encourages the CRAs to: (a) enforce policies and procedures that manage conflicts of interest, including implementing changes suggested by the SEC's broad review of conflict of interest issues; (b) publish sufficient information about the assumptions underlying their credit rating methodologies and models, so that users of credit ratings can understand how a particular credit rating was determined; (c) make changes to the credit rating process that would clearly differentiate ratings for structured products from ratings for corporate and municipal securities; (d) make ratings performance measures for structured credit products and other ABS readily available to the public in a manner that facilitates comparison across products and credit ratings; (e) work with investors to provide the information investors need to make informed decisions about risk, including measures of the uncertainty associated with ratings and of potential ratings volatility; and (f) ensure that adequate personnel and financial resources are allocated to monitoring and updating its ratings.
3. The rating agencies should be encouraged to conduct formal, periodic, internal reviews of criteria and methodologies for ratings of structured credit products.
4. The International Organization of Securities Commissions (IOSCO) should be encouraged to continue addressing credit rating issues through revisions to its "Code of Conduct."
5. The PWG will facilitate formation of a private-sector group (with representatives of investors, issuers, underwriters, and CRAs) to develop recommendations for further steps that the issuers, underwriters, CRAs, and policy makers could take to ensure the integrity and transparency of ratings, and to foster appropriate use of ratings in risk assessment.
6. The PWG member agencies will reinforce steps taken by the CRAs through revisions to supervisory policy and regulation, including regulatory capital requirements that use ratings.
7. The PWG will revisit the need for changes to CRA oversight if the reforms adopted by the CRAs are not sufficient to ensure the integrity and transparency of ratings.

D. Strengthening Global Financial Institutions' Risk Management Practices

Issues

1. The effectiveness of certain risk management practices was a key factor that differentiated institutions that sustained significant losses during the financial crisis from institutions that, while affected to some degree, avoided significant losses.
2. Firms that suffered significant losses tended to exhibit the following risk management weaknesses: (a) weak controls over potential balance sheet growth, including ineffective limits on the growth of business lines and poor monitoring of off-balance sheet exposures; (b) inadequate communications among senior management, business lines, and risk management functions; (c) dependence on a narrow range of risk measures that were based on assumptions that proved erroneous and on measurement processes that were difficult to alter once it became apparent that the underlying assumptions were wrong; and (d) insufficient attention to valuation issues, including excessive reliance on credit ratings and inadequate development of models for valuing complex or potentially illiquid securities.
3. These weaknesses were particularly evident with respect to the management of certain business lines: (a) CDO warehouses; (b) syndication of leveraged loans; and (c) conduit businesses (sponsorship or liquidity support for SIVs and other conduits that issued ABCP).
4. The root causes of valuation uncertainty were the failure of many financial institutions to develop sufficiently robust valuation models for complex, mortgage-related structured products and fundamental uncertainty about the ultimate performance of the underlying mortgage pools.
5. Losses from hedge fund defaults through year-end 2007 were negligible, but preliminary data indicate that hedge fund performance was poor in January, and in the last few weeks, a growing number of hedge funds have missed margin calls. Counterparties continue to monitor their exposures to hedge funds closely. Prior to the financial crisis, a multilateral review of major banks' and securities firms' counterparty risk management practices revealed some weaknesses with respect to the measurement of potential exposures and stress tests. In recent meetings with supervisors, financial institutions noted that some of those weaknesses remained.

Recommendations to Address Issues

1. Global financial institutions should promptly identify and address any weaknesses in risk management practices that the turmoil has revealed. These firms, and other financial institutions with similar types of weaknesses in their operations, should strongly reemphasize the importance of: (a) a strong, independent risk management function; (b) strategic planning with respect to balance sheet growth and utilization of capital and liquidity; (c) assessment of risks on an integrated basis across the enterprise; (d) ongoing communication among senior management, business lines, and risk management functions; and (e) the development of, and adherence to, strong operational and financial reporting controls over valuations.

2. The PWG will support formation of a private-sector group to reassess implementation of the Counterparty Risk Management Policy Group II's (CRMPG II) existing guiding principles and recommendations regarding risk management, risk monitoring, and transparency, and to modify or develop new principles and recommendations as necessary to incorporate lessons from the recent turmoil, including lessons regarding valuation practices.
3. Supervisors of global financial institutions should closely monitor the firms' efforts to address risk management weaknesses, taking action if necessary to ensure that weaknesses are addressed.
4. U.S. banking regulators and the SEC should promptly assess current guidance and develop common guidance to address the risk management weaknesses revealed by the recent market turmoil, including improvements to: (a) management information systems, including procedures that ensure aggregation of exposures across all business lines and ensure rigorous valuations of instruments and exposures; (b) concentration risk management, liquidity risk management, stress testing, and other risk management practices that are necessary to ensure that liquidity and capital cushions are sufficiently robust to absorb extreme system-wide shocks; and (c) governance of the risk management and control framework, including practices that address incentive problems in compensation policies.
5. U.S. authorities should encourage other supervisors of global firms to make complementary efforts to develop guidance along the same lines.

E. Enhancing Prudential Regulatory Policies

Issues

1. Various regulatory policies failed to mitigate some of the risk management weaknesses that have been identified.
2. Minimization of regulatory capital requirements by banks is an important driver of bank behavior. The limited risk sensitivity of Basel I encouraged banks to securitize low-risk assets and to support securitizations through facilities having low mandated capital charges. The securitization framework in Basel II is a more risk-sensitive approach that addresses many (but not all) of Basel I's shortcomings in that area. Existing capital requirements are not designed to address non-contractual exposures such as those arising from sponsorship of SIVs or mutual funds that firms may assume for reputational reasons.
3. Once firms experienced losses, their desire to maintain a capital buffer above regulatory levels significantly increased the risk that they would restrict credit availability and thereby add to stress in credit markets, with the potential for feedback on the real economy.
4. Authorities did not insist on appropriate reporting and disclosures of off-balance sheet vehicles.

Recommendations to Address Issues

1. Regulators should adopt policies that provide incentives for financial institutions to hold capital and liquidity cushions commensurate with firm-wide exposure (both on- and off-balance sheet) to severe adverse market events. These cushions should be forward looking and adjust appropriately through peaks and valleys of the credit cycle.
2. Regulators should enhance guidance related to pipeline risk management for firms that use an originate-to-distribute model.
3. Given the weak controls over balance sheet growth at some firms and the resulting liquidity pressures that those firms experienced, the Basel Committee on Banking Supervision (BCBS) should promptly complete its work to update the Committee's 2000 guidance on liquidity management, including the sound practice guidelines to be followed by regulated financial institutions as well as the oversight principles for supervisors.
4. The BCBS and IOSCO should review capital requirements for ABS CDOs and other resecuritizations and for off-balance sheet commitments, with a view toward increasing requirements on exposures that have been the source of recent losses to firms. In particular, they should reconsider the relationship between external credit ratings and capital charges under the "ratings based approach," especially for ABS CDOs and other securitizations of ABS, as well as the relationship between external ratings and capital charges under the "internal assessment approach" for exposures to ABCP programs.[4]
5. Supervisors should review the adequacy of guidance on Basel II's Pillar 2 with respect to the consideration of the reputational risks that conduit and asset management businesses entail and the implications for institutions' need for economic capital and their liquidity contingency plans.
6. To promote the maintenance of strong capital cushions and to mitigate the possibility that a more risk-based capital regime will heighten the potential for capital requirements to amplify credit and economic cycles, supervisors should rigorously assess banks' implementation of the Advanced Internal Ratings Based Approach to Basel II, especially the conservatism of estimates of losses from defaults during a downturn and the robustness of banks' stress tests.
7. Regulators should require financial institutions to improve their internal reporting and make more detailed and comprehensive disclosures of off-balance sheet commitments, including commitments to support ABCP conduits and other off-balance sheet vehicles.
8. Regulators should encourage financial institutions to improve the quality of disclosures about fair value estimates for complex and other illiquid instruments, including descriptions of valuation methodologies and information regarding the degree of uncertainty associated with such estimates.
9. State insurance commissioners should review the appropriateness of capital requirements for financial guarantors in light of changes in the firms' business lines.

[4] In the internal assessment approach the bank assigns an internal rating to the exposure and then maps the rating to an equivalent external rating.

Financial guarantors should strengthen their models for assessing the risks of new activities.

10. Regulators should review the current use of ratings in regulatory and supervisory rules. At a minimum, regulators should distinguish, as appropriate, between ratings of structured credit products and ratings of corporate and municipal bonds in regulatory and supervisory policies.
11. Authorities should encourage FASB to evaluate the role of accounting standards in the current market turmoil. This evaluation should include an assessment of the need for further modifications to accounting standards related to consolidation and securitization, with the goal of improving transparency and the operation of U.S. standards in the short-term. Additionally, authorities should encourage FASB and IASB to achieve more rapid convergence of accounting standards for consolidation of ABCP conduits and other off-balance sheet vehicles.

F. Enhancements to the Infrastructure for OTC Derivatives Markets

Issues

1. While the infrastructure of the financial markets generally has coped quite well with heightened price volatility and surging trading volumes, there have been issues with the accuracy and timeliness of trade data submission; the timeliness of resolutions of trade matching errors; documentation and cash settlement; electronic post-trade processing; backlogs; integrated processing, and reconciliation and valuation.
2. Although the industry has made significant progress in automating the infrastructure of the OTC derivatives markets over the last two years, the industry has not achieved a "steady state" in which events do not increase operational problems. This was evident in July and August 2007 when a spike in credit derivatives trades resulted in substantial increases in backlogs of unconfirmed trades throughout the industry.
3. Although the industry has developed a "cash settlement protocol" that can obviate the need for purchasers of credit protection to physically deliver obligations of the reference entity following a default or other credit event, standard industry trade documentation still requires physical settlement. Until the protocol is incorporated into standard industry documentation, there is a risk of significant market disruption if one or more major market participants chose not to adopt the protocol following a credit event. Of particular concern is the market impact such choices could have if multiple credit events were to occur simultaneously.

Recommendations to Address Issues

1. Supervisors should insist that the industry promptly set ambitious standards for the accuracy and timeliness of trade data submission and the timeliness of resolutions of trade matching errors for OTC derivatives.
2. Supervisors should urge the industry to promptly amend standard credit derivative trade documentation to provide for cash settlement of obligations stemming from a

credit event, in accordance with the terms of the cash settlement protocol that has been developed but not yet incorporated into standard documentation.

3. Supervisors should ask the industry to develop a longer-term plan for an integrated operational infrastructure supporting OTC derivatives that: (a) captures all significant processing events over the entire lifecycle of trades; (b) delivers operational reliability and scalability; (c) maximizes the efficiencies obtainable from automation and electronic processing platforms by promoting standardization and interoperability of infrastructure components; (d) enhances participants' ability to manage counterparty risk through netting and collateral agreements by promoting portfolio reconciliation and accurate valuation of trades; (e) addresses all major asset classes and products types; and (f) encompasses the buy side as well as the dealer community.

CONCLUSION

Market participants have begun taking steps to address many of the weaknesses that have contributed to the turmoil in global financial markets. Nonetheless, policy makers need to monitor their efforts closely and reinforce them where necessary. In most cases policy makers' efforts to promote implementation of these recommendations will require domestic or international regulatory cooperation. The PWG will work to ensure that U.S. federal regulators cooperate effectively with each other and with the relevant state authorities. Internationally, the PWG is working with foreign regulators, finance ministries, and central banks through the Financial Stability Forum (FSF) on a report to the G-7 Finance Ministers and Governors that will provide a diagnosis of the causes of global financial turmoil and an agreed-upon set of recommendations for addressing identified weaknesses in global markets and institutions. As part of that cooperative process, the PWG has shared with the FSF the diagnosis and recommendations set out in this statement.

The PWG plans to issue a follow-up statement in the fourth quarter of 2008 that will assess progress toward implementation of its recommendations and the FSF's recommendations and consider whether further steps are needed to address weaknesses in financial markets and institutions and related regulatory policies.

INDEX

H

I

Q

R

S

T

U

V

W

Y